DISASTER MANAGEMENT

M. Saravana Kumar

M.Com., M.B.A., M.S(IT)., M.Phil., Ph.D.,

Assistant Professor,

School of Management Studies,

Anna University,

Coimbatore.

Himalaya Publishing House

ISO 9001:2015 CERTIFIED

First Edition : 2010
Reprint : 2017
Reprint : 2023
Reprint : 2025

Published by : Mrs. Meena Pandey
for **HIMALAYA PUBLISHING HOUSE PVT. LTD.,**
"Ramdoot", Dr. Bhalerao Marg, Girgaon, Mumbai - 400 004.
Phone: 022-23860170, 23863863; **Fax:** 022-23877178
E-mail: himpub@bharatmail.co.in; **Website:** www.himpub.com

Branch Offices :

New Delhi : "Pooja Apartments", 4-B, Murari Lal Street, Ansari Road, Darya Ganj, New Delhi - 110 002. Phone: 011-23270392, 23278631; Fax: 011-23256286

Nagpur : Kundanlal Chandak Industrial Estate, Ghat Road, Nagpur - 440 018. Phone: 0712-2721215, 2721216

Bengaluru : Plot No. 91-33, 2nd Main Road, Seshadripuram, Behind Nataraja Theatre, Bengaluru - 560 020. Phone: 080-41138821; Mobile: 09379847017, 09379847005

Hyderabad : No. 3-4-184, Lingampally, Besides Raghavendra Swamy Matham, Kachiguda, Hyderabad - 500 027. Phone: 040-27560041, 27550139

Chennai : No. 34/44, Motilal Street, T. Nagar, Chennai - 600 017. Mobile: 09380460419

Pune : "Laksha" Apartment, First Floor, No. 527, Mehunpura, Shaniwarpeth (Near Prabhat Theatre), Pune - 411 030. Phone: 020-24496323, 24496333; Mobile: 09370579333

Cuttack : Plot No. 5F-755/4, Sector-9, CDA Markat Nagar, Cuttack - 753 014, Odisha. Mobile: 09338746007

Kolkata : 3, S.M. Bose Road, Near Gate No. 5, Agarpara Railway Station, North 24 Parganas, West Bengal - 700 109. Mobile: 09674536325

DTP by : HPH Editorial Office, Bhandup (Kalpana)

Printed at : Trinity Academy, Mumbai. On behalf of HPH.

PREFACE

The purpose of this book is fairly simple, to introduce and reflect on some of the key ideas, models and approaches of disaster management. It outlines some of the tools or models that are commonly used for thinking about or doing strategical moves in managing disaster. Moreover, the notion that anthropogenic disasters is planned then executed, by considering the models that explores the idea. Therefore, "hope for the best, but, be prepared for the worst" is the lesson that everyone must draw towards better managing the disasters.

Hence this text book provides a comprehensive overview of the most important topics covered in a disaster management subject at bachelors and MBA level. Throughout this, the theory is supplemented with enough necessary suitable examples and illustration.

Suggestion for the further improvement of this book is wholeheartedly welcome.

AUTHORS

Contents

CHAPTER 1 INTRODUCTION

Almost everyday, newspapers, radio and television channels carry reports on disaster striking several parts of the world. But what is a disaster? The term disaster owes its origin to the French word *"Desastre"* which is a combination of two words 'des' meaning bad and 'aster' meaning star. Thus the term refers to 'Bad or Evil star'. A disaster can be defined as "A serious disruption in the functioning of the community or a society causing widespread material, economic, social or environmental losses which exceed the ability of the affected society to cope using its own resources". A disaster is a result from the combination of hazard, vulnerability and insufficient capacity or measures to reduce the potential chances of risk.

A disaster happens when a hazard impacts on the vulnerable population and causes damage, casualties and disruption. Thus,

Disaster = Hazards x Vulnerability

Any hazard – flood, earthquake or cyclone which is a triggering event along with greater vulnerability (inadequate access to resources, sick and old people, lack of awareness etc.) would lead to disaster causing greater loss to life and property. For example; an earthquake in an uninhabited desert cannot be considered a disaster, no matter how strong the intensities produced.

There has been an increase in the incidence of natural disasters worldwide with increasing loss of life and damage to property. The risk of disasters can also be expected to rise in the future, particularly for developing countries' populations. There are two reasons for this trend: An increase in extreme natural events, primarily due to climatic change. Increased vulnerability of populations to these natural events, Natural disasters are closely bound up with the development status of a region: They disrupt or impair development and, at the same time, a low level of development increases the chances of them occurring. Supported in part by bilateral and multilateral donors, many countries are stepping up their efforts to prevent disaster. The idea is that effective precautions will avert future disasters or at least mitigate them. This in turn will help stabilize development in partner countries. We can lower disaster risk by containing the hazards and reducing vulnerability. The general economic and social conditions in a country are a major determinant for both factors. All measures must therefore be assimilated into the 'normal' institutional, regional and sectoral development strategies employed in threatened regions. Mainstreaming this issue in development cooperation sectors is a major challenge. Cooperation with projects for decentralization and/or community development, rural development, environmental protection and resource conservation, housing, health and education are of paramount importance.

The term 'disaster' may be defined as an unexpected happening, causing a huge loss of life and property. Major disasters may be defined as those causing at least one of three consequences which are as follows: (i) Causing damage to more than 1 per cent of Gross National Product, (ii) Causing deaths of more than 100 persons at a time and place, (iii) Affecting more than 1 per cent of the total population in an area.

According to an estimate during 1950-2001, about 6 lakh deaths took place due to major disasters out of which 1 per cent were in developed countries and 99 per cent in developing countries. Before 1950 the situation was quite different and at that time 30 per cent of total deaths took place in developed countries and 70 per cent in developing countries. These figures indicate the gravity of the situation and seriousness of the problem.

All said and done, the point remains as to how to prevent, predict and mitigate major disasters? So far through scientific and technological development the prevention of earthquakes and cyclones, floods, droughts, fires, etc., may be possible and can be predicted to some extent.

There is no doubt that a proper planning and effective management can reduce the effects and hazards of disasters, like earthquakes, since it is not the earthquake itself but the defective buildings, which cause loss of life and property.

A number of well documented studies show that there has been a significant increase in natural disasters over the last decade. There are also many small-scale, local disasters that are not recorded in official statistics. Even more pronounced than the increase in the numbers of disaster events is the magnitude of the physical damage caused and particularly the loss of human life. Natural disasters are caused by extreme occurrences in nature for which society is unprepared. They destroy the basic conditions of life for the victims, who lack the resources to recover in the short or medium term. Disasters often have a very significant detrimental impact on past development efforts.

Disaster Management is a management of crisis of unusual situation demanding commitment at all levels with clearly defined authorities to discharge assigned roles and identified structures to perform designated functions having also a support through appropriate budget and constituted of preparedness plans which would be more oriented to operations part, participatory skills and methods of handling than being generally descriptive.

Disaster Management is a continuous process which thrives on feedback, relies on resource planning and subsists on manpower plan based on the identification of the present strengths and weaknesses for a progression towards a better method and weakness free and fool-proof system.

As we all are aware of the fact that, it has got three components **— *rescue, relief and rehabilitation.*** The relief also includes recovery phase while rehabilitation in the present context also invites those for mitigation. The Government of India has been very concerned in planning to mitigate the disasters by constituting a High Powered Committee which has already given certain recommendations and this is backed up by an All Party Committee headed by the Hon'ble Prime Minister.

For instance, in the Uttaranchal State, a separate department for Disaster and the Disaster Mitigation Institution has been set up under the Ministry of Disaster Management which shows the concern of the State Government. In every Disaster Management, it is the district which is the focal point and every district needs to have advance contingency plan which shall have necessarily to include the disaster mapping of the place based on factors like disaster proneness, history sheet of disasters in the post and also local source and resource which are identifiable in the mitigation of the disaster.

DISASTER MANAGEMENT AND ITS EVOLUTION

The word disaster's root is from astrology: this implies that when the stars are in a bad position a bad event will happen. Disasters occur when hazards strike in vulnerable areas. A disaster is the impact of natural or man-made hazards that negatively affects society or environment. Hazards that occur in areas with low vulnerability do not result in a disaster; as is the case in uninhabited regions. It is often argued that all disasters are human-made, because human actions before the strike of the hazard can prevent it developing into a disaster. Hazards are routinely divided into natural human-made, although complex disasters, where there is no single root cause, are more common in developing countries. A specific disaster may spawn a secondary disaster that increases the impact. A classic example is an earthquake that causes a tsunami, resulting in coastal flooding.

Select Definitions

Disasters can be defined in different ways:

- A disaster is an overwhelming ecological disruption occurring on a scale sufficient to require outside assistance.
- A disaster is an event located in time and space which produces conditions whereby the continuity of structure and process of social units becomes problematic.
- It is an event or series of events which seriously disrupts normal activities.

The magnitude of the effects of the event will be viewed differently.

Disasters are classified in various ways:

- Natural disasters and man-made disasters
- Sudden disasters and slow onset disasters

The dividing line between these types of disasters is imprecise. Activities related to man may exacerbate natural disasters.

Although experts may differ in their definitions of disaster, many public health practitioners would characterise a disaster as a "sudden, extraordinary calamity or catastrophe, which affects or threatens health".

Disasters include

- Tornadoes,
- Fires,
- Hurricanes,
- Floods/Sea Surges/Tsunamis,
- Snow storms,
- Earthquakes,

- Landslides,
- Severe air pollution (smog),
- Heat waves,
- Epidemics,
- Building collapse,
- Toxicological accidents
  (e.g. release of hazardous substances),
- Nuclear accidents,
- Explosions,
- Civil disturbances,
- Water contamination, and
- Existing or anticipated food shortages.

Effects of Major Disasters

Disasters throughout history have had significant impact on the numbers, health status and lifestyle of populations.

- Deaths,
- Severe injuries, requiring extensive treatments,
- Increased risk of communicable diseases,
- Damage to the health facilities,
- Damage to the water systems,
- Food shortage,
- Population movements.

Health Problems Common to all Disasters

- Social reactions,
- Communicable diseases,
- Population displacements,

- Climatic exposure,
- Food and nutrition,
- Water supply and sanitation,
- Mental health,
- Damage to health infrastructure.

VARIOUS NATURAL DISASTERS AND ITS FORMS

Cyclone

The term "cyclone" refers to all classes of storms with low atmospheric pressure at the centre, are formed when an organised system of revolving winds, clockwise in the Southern Hemisphere, anticlockwise in the Northern Hemisphere, develops over tropical waters.

Cyclones are classified on the basis of the average speed of the wind near the centre of the system as follows:

Wind Speed	**Classification**
Up to 61 km/hr	Tropical Depression
61 km/hr - 115 km/hr	Tropical Storm
Greater than 115 km/hr	Hurricane

Hurricane

A hurricane is a low pressure, large-scale weather system which derives its energy from the latent heat of condensation of water vapour over warm tropical seas. A mature hurricane may have a diameter ranging from 150 to 1000 kms with sustained wind speeds often exceeding 180 km/hr near the centre with still higher gusts.

A unique feature of a hurricane is the eye. The eye provides a convenient frame of reference for the system, and can be tracked with radar, aircraft or satellite.

Classification: The Saffir/Simpson scale is often used to categorise hurricanes based on their wind speed and damage potential. Five categories of hurricanes are recognised:

- Minimal, Moderate, Extensive, Extreme and Catastrophic.

The destructive potential of a hurricane is significant due to the high wind speeds, accompanying torrential rains which produce flooding, and storm surges along the coastline.

Earthquakes

Definition and Measurement: "An earthquake is a sudden motion or trembling of the ground produced by the abrupt displacement of rock masses". Most earthquakes result from the movement of one rock mass past another in response to tectonic forces.

The focus is the point where the earthquake's motion starts. The epicentre is the point on the earth's surface that is directly above the focus. Earthquake Magnitude is a measure of the strength of an earthquake as calculated from records of the event made on a calibrated seismograph. In 1935, Charles Richter first defined local magnitude and the Richter scale is commonly used today to describe an earthquake's magnitude.

Earthquake Intensity: In contrast, earthquake intensity is a measure of the effects of an earthquake at a particular place. It is determined from observations of the earthquake's effects on people, structures and the earth's surface.

Among the many existing scales, the Modified Mercalli Intensity Scale of 12 degrees, symbolised as MM, is frequently used.

Earthquake Hazards: Earthquake hazards can be categorised as either direct hazards or indirect hazards.

Direct Hazards

- Ground shaking;
- Differential ground settlement;
- Soil liquefaction;
- Immediate landslides or mud slides, ground lurching and avalanches;
- Permanent ground displacement along faults;
- Floods from tidal waves, sea surges and tsunamis.

Indirect Hazards

- Dam failures;
- Pollution from damage to industrial plants;
- Delayed landslides.

Most of the damage due to earthquakes is the result of strong ground shaking. For large magnitude events, trembling has been felt over more than 5 million sq. km.

Tsunamis

Tsunamis are ocean waves produced by earthquakes or underwater land slides.

The word is Japanese and means "Harbour Waves". Tsunami is actually a series of waves that can travel at speeds from 400-600 mph in the open ocean. As the waves approach the coast, their speed decreases, but their amplitude increases.

Unusual wave heights of 10-20 ft high can be very destructive and cause many deaths and injuries.

Most deaths caused by tsunamis are because of drowning.

Associated risks include:

- Flooding;
- Contamination of drinking water;
- Fires from ruptured gas lines and tanks;
- Loss of vital Community Infrastructure [police, fire, medical];
- Areas of greatest risks are
  - Less than 25 feet above sea level;
  - Within 1 mile of the shore line.

Environmental conditions left by the tsunamis may contribute to the transmission of the following diseases:

From Food or Water

- Diarrhoea illnesses; Cholera, Acute Diarrhoea,

Dysentery;

- Hepatitis-A, Hepatitis-E;

- Typhoid fever;
- Food borne illnesses; Bacterial; Viral; Parasitic; Non-infections;
- From animals or mosquitoes.
  - — Leptospirosis, Plague, Malaria, J.E, Dengue, Rabies, Respiratory Diseases; Avian flu, Influenza, Measles.

Effects of Nuclear Holocaust

The effects of nuclear holocaust will result into blasts, heat storms, secondary fires, fire, ionising radiation and fall outs.

These effects fall into 3 categories:

(1). Immediate, (2). Short-term, and (3). Long-term effects.

1. The Immediate Effects: Include blast effects, heat effects, electromagnetic pulse (EMP) effects and radiation effects.

2. The Short-term Effects: Include problems connected with water supply, sanitation, food, dispersal of excreta, wastes and dead bodies, break down of vector control measures and outbreak of infections. Radioactive contamination of water and food are major concerns. The affected area creates a lot of other problems for the survivors and the rescue teams.

Major problem among survivors is of bone marrow depression resulting in leucopenia, which increases their susceptibility to infections.

3. Long-term Effects: The knowledge about the long-term effects is still incomplete. Some well known effects include radiation injuries due to radiation fallout, suppression of body immunity, chronic infection and other associated illnesses.

Persistent radiation hazards will lead to prolonged contamination of water supply, increased ultraviolet radiation, climatic and ecological disturbances, psychological disturbances and genetic abnormalities.

Current World Concern: In the light of the above facts the current world concern about the use of nuclear weapons is justified.

The world already possess an estimated total of 30,000 megatons of nuclear weapons with a total explosive power 50-100 times greater than that of all the explosives used during the Second World War.

Human Survival and Avalanche Rescue

Even small avalanches are a serious danger to life, even with properly trained and equipped companions who avoid the avalanche. Between 55 and 65 per cent of victims buried in the open are killed and only 80 per cent of the victims remaining on the surface survive. Research carried out in Italy based on 422 buried skiers indicates how the chances of survival drop:

- Very rapidly from 92 per cent within 15 minutes to only 30 per cent after 35 minutes (victims die of suffocation).
- Near zero after two hours (victims die of injuries or hypothermia).

Consequently it is vital that everyone surviving an avalanche is used in an immediate search and rescue operation, rather than waiting for help to arrive. Additional help can be called once it can be determined if anyone is seriously injured or still remains unaccountable after the immediate search (i.e., after at least 30 minutes of searching). Even in a well equipped country such as France, it typically takes 45 minutes for a helicopter rescue team to arrive, by which time most of the victims are likely to have died. In some cases, avalanche victims are not located until spring thaw melts the snow, or even years later when objects emerge from a glacier.

LAHAR

A lahar is a type of mudflow composed of pyroclastic material and water that flows down from a volcano, typically along a river valley. The term 'lahar' originated in Indonesia.

Lahars have the consistency of concrete fluid when moving, then solid when stopped. Lahars can be huge, the Osceola lahar produced 5,600 years ago by Mount Rainier in Washington produced a wall of mud 180 m (600 feet) deep in the White River canyon and extends over an area of over 320 km.

Lahars can be extremely dangerous, because of their energy speed. Large lahars can flow several dozen metres per second and can flow for many kilometres, causing catastrophic destruction in their path. The lahars from the Nevado del Ruiz eruption in Colombia in 1985 killed an estimated 21,000 in the city of Armero, buried under 8 m (26 ft) of mud and debris.

The 1953 Tangiwai disaster in New Zealand was caused by a lahar.

Several mountains in the world, including Mount Rainier in the USA, Mount Ruapehu in New Zealand, and Galunggung in Indonesia, are considered particularly dangerous due to the risk of lahars.

Several towns in the Puyallup River valley in Washington state, including Orting, the closest to Mount Rainier, are built on top of lahar deposits that are only about 500 years old. Lahars are predicted to flow through the valley every 500-1,000 years, so Orting, Sumner, Puyallup, Fife and the Port of Tacoma face considerable risk. The USGS has set up lahar warning sirens in Pierce County, so that people can flee an approaching debris flow.

A lahar warning system has been set up at Mount Ruapehu by the New Zealand Department of Conservation and hailed a success after it successfully alerted officials to an impending lahar on 18 March 2007.

The 1991 Mount Pinatubo eruption caused lahar as well, but it was due to the passing of a major typhoon over the Philippines which resulted in a torrent of volcanic ash and water down to the rivers surrounding the volcano. The lahar was caused by the mixing of settled ash and water from the monsoon which occurred the day after the volcano finished erupting. Although the eruption only killed 6 people, 1500 were killed in the resulting lahar, showing the destructive nature of lahars.

Causes

Lahars have several possible causes:

- Snow and glaciers can be melted by a pyroclastic flow during an eruption.
- A flood caused by a glacier, lake breakout, or heavy rainfall can release a lahar, also called glacier run.

ANTHROPOGENIC DISASTERS

Anthropogenic disasters are otherwise called as the human-made or man-made disasters.

A **man-made hazard** is a threat having an element of human intent, negligence, or error, or involving a failure of a man-made system. **Man-made disasters** are disasters resulting from the same factors.

Sociological Hazards

Crime

Crime is the breach of rules or laws for which some governing authority (via mechanisms such as legal systems) can ultimately prescribe a conviction. Individual human societies may each define crime and crimes differently. While every crime violates the law, not every violation of the law counts as a crime; for example: breaches of contract and of other civil law may rank as "offences" or as "infractions".

Arson

Arson is the criminal intent of setting a fire with intent to cause damage. The definition of arson was originally limited to setting fire to buildings, but was later expanded to include other objects, such as bridges, vehicles, and private property. Arson is the greatest cause of fires in data repositories. Sometimes, human-induced fires can be accidental: failing machinery such as a kitchen stove is a major cause of accidental fires.

Civil Disorder

Civil disorder is a broad term that is typically used by law enforcement to describe forms of disturbance. Although civil disorder does not necessarily escalate to a disaster in all cases, the event may escalate into general chaos. Rioting has many causes, from low minimum wage to racial segregation.

Terrorism

Terrorism is a controversial term with multiple definitions. One definition means a violent action targeting civilians exclusively. Another definition is the use or threatened use of violence for the purpose of creating fear in order to achieve a political, religious, or ideological goal. Under the second definition, the targets of terrorist acts can be anyone, including civilians, government officials, military personnel, or people serving the interests of governments. In the early 21st century, terrorism has been considered by some a constant threat to all people of the world, after the worst disaster of its kind struck on September 11, 2001 (known primarily as 9/11).

War

War is conflict between relatively large groups of people, which involves physical force inflicted by the use of weapons. Warfare has destroyed entire cultures, countries, economies and inflicted great suffering on humanity. Other terms for war can include armed conflict, hostilities, and police action. Acts of war are normally excluded from insurance contracts and disaster planning.

Technological Hazards

Industrial Hazards

Industrial disasters occur in a commercial context, such as mining disasters. They often have an environmental impact.

Structural Collapse

Structural collapses are often caused by engineering failures. Bridge failures may be caused in several ways, such as under-design (as in the Tay Rail Bridge), by corrosion attack (such as in the Silver Bridge), and by aerodynamic flutter of the deck (as in Galloping Gertie, the original Tacoma Narrows Bridge). Failure of dams was not infrequent during the Victorian period, such as the Dale Dyke dam failure in Sheffield, England in the 1860s, causing the Great Sheffield Flood. Other failures include balcony collapses.

Bush Fires

Bush fires, forest fires and mine fires are generally started by lightning, but also by human negligence or arson. They can burn thousands of square kilometers. If a fire intensifies enough to produce its own winds and "weather", it will form into a firestorm. A good example of a mine fire is the one near Centralia, Pennsylvania. Started in 1962, it ruined the town and continues to burn today. Some of the biggest city-related fires are The Great Chicago Fire, The Peshtigo Fire (both of 1871) and The Great Fire of London in 1666.

Through Hazardous Materials

Radiation Contamination

When nuclear weapons are detonated or nuclear containment systems are otherwise compromised, airborne radioactive particles (nuclear fallout) can scatter and irradiate large areas. Not only is it deadly, but it also has a long-term effect on the next generation for those who are contaminated. Ionizing radiation is hazardous to living things, and in such a case much of the affected area could be unsafe for human habitation. During World War II, United States troops dropped atomic bombs on the Japanese cities of Hiroshima and Nagasaki. As a result, the radiation fallout contaminated the cities' water supplies, food sources, and half of the populations of each city were stricken with disease. The Soviet republics of Ukraine and Belarus are part of a scenario like this after a reactor at the Chernobyl Nuclear Power Plant suffered a meltdown in 1986. To this day, several small towns and the city of Chernobyl remain abandoned and uninhabitable due to fallout. In the 1970s, a similar threat scared millions of Americans when a failure occurred at the Three Mile Island Nuclear Power Plant in Pennsylvania. The incident was fortunately resolved, and the area retained little contamination.

CBRNs

A catch-all initialism meaning **Chemical, Biological, Radiological,** and **Nuclear.**

The term is used to describe a non-conventional terror threat that, if used by a nation, would be considered use of a weapon of mass destruction. This term is used primarily in the United Kingdom. Planning for the possibility of a CBRN event may be appropriate for certain high-risk or high-value facilities and governments.

Transportation Hazards

Aviation

An aviation accident is defined in the Convention on International Civil Aviation Annex 13 as an occurrence associated with the operation of an aircraft which takes place between the time any person boards the aircraft with the intention of flight and all such persons have disembarked, in which a person is fatally or seriously injured, the aircraft sustains damage or structural failure and/or the aircraft is missing or is completely inaccessible.

An accident in which the damage to the aircraft is such that it must be written off, or in which the plane is destroyed is called a *hull loss accident*

The deadliest aviation-related disaster of any kind, considering fatalities on both the aircraft and the ground, was the destruction of the World Trade Center in New York City on September 11, 2001 with the intentional crashing of American Airlines Flight 11 and United Airlines Flight 175 by Al-qaeda terrorists. The crashes killed 2,988, most of them occupants of the World Trade Center towers or emergency personnel responding to the disaster.

Statistics from Aircraft Crashes Record Office (ACRO)

The Geneva-based Aircraft Crashes Record Office (ACRO) compiles statistics on aviation accidents of aircraft capable of carrying more than six passengers, not including helicopters, balloons, or fighter airplanes. The ACRO announced that the year 2007 was the safest year in aviation since 1963 in terms of number of accidents. There had been 136 accidents registered (compared to 164 in 2006), resulting in a total of 965 deaths (compared to 1,293 in 2006). 2004 was the year with the lowest number of fatalities since the end of World War II, with 766 deaths. The year with most fatalities was 1972, with 3,214 deaths.

year	deaths	No of accidents
2009	1,103	122
2008	884	156
2007	971	147
2006	1,294	166
2005	1,459	185
2004	771	172
2003	1,230	199
2002	1,413	185
2001	1,534	200
2000	1,582	189

Railroad Disasters

A train wreck is a type of disaster involving one or more trains. Train wrecks often occur as a result of miscommunication, as when a moving train meets another train on the same track; or an accident, such as when a train wheel jumps off a track in a derailment; or when a boiler explosion occurs. Train wrecks have often been widely covered in popular media and in folklore.

Space Disasters

Space disasters, either during operations or training, have killed around 20 astronauts and cosmonauts, and a much larger number of ground crew and civilians. These disasters include either malfunctions on the ground, during launch, or in orbit with technology, or of natural forces. Not all space disasters result in human fatalities, for example, unmanned orbiting satellites that drop to the Earth can incinerate and send debris spewing across the sky. One of the worst manned space disasters, the Space Shuttle Challenger explosion of 1986, cost all of the lives on board. The shuttle exploded several seconds after taking off from the launch pad in Cape Canaveral, Florida. Another example is the Space Shuttle Columbia, which disintegrated during a landing attempt over Texas in 2003, with a loss of all 7 astronauts on board.

The worst case in climate destabilization for the long term will result from either a ***"business as usual"*** mode of operation or from *superficial mitigation efforts* that do not radically address the problems. It encompasses both a series of catastrophic impacts to humanity and Planet Earth, and runaway behavior in a dynamic system. Though the catastrophic impacts occur in a number of specific arenas, they must be understood to interact with each other, often resulting in acceleration of effects.

Climate change has begun to affect human health worldwide, with the extent of impacts expected to increase with increasing climate change. Replicable climate models indicate that the concentration of carbon dioxide in the Earth atmosphere may reach approximately 1,000 parts per million (ppm) by the end of the present century and remain above this level for thousands of years. At present, 400 to 600 ppm is considered a "red zone" of danger, and current levels are already approaching 400 ppm; in fact, one participant proposed that adding in CO2 equivalents puts current levels already at 445 to 450 ppm. Scientists believe that once the red zone has been entered, the planet will likely remain within or above the red zone range long enough that both the Greenland and Antarctic ice sheets will melt completely. Unlike the popular literature that suggests that CO2 in the atmosphere is a century-timescale issue, in fact, CO2 recovers on a timescale of 100,000 years. After an equilibration with the oceans, which itself requires a few centuries, there is still a remaining percentage that is neutralized only in reaction with rocks in a process requiring hundreds of thousands of years.

According to the Climate modeler Dr. Andrey Ganopolski, "It should be borne in mind that present-day climate models do not tend to overestimate or exaggerate the magnitude of climate changes in the past. Instead, there is reason to consider climate model simulations as conservative." Accordingly, it is doubtful that the model projection of 1,000 ppm should be dismissed as unlikely or lacking credence, even though it is understood that past climate changes are not a direct analog for the future.

NASA risk assessment expert Dr. Feng Hsu pointed out that an implication of 1,000-ppm concentration of CO2 in the atmosphere, which is approximately two times or more over the tipping point, is clearly an unacceptable level of catastrophic risk that will likely lead to the extinction of humanity. This catastrophic end would be the consequence of either no global strategic adaptation measures for risk averting or ineffective mitigations in today's human activities that affect CO2 levels in the atmosphere.

The direct consequence of the increase of CO2 concentration in the atmosphere is rising temperatures on the globe. By the end of this century, global average temperatures will rise by more than 5 degrees Celsius, with regional rises of more than 10 degrees Celsius, and will continue to rise for centuries. In coming decades typical summer temperatures in Southern Europe and the United States can be expected to rise from 30 degrees to 40 degrees Celsius (105 degrees Fahrenheit). An early taste of this elevation of heat was the 40 degrees Celsius that was considered anomalous in the 2003 heat wave in Europe, when 15,000 deaths in France alone were directly attributable to the heat. Some natural cooling that might be expected from the natural progression of the Earth orbital cycles is not going to ameliorate the warming from fossil fuel CO2.

Indirect effects of the increasing heat are also already evident on the globe. A recent study found that the maximum speed of the strongest hurricanes of the last 25 years increased by 5 meters per second per 1 degree of ocean warming. Since the power and destructive potential of hurricanes are proportional to the cube of velocity, a 50 percent increase in speed would imply a tripling increase of destructive potential. Presently a Category 3 hurricane has a maximum speed of 50 meters per second; a 50 percent increase to 75 meters per second raises the level to a Category 5 hurricane – the most severe category. It is likely that new categories for measuring hurricanes must be introduced, as well as new language, since Category 5 is now considered "catastrophic." Sea levels will also be affected by rising temperatures as ice masses gradually disappear from the planet, melting into ocean and other water bodies. Scientifically based estimates suggest that sea level could rise by up to two meters during the present century, and increases will be measured in meters, not inches, over the next few centuries. Even a one-meter rise, which many scientists anticipate by 2100, will affect at least 150 million people, most of them in Asia, though North America will also experience significant flooding. If a large percentage of the population of Bangladesh is forced to move, where will those people go?

A sea-level rise of 10 meters in coming centuries will affect about 500 million people and submerge 5 million kilometers of land, including loss of most of the Netherlands, to mention just one impacted region. When both the Greenland and Antarctic ice sheets have melted completely, sea levels will have increased by 70 meters. Even 3 degrees C of warming that persists for thousands of years will ultimately result in tens of meters of sea-level change. As mentioned, effects will vary from region to region; in fact, it is possible that some regions will experience rapid cooling at the same time as others record rapid heating. The Atlantic thermohaline circulation is a dangerous component of the climate system because it is capable of rapid reorganization resulting in abrupt climate change, with temperature shifts either up or down by as much as 10 degrees Celsius in a matter of decades. The melting of the ice sheets has an indirect impact on thermohaline circulation; however, it is not possible to say from modeling what the probability of a meridional overturn in circulation is, either in this century or subsequently. Water-related effects will also vary from region to region, with some areas experiencing extraordinary flooding while others see deep, long-lasting droughts.

There are scientists, namely, David Wasdell, who uses a systems dynamics approach based not on modeling but on tracking complex feedback dynamics, said that climate stabilization is not about stopping catastrophic impacts but about stopping runaway behavior in a dynamic system, and he believes that the early stages of runaway climate changes have already commenced, with no naturally occurring negative feedback process able to contain the effect. Most of the systems are already in net amplifying feedback, so *"the hotter the Earth gets, the faster it gets hotter,"* he said. In order to deal with the worst case, humankind will have to generate a negative feedback intervention of sufficient power to overcome and reverse not just what has already occurred, but what continues to occur.

The environmental scientists firmly believe that, in the global heating now under way, the gap between energy received by the Earth from the Sun and energy radiated back out is running at approximately two watts per square meter, and the amount is increasing by about 25 percent per decade, under "business as usual." There was, however, some disagreement about whether climate destabilization is already being accelerated by the feedbacks to a runaway status. However, three tipping points already passed, apparently irreversibly, were identified: (1) the pine bark beetles in northern United States and Canada. The winters are no longer cold enough to kill off the larvae of the beetle, which is killing vast areas of pine trees, adding yet more carbon to the atmosphere; (2) the acidification of the oceans, leading to massive changes in the lower part of the ocean food chain, and (3) the disappearance of the coral reefs in the Caribbean Sea due to increasing temperatures. Other indicators that climate change is already affecting ecosystems were also cited, including changes in hardiness zones for plants.

Dr. Kristie Ebi, an independent consultant and a lead author for the IPCC Fourth Assessment Report on human health, has conducted research on the impacts of climate change for more than a dozen years. She stated: "I am more concerned about health impacts in the next few decades than later this century because the lack of current preparedness suggests that impacts may be larger in the short term, until programs and activities are implemented to increase resilience to extreme weather events and other changes projected to occur with climate change." There are not enough people trained to cope with current climate variability, and funding for training and capacity-building is inadequate. Changing temperatures and precipitation patterns will alter ecosystems, as well as change the geographic range and intensity of transmission of a range of infectious diseases. At present approximately 150,000 people die every year due to climate change impacts; most of these deaths are in children under the age of five living in Africa and Asia. Worldwide, the major climate-sensitive health outcomes of concern are malnutrition, diarrheal disease, and malaria. Other health impacts to expect are increasing illnesses and deaths due to increases in the frequency and intensity of heat waves, flooding events, and other extreme weather events, increases in adverse health outcomes due to air pollution, and increases in the geographic range and incidence of a wide range of food - water-, and vectorborne diseases. Sudden and severe declines in crop yields could lead to large numbers of refugees. In some areas, there is the possibility that climate change could affect the national security.

In is concluded by emphasizing that the real problems today are the speed of the change in climate and where the tipping points are, rather than the size of the change itself, and the wider perspective of global catastrophic risks in which climate change is only one of the problems.

What to do?

How to represent the worst case in a way that communicates effectively to the public and results in action was so important and all of which assume comprehension by ordinary citizens, included:

1. A graphical representation of global population as affected over time, depicting the impact of actual past events as well as anticipated future climate-related vents.
2. A SIM City simulation game that connects the present with future conditions through interactive cause-and-effect linkages. Computer games, films, and similar media created for the purpose of communicating the climate destabilization story should encompass the entire civilizational impact and require, for legitimacy, the backing of solid science as well as oversight by climate scientists.
3. A "disaster yardstick" to graphically depict the response to the question: "How bad could it get, really?" Levels described on the downward course of the yardstick would include breakdown of the social order, failed states and anarchy, and ultimately human extinction. Narratives of regional impacts might be associated with differing levels.
4. Narratives or stories or cartoon-style books to illustrate health issues and detailed regional impacts related to, for example:
   a. Extended drought in sub-Saharan Africa, including disease impacts and the world's response to 5 million climate refugees.
   b. Water issues, showing different regions impacted by too much, too little, wrong place, wrong time, including a Category 5 hurricane striking Miami, Florida; storm surge activity in Bangladesh that puts 200 million Bangladeshis on the move, with ramifications for food and water supplies

as well as disease epidemics; the impact to cities that would be vulnerable in a 6-meter sea-level rise, with millions of people hit simultaneously; water wars in places on the globe where complex border issues and mixed populations have already created extremely tense relations.

c. Disappearing ice on the planet and what this means to different places on the globe. For example, a roughly 17 per cent loss of ice in recent years in the Tibet and Himalayan region will have cascading effects to people downstream in India and China, such as acute freshwater shortages, loss of agricultural production and hunger crises, eventually leading to global-scale chaos and wars, likely triggered by panic mass migration.

d. The thermohaline circulation of the Atlantic Ocean and how a sudden reorganization of it would result in abrupt climate change, with varying impacts to different locales. The participants felt that there is a need for good specification of scenarios, timelines, and stories identifying the worst case. A useful project would be mapping out the time frames for the worst case in drought, hurricanes, sea-level rise, tropical disease, and so on.

Any graphical representation created for the public should be usable by policymakers and governmental decision-makers. Additionally, "cyberspace situation rooms" would improve information and knowledge coherence for decision-makers.

Representations of physical extremes should emphasize not only the magnitude of the individual event but, more importantly, that unprecedented events will occur in number, in parallel, exacerbating nonlinear patterns. It is likely to be most effective to focus representations on near-term events, while noting the longer-term risks and citing historical analogs. Risk assessments must be performed to determine the likelihood of various possible events, and a ranking of events according to the assessed risk would be helpful.

Critical element in the response to climate destabilization was identified as *"thinking differently."* Humankind today must begin thinking differently about a proper response to climate destabilization.

REVEIW QUESTIONS

Short Answer Type Questions

1. What do you understand by the term 'disaster'?
2. Define disaster management
3. Write a note on the hazardous effects of major disaster
4. List down the forms of natural disaster
5. List down the forms of various man-made disaster
6. Write a note on lahar.
7. What is meant by an avalanche risk?
8. Write a note on CBRNs.
9. Write a note on threat imposed by nuclear and biological weapons
10. Illustrate space disasters with an example.

Essay Type Questions

1. Trace the evolution of disaster management.
2. Explain the various forms of natural disaster and its vulnerability.
3. Explain the various forms of man-made disaster and its hazardous impacts.
4. Critically analyze what to be done from the humans' side for not being at the receiving end of a disaster.

CHAPTER 2

DISASTER RESPONSE

REASONS FOR CONCERN

The international humanitarian relief system is just now beginning to meet the challenge of working with the displaced. There are three principle reasons for concern by relief agencies. One is that displaced persons are often ineligible to receive relief and assistance available to refugees (individuals who have crossed an international border seeking protection). A second reason is that the displaced are often insecure about relying on their own government for protection. A third reason is the obstacle of national sovereignty that limits outside agencies to assist this population.

The variety of possible situations generating displaced persons makes generalisations difficult, but the following may be experienced in varying degrees.

- Loss of means of livelihood.
- Communities becoming separated from any services previously provided.
- Loss of normal sources of food.
- Lack of shelter and household necessities.
- Lack of fuel for cooking.
- Lack of potable water.
- Communicable diseases and overcrowding.

- Additional burdens particularly for women heads of households.
- Possibly large numbers of unaccompanied children.
- Loss of land tenure.
- Possible communication and logistics problems.
- Insecurity due to tensions and military activities.

Not to be forgotten is the population that may remain at home and, even though they are not "trapped in combat areas", they nonetheless are in places that are hard to reach because of political, logistical and/or security obstacles. They may suffer many of the above problems and be isolated from international humanitarian relief.

Disaster Response Objectives

- Appropriate application of current technology can prevent much of the death, injury and economic disruption resulting from disasters.
- Morbidity and mortality resulting from disasters differ according to the type and location of the event.
- In any disaster, prevention should be directed towards reducing
  - (1) Losses due to the disaster event itself;
  - (2) Losses resulting from the mismanagement of disaster relief.

Therefore, the public health objectives of disaster management can be stated as follows:

1. Prevent unnecessary morbidity, mortality and economic loss resulting directly from the disaster.
2. Eliminate morbidity, mortality and economic loss directly attributable to mismanagement of disaster relief efforts. Significant aspects in development, an important issue which deserves consideration in the context of Disaster Management is the bottlenecks of the development processes of the planned development.

All plans for development have greater chances for success if the relevant cultural and social factors are integrated into the planning. That integration, however, should not add yet another extraneous load on already overburdened planners. Social and cultural considerations must be so presented that they are plainly appropriate to the problems at hand and are clearly useful for makers of development decisions. There is no gain from deluging planners with data they cannot deploy, with recommendations too wordy to be carefully read or too abstruse to be readily understood. There is, however, great potential gain in broadening development policies so that they include significant forces that have hitherto been largely overlooked (Mandelbaum, 1981).

All the social and behavioural sciences can be tapped for this purpose. Anthropologists have special resources to offer (Mandelbaum, 1978). Their emphasis on a holistic view disposes them to take into account the social matrix in which particular problems are embedded. Their practice of fieldwork directs attention to development as perceived from within, how the people understand, accept or reject introduced innovations (C.F. Srinivas, 1977; Wallmen, 1977). Anthropologists are also inclined to relate what they learn in the microview to the macroview, to some general perspective on the human career (c.f. Patch and McMorrow, 1977).

The concept of development is illusive. To some it may mean change; (but all changes are not necessarily development) to others it may be alleviation of poverty and well-being. Still to some others 'development' represents an increase in the capacities of a society to organise for its own objective and to carry out its programmes more effectively. Some hold the Marxian conception. Thus, many of us speak of development with reference to 'social', 'cultural', 'political' and 'economic' with the qualifying connotation or adjective or of a complex amalgam of all these. However, our reference is to the tribal society and with their problems, the resolution of which is so-called tribal development.

There is no one road to development and certainly not the identical sequence traversed by countries now deemed to be developed. Whatever course is urged or coerced by planners and political leaders, each major group within a nation, eventually judges what the purpose of development is for them, and for whom the development bells toll. The outcome of any model of development depends ultimately on the effectiveness of their participation (De Kadt, 1974; Eisenstadt, 1977).

The past decade has witnessed an extraordinary increase in the number and extent of natural disasters. As Kofi Annan, Secretary General of the United Nations, points out, "The facts are startling. The costs of weather-related disasters in 1998 exceeded the costs of all such disasters in the decade of the 1980s. In the Caribbean, the hurricanes designated George and Mitch, killed more than 13,000 people, with Mitch being the deadliest Atlantic storm in 200 years. Major floods hit India, Nepal, Bangladesh and much of East Asia, with thousands killed. Two-thirds of Bangladesh was inundated for months, leaving millions homeless. There were three times as many great natural hazards in the 1990s as in the 1960s, while disaster costs increased more than nine-fold in the same period."

It is true that before other measures for development can be effective, certain basic conditions must prevail. People cannot do much construction for the future if many of them are struggling for more subsistence survival. Nor can development programmes take shape if a state is torn with turmoil, its land more the scene of battles than of building. But given such basic requirements, people do respond effectively to programmes for development if the programmes are presented in terms they can understand and accept (Mandelbaum, 1981). When the people of a country become assured that their basic material needs are reasonably well available, then their aspirations for development are likely to turn to the quality of their lives.

Anthropologists now have more opportunity than before to contribute to development. Their own ethical and procedural problems in the field have been sufficiently arised to permit such work to proceed at a fast pace. Planners and administrators are coming to realise that their previous models have slighted some critical elements, namely the cultures and societies of the people whom and on whom development plans were enacted (cf. World Bank, 1978: 33-42). Anthropologists not only view development problems from the perspective of the people, they also try to understand particular projects as parts of a larger system. And very frequently, it is the system of social relations and cultural understandings that is critical for the success or failure of projects. For, as, we now recognize, development is not only the adaptation of advanced technology and economic programming, nor is it just another term for change. Development consists of purposive efforts by a people, led by public figures and planners, to organize themselves in new technical, cultural, and social ways. These are ways that will enable them to achieve the style and quality of life which they aspire. When their aspirations shift, the direction of development efforts much shift accordingly (Mandelbaum, 1981).

India is one of the few nations of the world noted for its tribal concentration. According to the 1981 census, the tribals in India account for 7.18 per cent of the total population. About 80 per cent of'them live in remote forest areas and hill tracks without any access to modern socio-economic inputs.

Although there are ethnographic variations in terms of their 'anthropological identity', most tribals share certain characteristics: nature of rurality, speciality of illiteracy, economic backwardness and social deprivation. Their standard of living, judged by the standard measures of income position, calorie-intake, nutritional norms, educational standards and 'Physical Quality Life Index' (PQLI), does not fit anywhere within the scope and ambit of the Planning Commission's stylised standards, the employment problem of these communities cannot be discussed in isolation, for most of them are unemployed and a very few are engaged in traditional occupations.

Their earnings, apart from the monetary angle, do not even conform to the barest minimum necessary for their sustenance. The expert definitions of the 'poverty line' or 'poverty gap' for these groups have yet to be defined or redefined.

The origin of the present day Integrated Tribal Development Projects (ITDP) can be traced back to 1950, when the Government of India initiated the National Extension Schemes (NES) in 1951, with the intension of intensifying the block level development activities to raise the general standard of living of the weaker sections. When the Block level activities became a blockade to the development of the weaker sections therein, a new scheme was reinstated in the name of the Tribal Development Block (TDB) in 1962. These blocks were able to initiate some efforts on the social welfare front of tribals.

However, since these programmes were patterned after the development efforts attempted in the earlier periods, they turned out to be not in tune with the tribal context and culture. But, the experiment over a period often years or more proved that the emancipation of tribal communities was a "complex" process with serious socio-political and economic implications. The powerful feudal and vested economic interests, therefore, had to be fought against and new modes of role relations had to be established to ensure tribal claims.

Consistent with the norms and directives of concerned departments, the Pilot Report, Preliminary Report, Primary Report, Pre-revised First Draft Report, Revised Confidential Report and Final Reports (strictly confidential and official) were prepared in all States. The State Planning Boards and Tribal Welfare Departments were entrusted with the task of preparing periodic reviews and studies on 'specific problem oriented tribal development issues'. Inspired by the heavy budget allocation for tribal development, the experts in the field were eager to conduct national and international seminars and conferences at the cost of the half appeased starving tribals. 'Action-oriented' researches were held under the expert guidance of eminent scholars in the field weeded to tribal life and dedicated to the welfare of the weaker sections of society. Resultantly, the volume of 'Reports' increased at an alarming pace along with the number of Institutes and 'Directors', Joint Directors, Deputy Directors, Additional Directors, Assistant Directors, Acting Directors and Special Executive Directors. But at the end of it all, the truth is sad indeed for the only comment that can be made is: 'poor are my tribals, rich are their protectors'. This is a fact that, the more the plans, the more are the tribals moving from 'poverty to absolute pauperism'. What they needed is not expert seminars, comprehensive reports or directives from ministers and ministries, but a time bound solution to their century old socioeconomic problems with which they are struggling. Nevertheless, credit does go to the planners for what they have planned, rather than for what they have been able to do.

It is a fact that in all ages those who think must act for and govern those who toil for them. The people at the grassroots level must feel proud of their more fortunate countrymen whose vision and learning can be of benefit to the more unfortunate masses. But the most distressing fact of our present day nationalism is that, instead of the elite and educated community representing the 'brain, and consciousness of a nation', as the legitimate spokesmen of the illiterate masses — their dream, the custodians of their interest we have become actually anxious to exploit whenever and wherever possible. Now we are aliens within our own national boundaries, strangers to each other and even to our own people. The ideas and beliefs of the nation are not shared by the masses or the people at the lower rung of the ladder, but only by a small class of affluent few for whom there is nothing more appealing than acquisition at any cost. They are clear about their own ends but not the means, thus shattering the fond dreams of the destitute millions who recoil with horror and dismay at what is generated by the liberal leaders of our political economy.

We are taught to be obedient to the law of the land 'but not to be against the power of the few'. We are taught that 'the law will take care of us', but not 'who will take care of the law' the 'masses or the mightly few'. If the achievement of political freedom is a proven historical and necessary event, the achievement of economic freedom is the natural right of every human being, a matter of the utmost urgency.

The genuine question that arises now is: should the government of the country be left to the elected representatives of the minority (in the factual sense) of their own party without any ideology to represent the masses. Should it be reduced to the level of street demonstrations and conspiratorial meeting? Even then, the masses are supreme. They must be trusted to define their economic objectives and to work for their strategies of development. The theories and models must become relevant to their needs and not become objects for 'soap bubble oratory', we must test our development theories so that we do not degenerate into a twentieth century off-shoot of nineteenth century imperial legalits.

When social thinking is tardy and parochial, the power structure tends to keep an ambivalent attitude to institutional changes. This fact is evident in many fields of the development process in India. Thus, the social thinkers always become the worst enemies of a society which lives on the wages of exploitation. Pretence of action is worse than inaction. Inaction generates resistance and pretence distrust. Thus, there is a fundamental difference between organised resistance and organised distrust. Both lead to conflict. But the latter invariably introduces an element of perversity.

When programmes of development are initiated without certain institutional changes, one of the inevitable outcomes to begin with, is the strengthening of already entrenched social interests. This is what is happening in the case of tribal development in India. It is a game without rules. The brave words of the Planning Commission, except for sentimental potentialities, have failed to come to grips with the entrenched interests of tribal planners and protectors.

The party in power was unable to create any new and more effective instrument for the implementation of its social and economic policies than 'the crushing bureaucratic machinery' which has proved unsuitable beyond all doubt. In this context, advocacy of radical policies at the highest level of plan action does not get translated into fact. In fact, as policy declarations become more radical, the gap between the preaching and the practice becomes strikingly evident. So it is wiser to retreat to realistic plans rather than radical phraseology to which partymen are heroically accustomed. Therefore, it is not surprising that the present mode of development which has been stimulated over the years can only meet with failure.

The positive discrimination policy of the state on behalf of the disadvantaged groups and weaker sections of the society is the most effective way to help the tribals and weaker sections enter the modern mainstream. However, the quasi-structural frame, when linked with abstract development theories with the inbuilt institutional flavour, can only thwart the various measures for poverty eradication. The feasibility of measures of development through the superimposition of democratic institutions on a non-egalitarian social structure, is questionable; it stems from cynical and quacks, really, who believe in the self-percolation effect of the benefits of development towards the lower strata of the society. Such practice based on abstract theories has proved that well intentioned state intervention often ends up in accomplishing the very opposite of the objectives laid out in the plans and proposals. Any number of solutions to the problem of economic development of weaker sections in areas perennially handicapped by basic infrastructural constraints, coupled with gross financial misuse, organisational impotence, incorrect priorities and faulty identification processes will only help to aggravate the socio-economic tension which prevails within the backward tribal regions. Finally, the eruption of violence and bloodshed, in whatever form that we see in India, is not an accident but the inevitable outcome of the development experience.

Over the last three decades now, we have been planning, doing research and making policies for positive state intervention towards the most obviously disadvantaged groups in the society. But, by and large, the sad truth prevails that, by now the lack of political will has been amply demonstrated and gaps exist between the policy and the legislations, between the law and its implementation. Perhaps, there is no sphere of government action in our country which has shown such a deep hiatus between precept and practice as in the domain of planning for the weaker sections and socially deprived groups.

Despite all our integrated plan programmes and concerted efforts, the tribals still remain mostly disintegrated within our society. Unfortunately, planners are yet to define how to integrate and what to integrate, and why at all to integrate, if integration is a self-permeating process of economic development. But, it provokes us to think that if disintegration is the basic concealed objective under the disguise of integrated development, then nothing could be better done.

To bring the tribals into the mainstream of modern life, still a large gap has to be made up. But it is a reality that the tribals are much more socio-economically isolated and even if development is ensured, they are often dragged into subproletarian servitude by the reactionary forces of a society which lives on the wages of exploitation. The statutory reservations, discriminations, special provisions, guarantee of minimum needs, etc., as a means of social change is, no doubt, a welcome approach. This will bring about change in educational programmes, occupational mobility, cultural conditioning, redistribution and would also raise the overall competitive level of disadvantaged groups in what they are able to attain by their own effort and means.

No doubt, schemes and special provisions are obviously a help towards this end, but in the absence of comprehensive remedial measures to check the alteration processes of exploitative organs, they can only lead to social conflict and structural dislocation within already wounded social patterns. The reality is that the tribal plans look elegant and egalitarian, in appearance but the conspired practise makes the approach shabby and inegalitarian, as now the areas of elite catchment have widened to enlightened towns of 'integrated social groups'.

So the existing measures to improve the socio-economic condition of tribals must dissolve into a cohesive whole of the society of which the whole is larger than the sum of its part. But the question is, how to dissolve and what are the norms of division. Even otherwise, the virtual exclusion of wider objectives and substitution of temporary devices is only a conditional measure which makes the returns negative through shortsighted and misconceived policies which are objectively questionable and practically refutable (Verghese, V. Alexander, 1983).

Sometimes, the uncertainty of consequences of change among the tribals also block the developmental processes meant for them. They would rather go through a life which is known or familiar, than make a change where the consequences are uncertain. Fear of failure in the new ventures or new roles may deter them from taking advantage of the whatever little new opportunities provided to them. However, it does not mean that they do not like to live and lead the changed way of life, but the element of fairness sometimes resists the development process. An attempt towards the solution of the issues of why to approach and what to approach, may facilitate the tribal development process.

Moreover, a study covering about eleven countries, revealed some interesting trends in the context of social structures. Those who held positions in the centre (the top) were 'open-minded' but sceptical, they possessed all the intellectual means for reconsidering their strategy, but they were not willing to introduce or accept major changes especially if those endangered their position. On the other hand, it was found that those at the periphery (bottom) were dogmatic, less educated, dissatisfied with their situation but without the initiative to change it, often not even aware of their own interest but eagerly advocating changes which they assumed would imply a development for the better. The 'top' predicted developments and achievements for which they did not show enthusiasm whereas those at the 'bottom' expressed their hopes for what they did not really believe would happen.

The 'top' who are close to the instruments of communication and decision-making would be the ones to take initiatives, to plan and appear to be effectively in charge of what had to be done to meet the future. At the same time, those at the "bottom", convinced that their ideas would not be realised anyhow, would do little to promote them. What they did would matter little anyhow, so long as they did it only at the individual level. One of the major stumbling blocks in the way of united action by those at the bottom is that while they do have quite a bit of change-oriented, thinking, it is rarely that the same idea prevails throughout those who constitute the periphery.

These are some observations based on a study across eleven nations which hold true in most of the hierarchical structures. In this context, any socio-economic change planned for groups occupying positions which are economically, socially, or both, vulnerable should take into account their feelings, their attitudes and the role of the structures — social, cultural, political, administrative — in shaping and reinforcing them. Therefore, improvements sought to be brought about among disadvantaged groups of people should not only take measures to unsettle the existing social structure but also modify the attitudes reflecting the dictates of that social structure (Muthayya, B.C. 1983).

Lack of interest in the tribal development by the administrative and executive personnel have also held up the developmental processes to a great extent along with lack of proper training to the administrative personnels, meant to implement the ambitious tribal development. No doubt, statistics tell us an impressive story of tribal development. Thus, each five-year plan allocation in respect of their preceding one reveals an increase in the outlay and the fifth plan allotment of a sum of Rs. 1182 crore marked a phenomenal increase from earlier plan outlays. But an increase in the allocation of the outlays is no longer, a real achievement in the field of tribal development. And it may be remarked in the words of Adelmann and Morris that "hundreds of millions of disparately poor throughout the world have been hurt rather than helped by economic development". We often identify the tribal development with that of the economic development. We often assume that without economic development, the real development cannot be achieved. No doubt, we cannot expect too much of the success of developmental schemes of the tribals when the basic needs are not assured to them. But it happens so that in doing it, we overemphasise the economic development as if the tribal development is wedded to the economists and divorced from anthropologists. In absence of social and cultural heritage of the tribal population, the schemes result into failure. It is not seriously taken into account both by the public and bureaucracy because of the fact that government schemes need not always succeed.

Moreover, the developmental programmes meant for the tribals are uniformly planned not keeping in mind the fact that there is a differential development among the tribals themselves and consequently of their needs. It may be observed that there is a well-marked differential development among those tribes who have adopted or are practising Christianity and those who are non-Christian. It may be added here again that the tribals who are still primitive or have dwellings on the hill, forests, and are not much in contact with the forces and agents of change of the plains, still show a poor state of affairs in contrast to the tribes which are on plains and to those who are exposed to the forces of industrialisation and urbanisation. It is evident from these facts that the developmental plans for the tribals should have a wide range of variability and should be formulated accordingly. Thus, the uniformity in the frames of plans, being away from the needs of a particular tribal community and its differentiation from the needs of another particular tribal group has also resulted in their failure. What it requires is not a separate plan for each tribal group, a long agenda, but must be in conformity with the classificatory tribal communities.

When we look at the tribal development in the state of Bihar, we are soon confronted with the sad picture emerges even after a concerted effort made in the last 30 years planning. It is still an experiment in the held, the cause and effect relationship remains to be inhibitory and inferences are far ahead to be drawn.

Studies conducted recently to examine the tribal participation in the developmental schemes through the institution of Panchayati Raj in the four Blocks of Ranchi district, reveal an increased participation. The latter is of utmost importance for the successful implementation of the developmental schemes meant for them. The figure that we have well explains the developmental efforts of the tribals for whom the developmental schemes are meant, but the stray cases cannot take the place of generalisations. Moreover, the fruits of the project are taken by the non-tribals as the study reveals instead of the tribals.

Studies conducted on the Sauria Paharia of Jharkhand reveal a distressing picture. The tribe is facing extinction but no tangible solution has come up uptil now. The bureaucratic display of development achievement is a misnomer and bleak. There should be a close understanding between the implementing officials and the poor tribals in order to attain the goal of real development. There should be no gap between the officials and the tribals. Sometimes the tribal elite acts as a 'mediator' between the tribals and the officials, the bulk of the fruits of the schemes go in the share of the so-called elite group rather than those who really deserve it. Moreover, there should be a close understanding between the economists and anthropologists not at the planning level but also up to the evaluation stage. Such a wedding is not only inevitable but also realistic in the sense of improving in present state of affairs. A training to the officials for a fixed period is no longer a parameter to the fact that he/she has become competent enough to undertake the project and its success is imminent. A coach of class and an operation in the field are two distinct identities and cannot replace or clash but rather reinforce each other. The symbiosis can be of immense value for the effective launching of the schemes and its success is the objective before us to improve their lot.

The cooperative credit movement was started to get the farmers out of the clutches of the money lenders. Now the problem is how to get the cooperative movement out of the 'clutches' of the vested interests. It seems nobody has a solution to this. Panchayati Raj was introduced with a view to increasing people's participation in development efforts. The basic idea was to get the development activities out of the 'clutches' of bureaucracy. Now, the problem is how to keep local bodies out of the 'clutches' of the local power-oriented politicians. In short, the obvious conclusion is that the failure to improve the lot of the tribals in the tribal areas, so far, has been the result of a complex interplay of economic and political forces and many maladies in the administrative machinery. It seems the failure has been partly due to wrong policies and partly due to interest weakness in the political and economic institutions and administrative machinery, in addition to the faulty planning. All need careful investigations and corrections to realise the fruits of the tribal development in real sense. If we are really concerned for the development of the tribe then we have to think for their development in terms of their 'Felt' need and not in terms of their

'Assessed' need. What is being done till todate is that the needs are assessed by those who are strangers to them, which results into negative development. Data gathered from various departments of the State and Central Governments engaged in the development of tribes and reveal that approximately Rs. 3.75 lakh has been spent so far per square metre on their development. Density of population per square metre is two in tribal Bihar. Even if this amount would had been given as dole to each tribe, which comes to approximately Rs. 1.87 lakh it would have helped and reached each tribal.

An example of providing safe drinking water to Paharias without any cost but on which crores of rupees were spent and the result was zero, well explains the intentions and motive of the authorities involved. Providing drinking water through experiment did not involve any expenditure as it was made available with the indigenous materials. Bamboo is available in abundance among Sauria Paharia. Inner portion of the bamboo is hollow. One piece of bamboo was jointed with another and in this way 20 to 30 bamboos, sometimes more than this helped in bringing safe drinking water to the doorstep from the natural spring. These bamboos are periodically changed in order to keep the water safe. Likewise use of milk was also introduced in the community. These examples demonstrate that if the 'Felt Need' of the community is designed and implemented through participatory development then the chances of 'positive development' in the community is higher. These days a good number of national and regional seminars are organised for the development of various state including Bihar and a good number of recommendations are being made. But the pre-condition for any development is the human behaviour and its management which is missing the 'participatory development' or the 'empowered development' is a development from within the community for which understanding of human feeling is a must probably here anthropologist have a great role to play.

Thus it is evident from the foregoing discussions that the Anthropology of Disaster Management broadly discusses the Natural Disaster as well as the man-made disaster. At the beginning of 21st century the anthropologists are more concerned with the man-made disasters. Researches and development in science have minimised the occurrence of natural disasters but through planned development the occurrences of man-made disasters have maximised. Death of innocent people in explosions and bomb blasts, proxy wars, sex scandal of USA President, Bill Clinton, spread of HIV and AIDS, ethnic violence in Canada, etc. are a few glaring examples of man-made disasters. In course of time we learnt the art of controlling the natural disasters but we are yet to learn the management of disasters caused by man. Majority of disasters of 21st century will be due to human failure. The emotions, human feelings, fellow feelings, compassion, fear from God, etc., have evaporated and have been dried in human beings due to scientific and planned development. If anthropology has to survive it has to take care of such disasters and UNESCO has rightly declared the 21st Century as the century of Anthropology.

We must, therefore, stress at world level meetings of anthropologists that development is for mankind rather than mankind being there for development.

R.K. Celly and T.N. Gupta in their article "Dimensions of Natural Disaster Management in India" in Shelter (Oct. 12,1999) observe that "a natural hazard is an event of nature, which causes sudden disruption to the normal life of a society and causes damage to life and property, to such an extent that normal, social and economic mechanisms available to the society are inadequate to restore normalcy". Viewed in this manner, a host of natural phenomena cause disasters to a society, whether they are related to an occurrence in microenvironment or not. In macro terms, the hazards, which cause widespread damage and disruption in India are floods, cyclones, earthquakes and landslides.

The humanitarian community does a remarkable job in responding to disasters. But the most important task in the medium and long-term is to strengthen and broaden programmes which reduce the number and cost of disasters in the first place. While we should continue to improve and strengthen our response capacity, we need to engage in working together to build a "global culture of prevention". This means greater efforts to reduce vulnerability to natural hazards in the first place.

As we enter the beginning of the new millennium, the International Decade for Natural Disaster Reduction (IDNDR) is proved to have contributed, with all its partners worldwide, to fostering a "global culture of prevention" for the 21st Century. To build on the progress achieved during the IDNDR, we have to act decisively, so that disaster reduction becomes an essential element of government policies. Recalling the Geneva Mandate adopted at the IDNDR Programme Forum, we have to adopt and implement policy measures at the international, regional, national and local levels aimed at reducing the vulnerability of our societies to natural disasters. These measures should have as main objectives the establishment of hazard resistant communities, the protection of people from the threat of disasters and the safeguarding of our natural and economic resources and of our social well-being.

Mr. K. Rajan, Adviser, Planning Commission, in his Article, "Natural Disaster Management in National Development— An Indian Perspective" outlines the following adversities, which befall people and the area.

- Loss of crops and availability of essentials like food and agricultural commodities;

- Loss of employment opportunities in the area where natural disaster occurs, particularly rural employment;
- Problems of health and diseases arising both from insufficient availability of the basic necessities causing malnourishment, hunger, etc., or lack of the availability of good and hygienic drinking water;
- Financial distress caused to the farming community and those dependent on land which affect their ability to withstand hard conditions immediately following the occurrence of the natural disaster but also importantly, their ability to recover well enough before the next cropping season and take full advantage of normal conditions which may prevail;
- Impact on industrial sector due to loss of production of raw materials, reduce generation of power, etc.; and
- Lastly, the impact of the disaster on the cattle wealth. V. Suresh has rightly summed up that natural disasters, which damage national economies and produce hardships for large sections of the population, are one of the single largest concerns for most nations. Human settlements are frequently affected by natural disasters — earthquakes, floods, hurricanes, cyclones, landslides, sea erosions — which take a heavy toll on human lives, destroy buildings and infrastructure and have far reaching economic and social consequences for communities.

Select Tragic Incidents

When all over India, people were celebrating their Republic Day, Gujarat experienced its worst natural calamity after independence. The earthquake which struck on 26th January 2001 at 8.46 hours measuring 6.9 on the Richter Scale, hit certain regions of Gujarat state, very hard. The tremor left behind huge devastation of life and property, both private and public and created utter panic, chaos and trauma among the people.

It has been 50 years since Gujarat witnessed an earthquake and therefore most of the people did not know what to do, except that those who could rush out of their houses in whatever state they were in.

It was only after getting over from the terror and shock of the earthquake tremor that the people began to think about the situation of neighbours, other cities, and other areas of the state and the country. Gradually, the disaster sinked, the cries of the injured and bodies trapped inside the debris began to be heard by others.

It was a calamity of unprecedented magnitude which caused large-scale damage to houses over extensive areas in Gujarat and also resulted in the break-down of vital infrastructure.

Gujarat Earthquake

- Severe earthquake of magnitude 6.9 on Richter scale occurred at 0846 hours.
- Epicentre 20 km. Northeast of Bhuj.
- Impact felt in various parts of the county; Many parts of Gujarat severely affected.
- Colossal damage to life and property in Gujarat; Kutch district adversely affected. No reports on damage from other parts of the country.
- After shocks still being received; more than 400 already received.

Damage at a Large Scale

- 7904 villages in 182 talukas in 21 districts affected.
- 7633 affected villages in Zones III to (5690 in Zone III, 1062 in Zone IV and 881 in Zone V).
- 1.59 crore out of 3.77 crore population affected.
- More than 19800 deaths so far; about 18200 in Kuteh district alone.

Affected Areas by Calamities

Districts Affected	Talukas families	No. of Villages	No. of affected
Surendranagar	Chotila	112	4919
Dhangadra	64	8043	
Lakhtar	43	2023	
Limbdi	60	715	
Malwad	67	8790	
Sayla	67	620	
Patdi	89	9198	
Vadhwan	35	11012	
Mudi	58	4593	
Chuda	38	520	
Jamnagar	Bhanvad	7	432

Jamjodhpur	15		
Kalawad	5	1195	
Jamnagar	13	2064	
Okhamandal	24	886	
Kalyanpur	12	327	
Bharuch	Amod	22	84
Vagra	56	653	
Jambusasr	71	6585	
Rajkot	Malia	7	700

Source: Ministry of Agriculture, GOI, New Delhi.

- 1.66 lakhs injured (1.36 lakh in Kutch district); 20,717 seriously injured.
- 232 persons missing in Kutch; Cattle deaths— 20712.
- Houses destroyed — 1.72 lakh (pucca), 1.67 lakh (kachcha) and 1.16 lakh (huts); Houses partially damaged — 4.88 lakh (pucca), 3.45 lakh (kachcha) and 0.34 lakh (huts).
- Preliminary estimates of damage — Rs. 21,262 crore as indicated here.

	(Rs. in crore)
Personal properties	387.00
Household properties	11195.00
Public utilities	600.00
Public infrastructure and amenities	1080.00
Industrial establishment	5000.00
Commercial establishment	3000.00

GOVERNMENT OPERATIONS IN DISASTER RESPONSE

Central Government Operations

- National Crisis Management Committee (NCMC) under Cabinet Secretary and the Cabinet met immediately on 26.1.2001 for taking immediate measures.
- Krishi Control Room was activated and started functioning round the clock from 26.1.2001.

- Armed and Para-military Forces were deployed immediately on rescue and relief operations.
- 23,500 Army troops and 3,000 Para-military Force personnel were deployed.
- Air Force deployed 48 aircrafts including helicopters and carried over 950 sorties for evacuating injured persons and for carrying relief, teams, equipments/material, etc.
- Navy made available 3 ships and 2 ships were converted into hospitals.
- Satellite phones, hotlines, HAM radios and mobile phones were pressed into services.
- Teams of doctors and medicine/equipments arranged and sent immediately.
- Empowered Group of Ministers (EGoM) under Home Minister was set up; 4 meetings of EGoM held within 15 days.
- EGoM and NCMC were regularly monitoring the situation.
- Prime Minister held meeting with leaders of all parties/groups on 3.2.2001.
- As a follow-up, 37-member National Committee on Disaster Management (NCDM) setup under Chairmanship of PM; 1st meeting of NCDM held on 18.2.2001.
- All Central Ministries/Departments and agencies were assisting in relief operations.
- Immediate assistance of Rs. 500 crore from NCCF was released by GOI on 30.1.2001.
- Railways have restored the damaged tracks in BG/MG sections.
- Telecom service was restored in all 147 exchanges by - 2.2.2001.
- Civil Aviation arranged free transportation of relief materials and arranged transportation facilities for relief materials from abroad.
- External Affairs made arrangements for issue of 15 days visa at entry point without delay, to the relief teams from foreign countries.
- Ministry of Finance (Deptt. of Expenditure) arranged relaxation of Overdraft Regulation Scheme.
- Rs. 10 crore was released from PM's National Relief Fund.

- Deptt. of Food & Public Distribution allotted 1 lakh tonnes of foodgrains and released in advance 10,000 MTs of levy sugar.
- Regular monitoring of medical facilities at DGHS Headquarters, New Delhi.
- Adequate quantities of diesel and kerosene allotted.
- Ministry of Power arranged 19 large DG sets for utilisation of GEB at Bhuj/Anjar.
- Powergrid/NTPC were engaged in repair/recommissioning of 10 GEB major sub-stations.
- PEC sanctioned loan of Rs. 100 crore for rehabilitation/reconstruction of transmission and distribution system; REC sanctioned loan of Rs. 100 crore to GEB.
- Ministry of Rural Development made additional allocation of Rs. 250 crore for constructing earthquake resistant houses for BPL families; assistance of Rs. 22,000 per dwelling unit was proposed for the affected districts.

State Government Operations

(a) Relief

- In death cases, payment of Rs. 1 lakh to adult and Rs, 60,000 to minor.
- Rs. 13.23 crore death compensation paid within one month.
- Cash dole paid — Rs. 50.43 crore to 7.55 lakh families.
- 45 damaged sub-stations and 255 damaged feeders fully energised/restored.
- Power supply restored in all 925 disrupted villages.
- Water supply restored in all 1340 affected villages through pipes (994), tankers (277) and other sources (69).
- Heavy equipments, namely cranes/JCBs, bulldozers/excavators, loaders/dumpers/trucks, jeep/ambulances, gas cutters deployed in large numbers.
- All ration shops operational; Essential commodities (foodgrains, vegetables, edible oil, kerosene, diesel, petrol) supplied.
- Shelter material (tents — about 51,000 and tarpaulin/GC sheets — 2.84 lakhs) supplied.
- Grass supplied free of cost for 30 days @ 4 kg. per day per animal in affected areas.

(b) Rehabilitation and Reconstruction

- Senior officers deployed to oversee relief and rehabilitation measures.

  New Department of Earthquake Relief set up.

- Gujarat Disaster Management Authority (GDMA) under Chief Minister set up to implement rehabilitation packages.
- 229 identified for relocation; package for 4 towns (Bhuj, Anjar, Bhachau and Rapar) being worked out.
- 4 packages of rehabilitation declared:
  - (i) Relocation and reconstruction of completely destroyed villages,
  - (ii) Assistance in severely affected areas in Zones IV and V for in-situ reconstruction,
  - (iii) Scale of assistance for destroyed/partially destroyed houses in areas away from epicentre,
  - (iv) Corporation/Area Development Authority (except Bhuj, Anjar, Bhachau and Rapar).
- There is no separate adoption policy and it is part of the rehabilitation/ reconstruction package.
- Restoration at new sites with essential infrastructure.
- All damaged/destroyed huts to be replaced by dwelling units.
- Repair/reconstruction of required public infrastructure conforming to earthquake resistant standards by the State.
- Plan of Action for adoption of affected villages.

Package for Industries

- Comprehensive package for damaged industrial units announced on 25.2.2001.
- Benefits include royalty exemption, concession for construction materials.
- Package also includes concession for cottage industries.
- Timely relief requirement of 3.27 lakh temporary shelters projected.
- About 2.75 lakh families covered.
- 48327 tents, 2.50 lakh tarpaulin and 2.06 lakh GC sheets distributed.

Various State Governments' Aid

- Contributed total financial assistance of Rs. 48.68 crore (Andhra Pradesh, Assam, Bihar, Chhattisgarh, Delhi, Daman & Diu, Himachal Pradesh, J & K, Karnataka, Kerala, Madhya Pradesh, Maharashtra, Manipur, Meghalaya, Rajasthan, Tamil Nadu, Tripura, Uttar Pradesh, West Bengal).
- Also provided assistance in kind — food, food materials, shelter material (tents, blankets, plastic sheets), medicine, medical teams, water, equipments, etc.
- Assisting in relief operation with men and material.
- Despatched several loads of relief material.
- Assisting in adoption of affected villages.

Foreign Aid

- International community responded generously.
- More than 70 countries and 17 international organisations provided assistance to the State Government to the tune of Rs. 178 crores.
- Assistance provided includes:
  - (i) Financial assistance.
  - (ii) In kind in the form of food items, shelter material,
  - (iii) Rescue teams with sniffer dogs.
  - (iv) Medical facilities by setting up mobile hospitals with surgical facilities.
  - (v) Messages expressing deep regrets on loss of lives.
- US $ 300 million announced by World Bank.
- US $ 350 million announced by Asian Development Bank.

Role of Military or Armed Forces

To understand fully the military's role in domestic crisis response it is necessary to explore the national-level structures and response options prior to the involvement of military forces. In general, the laws of the United States assign primary authority to the federal government to prevent and respond to terrorism. The FBI, through DoJ, is designated the Lead Federal Agency for crisis management of threats or acts of terrorism that take place in the United States or in international waters that do not involve the flag vessel of a foreign country. Crisis management is predominately a law enforcement function that manages the resources necessary to prevent or resolve a terrorist incident including intelligence gathering, surveillance, tactical operations, negotiations, forensics, and follow-on investigations. It also includes technical missions involving WMD such as search, render safe procedures, transfer and disposal of a device, and limited decontamination if necessary. The federal response to a terrorist incident is seen as a highly coordinated interagency operation that can include federal, State, and local participation. Primary federal agencies besides the DoJ and the FBI are the Federal Emergency Management Agency, DoD, the Department of Energy, the Environmental Protection Agency, the Department of Health and Human Services, and now the Department of Homeland Security.

National Level Crisis Management Structure

Past experience has shown that non-federal local authorities are normally the first to respond to most emergencies or threats. Once it is determined that federal authorities should enter the coordination and decision process, those same authorities will ultimately decide if or when the federal government will begin coordination of the entire process. Some of the factors, that determine how fast and to what extent federal intervention takes place are the nature of the incident, the intended target, the potential consequences of a successful incident, and the capabilities of the local authorities. *The United States Government Interagency Domestic Terrorism Concept of Operations Plan (CONPLAN)* states that the "laws of the United States assign primary authority to the federal government to prevent and respond to acts of terrorism or potential acts of terrorism." The federal response will surely come sooner than later if the possibility exists that a WMD is involved in the incident. Additionally, if WMD is involved, the FBI may look to DoD for assistance in earlier stages of the crisis.

Road Transport and Highways

Out of 650 km of national highways damaged, 100 km were severely damaged. Most of the minor/major bridges were damaged. Surajbari bridge was damaged and repaired on war-footing and restored. National highways were made traffic worthy.

Telecommunication

Telecommunication facilities were disrupted. Number of exchanges damaged was 147 and total lines damaged were 82,000. Optical Fibre system from Bhuj-Bachau-Rajkot was damaged. Exchanges started choking due to heavy traffic. Estimated cost of damages was nearly Rs. 200 crores.

Railways

Costs	Track	25 crores
	Signal & Tele	15 crores
	Electrical	7 crores
	Misc.	3 crores
	Total	50 crores

Heavy damage to station buildings, station cabins, residential quarters, bridges in the affected sections. Signalling equipments at 25 stations and control communications on Viramgram-Gandhidham section damaged.

The Prospects

Mankind has survived and lived with natural disasters right from the days of the mythical universal deluge. Floods, volcanic eruptions and earthquakes have plagued and devastated humanity since time immemorial. Recurring floods are believed to have contributed, among other factors, to the extinction of the flourishing Indus valley civilization of South Asia in ancient times. You can do nothing about shifting of tectonic plates beneath the oceans causing devastating earthquakes or lava simmering underneath the earth's crust to erupt violently. And if our astronomers are to be believed, our planet is facing the dire prospect of total annihilation by the Haileys comet striking it in less than one and a quarters century from now. The exact year of their dark prediction is — 2116. Human endeavour in respect of such natural disasters, which are beyond human control and regulation, is limited to deep study, fact-finding and forewarning by natural scientists concerned. These are beyond the perview of social scientists. There is another category of disasters facing humanity today which is very much in the agenda of social scientists. This is the category of man-made disasters which calls for earnest attention of researchers in humanities, if mankind has to be saved from much avoidable damage. Some of these are almost as deadly and certainly more frequent than natural disasters. As man approaches the 21st century he is more and more exposed to the threat of man-made disasters almost invariably resulting from mismatch between the ever proliferating technological innovations and man's capacity to handle them.

It is not meant to decry technological innovations in production of goods and services or call for a halt to revolutionary changes they entail in the affairs of human beings. Rapid technological advance is an irreversible process and, if anything, it is only going to accelerate in future. The objective behind any in-depth study of man-made disasters could only be to increase the awareness about the inherent dangers, which is lacking at present and evolve effective damage control policy.

Before talking about the strategy in abstract, some of the well-known and not so well-known flash points of disasters may be identified and dwelt upon. This study deals with two such flash points — environmental disaster, and industrial disaster. Some factual indicators are being provided in respect of environmental disaster to highlight the dangers involved, which is meant to be only illustrative. Facts about the less known kind of industrial disasters have been derived largely from the Bhopal Gas Tragedy of India which was perhaps the worst industrial disaster of history.

REVIEW QUESTIONS

Short Answer Type Questions

1. List down the reason for concern soon after a disaster happened.
2. In a disaster situation, how preventive measures should be directed.
3. What are the lessons that one has to drawn out of Gujarat earthquake event.
4. Name the major relief operations initiated by the central government in response to a disaster
5. What was the state government operations in response to a disaster.
6. Write a note on the impact of foreign aid towards disaster response.

Essay Type Questions

1. What are all the areas to be focused while executing rescue operations, in response to a disaster?
2. Critically analyze the impact of adversities, which befall people and the area.
3. Discuss the relief and rehabilitation measures taken by the respective various state, towards recovery and reconstruction.
4. Explain the role of armed forces in managing the disaster and the functions of nation level crisis management structure I detail.

CHAPTER 3

DISASTER MANAGEMENT AGENCIES AND ITS FUNCTIONS

The sporadic and isolated attempts in response to a disaster could have only nominal impact on the welfare of the recovery stage after being at the receiving end. When it was found that the agencies created and appointed for same were ill-equipped to restrain the exploitation by powerful local forces the Integrated Area Development Programme (IADP) was baptised in 1972 by the special convocation of the Tribal Development Department of the Ministry of Home Affairs with the consultation of various state level tribal development agencies. But, following the same line of experience as over the preceding years has proved that without developing the tribals therein cannot succeed. Yet, all of this seems to have got concealed in the new label of Sub-plan Scheme for Tribal Development (SSTD) in 1976 without defining the area coverage and plan objectives.

The new sub-plan under the main plan (of State and Union Government) started functioning in almost all states under the new name of Integrated Tribal Development Projects (ITDP) without 'project officials' to control, direct and manage the development activities of the various State and Union Government Departments.

According to the new strategy, Area Sub-Plans comprising several projects are prepared for each such 'sub-plan area'. For each one of these projects, IADP focusing attention on the specific problems of the tribal people in that area has been formulated.

ORGANISATIONAL TASKS AND GENERAL ROLES

Primary responsibility for all aspects of disaster management rests with the Government of the affected country. This includes: planning and implementing long-term risk reduction and preparedness measures; requesting and administering disaster relief and rehabilitation operations, requesting international assistance if required; and coordinating all disaster-related assistance programmes, both nationally and internationally-funded. Each UN organisation or agency is responsible for providing advice and assistance to the Government of a disaster-prone or disaster-affected country, in accordance with its mandate and the resources available to it. In so doing, each agency is accountable to its own governing body, but it is also called upon to act as a member of a united team. In the case of refugee emergencies, UNHCR remains responsible for their protection and the coordination of international assistance for the refugees.

In relation to disaster relief and other post-disaster assistance, each organisation and agency of the UN system is called on to: "Mobilise and provide timely technical assistance and material support to disaster-affected countries, according to its own mandate and the resources available to it".

Roles and Resources of UNDP, UNDRO and other UN Agencies UNDP focuses primarily on the development-related aspects of disaster risks and occurrences, and on providing technical assistance to institution-building in relation to all aspects of disaster management. Its emphasis is therefore on:

(a) Incorporating long-term risk reduction and preparedness measures in normal development planning and programmes, including support for specific mitigation measures where required,

(b) Assisting in the planning and implementation of post-disaster rehabilitation and reconstruction, including the definition of new development strategies that incorporate risk reduction measures relevant to the affected area.

(c) Reviewing the impact of large settlements of refugees or displaced persons on development and seeking ways to incorporate the refugees and displaced persons in development strategies.

(d) Providing technical assistance to the authorities managing major emergency assistance operations of extended duration (especially in relation to displaced persons and the possibilities for achieving durable solutions in such cases).

In addition, UNDP provides administrative and operational support to the resident coordinator function, particularly at country level, but also at headquarters.

In the event of a disaster, UNDP may grant a maximum of $50,000 from SPR funds to provide immediate relief. UNDP is not otherwise involved in the provision of "relief" using any of its own resources or other funds administered by the Programme.

Where a major emergency substantially affects the whole development process within a country, IPF resources may be used to provide technical assistance to plan and manage the operation, with the agreement of the Government. Technical and material assistance in support of long-term risk reduction and preparedness measures is included in the country programme and may be funded from IPF resources or from other UNDP-administered funds. The same can also be used to assist rehabilitation and reconstruction. Special additional grants (up to $1.1 million) may be made from SPR funds for technical assistance to such post-disaster recovery efforts following natural disasters.

The particular responsibilities of the UNDP resident representative are summarised in the following panel.

Disaster management responsibilities of the UNDP resident representative. The resident representative is responsible for:

(a) Ensuring that all concerned in planning development programmes are aware of any known or potent hazards and their likely effects, and that these are appropriately taken into account in the country programme.

(b) Designating a "disaster focal point", and ensuring that the field office is adequately prepared to respond to emergency.

(c) In the event of a disaster:

Mobilising UNDP staff and technical assistance personnel and other resources that meet the needs of the situation, particularly those needed for the initial assessment and immediate response.

Ensuring that UNDP assistance is used to good effect, and the capacity of the office is strengthened if necessary to ensure effective response. In all disaster-prone country field offices, a senior national officer is designated a "disaster focal point" for all disaster-related matters including mitigation, response and international UN/ UNDP preparedness.

In a major or complex emergency of extended duration (typically involving displaced populations), UNDP may temporarily assign an additional deputy resident representative. That deputy may either manage normal UNDP business while the resident representative concentrates on the resident coordinator functions, or may take day-to-day responsibility for matters relating to the emergency which are within the UNDP mandate. In the countries with the most severe or prolonged emergencies UNDP has established UN Emergency Units. These units are able to focus exclusively on addressing the emergency and are often staffed by persons seconded from sister UN agencies that are operational in that country. In the event of a sudden influx of refugees into a country in which there is no UNHCR representation, the resident representative immediately notifies UNHCR and initiates the assessment process on behalf of the UNHCR.

ROLE OF UN IN COMPLEX EMERGENCIES

In light of the issues created by complex emergencies and the special needs of displaced populations, the United Nations has determined to strengthen and make more effective the collective efforts of the international community, in particular the UN system, in providing humanitarian assistance. This determination is reflected in the implementation of General Assembly resolution 46/182, passed in December of 1991.

This resolution affirms that humanitarian assistance must be provided in accordance with the principles of humanity/ neutrality and impartiality. Accordingly the UN has a central and unique role to play in providing leadership and coordinating the efforts of the international community to support the affected countries.

The implementation of resolution 46,182d includes the creation of a contingency funding arrangement, that is, a central emergency revolving fund of US $50 million as a cash-flow niechanism to ensure the rapid and coordinated response of the organisations of the system. The UN will also establish a central register of specialised personnel and teams of technical specialists, supplies and other resources that can be called upon at short notice by the UN.

The leadership of this UN initiative will be provided by a high level official, the emergency relief coordinator, designated by the Secretary-General, to work with the entities of the UN system dealing with humanitarian assistance. This position combines the functions previously carried out in the coordination of UN response by representatives of the Secretary-General for major and complex emergencies, as well as by the United Nations Disaster Relief Coordinator.

This emergency relief coordinator, among other duties, is charged with facilitating the access by the operational organisations to emergency areas for the rapid provision of emergency assistance. In cases of complex emergencies this may require negotiation with all parties concerned to obtain their consent and, where needed, the establishment of temporary relief corridors, days and zones of tranquillity and other forms.

Safety of Relief Teams in Conflict Zones

There are many operational considerations in complex emergencies. One of the most crucial is that of the safety of relief teams in conflict zones. As coordinators of assistance for the displaced, the UN staff bears a special responsibility for ensurirtg that all personnel operating in or adjacent to conflict zones work in conditions of minimum risk and maximum security. Guidelines and procedures for personnel should be established in conjunction with the host government and, where possible, with insurgent groups. The UN is often charged with the responsibility of notifying relief workers and other sanitations about the risks they may face from military operations in or near their relief activities. In this regard, the UN is often able to obtain clearances for special flights into contested areas on aeroplanes bearing United Nations markings to arrange for safe transport through the frontlines in specially marked UN vehicles, and to establish special relief corridor whereby food and relief supplies can be delivered under flag of truce or through designated corridors, without understanding. It is important for the UN to carefully assess the risk before encouraging relief organisations to commit personnels and resources to operations in non-secure areas.

Two of the most important aspects of working in remote and insecure areas are communications and standby evacuational support. To the greatest extent possible, UN coordinators should ensure that relief personnel have immediate and 24-hour access: to telecommunications facilities and that suitable means and immediately available to evacuate personnel in case of an emergency. This may entail the assignment of light aircraft to be available on short notice to evacuate staff.

The scope of disaster management, therefore, can include all disaster-related activities. These activities become so inclusive that no one individual is responsible for the entire range. Instead the responsibility is divided according to the descriptions and limited by the organisation's primary functions. The Red Cross/Red Crescent Societies, for example work mainly in preparedness and emergency response phase; and less often in reconstruction. Some NGOs work only in reconstruction. Even government, with its broad responsibility for overall aspects of disaster management, breaks down these components to be managed by several of its agencies. The UN has similar allocations of responsibility as a function of it; agencies' mandates and sectoral expertise.

THE UN DISASTER MANAGEMENT TEAM

The United Nations General Assembly believes that the objectives of team management are applicable to the the agencies oriented to emergencies.

They have mandated that a standing UN Disaster Management Team (UN-DMT) be formed in each disaster-prone country, convened and chaired by the UN resident coordinator. The composition of the UN-DMT is determined by taking into account the types of disaster to which the country is prone and the organisations present, but should normally include a core group consisting of the country-level representatives of FAO, UNDP/UNDRO, UNICEF, WFP, WHO and, where present, UNHCR. It may be enlarged to include additional representatives or project personnel from other relevant agencies when an emergency arises.

The original and primary purpose of the UN-DMT is to ensure a prompt, effective and concerted response by the UN system at country level in the event of a disaster. The team should also ensure similar coordination of UN assistance to the Government in respect to post-disaster rehabilitation and reconstruction, and relevant disaster mitigation measures through long-term development programmes. It should be emphasised that for all aspects of disaster management the UN-DMT is in a support role of the government.

The UN-DMT recognises and in no way supersedes the mandates and specific functions of the various organisations in the exercise of those mandates.

It supports and assists the office of the resident coordinator in the exercise of its system-wide functions. In line with General Assembly resolution 46/182, the latter will maintain close contact with, and receive leadership from the Emergency Relief Coordinator.

COUNTRY DISASTER MANAGEMENT TEAM

Most disaster prone countries already have a formal or informal disaster management team. It is typically headed by a national disaster focal point body. This body functions in liaison with the Office of the President or Prime Minister, with civil defence organisations, key government ministries, the Red Cross/Red Crescent, and other NGOs and major donors.

The UN-DMT needs to interface with this team and, where practical, to be a team member. Where national officials do not participate in UN-DMT meetings or activities, the resident coordinator should ensure that they are consulted and briefed on all relevant matters. In practice it is vital that the policies of the DMT relate to those approved by the Government even under the pressure of event.

The main reason why the agencies and the helping hand rendered by them are absolutely necessary, may clearly be understood by anyone, only when they are either witnessing or came to know about the atrocious outcomes on environmental as well as industrial disasters.

Environmental Disaster

Global warming is the most important component of environmental disaster that mankind is facing today. Unprecedented increase in world population, coupled with even faster increase in economic activities is threatening to disrupt the finely balanced ecosystem which sustains life on earth. In 1900 the world population was about 1.6 billion which rose to 2.5 billion by 1950. But during 40 years from 1950 to 1990, the world population more than doubled. What is more, world economic activity increased more than four times in the same period.

The need to support more people and rapid technological advance to enable them to live better have been steadily eroding the fine ecological balance. Hyper industrialisation is leading to abnormal rise in the level of CO_2 emissions—CFCs (Chlorofluro-carbons), acidified forests, polluted rivers, etc. This has such a disturbing effect on the ecosystem that more of sun's radiant energy or heat gets trapped within the earth's atmosphere, as inside the glass of a greenhouse. This results in warming up of not only the atmospheric gases but of everything else on earth.

At the same time, chemical emissions like CFCs are adding up to the harmful effects of solar radiation in another way. The Ozone layer, situated about 20 kilometres above the earth's surface, protects the earth from the harmful effects of sun's rays. Chemicals like CFCs widely in use in refrigeration, air-conditioning, etc., cause depletion of the Ozone layer, resulting in what has come to be known as 'Ozone hole'. The wider the management ***'Ozone Hole'***, the greater the danger of sun's rays directly penetrating the earth's atmosphere unfiltered by the protective shield of ozone, resulting in serious consequences for global population.

Galloping population and even faster pace of industrialisation are thus slowly but steadily leading to a rise in earth's temperature through greenhouse effect and ozone depletion. This could prove to be disastrous for large chunks of inhabitants of our planet. It is estimated that average increase in global temperature in course of the last one hundred years was only to the extent of 0.3° celcius to 0.7° celcius. As against this insignificant rise, it is estimated that double the CO_2 emission levels, consequent upon accelerated population growth and industrialisation, will produce an average temperature increase of between 1.5°celcius to 4.5°celcius by the middle of the 21st Century. One of the consequences of this abnormal increase in global warming could be perceptible rise in earth's sea levels. This would be inescapable because a warmer liquid has more volume than an equivalent mass of cold liquid.

In concrete terms, any significant rise in sea level during the 21st Century may spell disaster in many countries of the Third World. For instance, a one-metre rise in sea-level would submerge about 11.5 per cent of the land of Bangladesh containing a population of about 8.5 millions. Similar would be the fate of large populations residing on low-lying deltas in Egypt and China. A two-metre rise in sea level would completely swallow up the Maldive islands, inhabited by about two hundred thousand people, as well as many atolls in the Pacific ocean.

Although the potential damage caused by global warming may be less severe in developed world, it cannot escape the disastrous consequences altogether. Low-lying regions of Louisiana, New Jersey, the Netherlands, etc., would remain vulnerable to varying degrees of devastations through rise in sea levels. In the USA alone, a rise of one metre in the sea level would devour up to eight thousand square miles or thereabouts and ten thousand square miles of dryland. The vintage city of Venice and many other towns and habitations located near water's edge would be seriously threatened.

Industrial Disaster

While there is growing awareness about the threat of environmental disaster looming large over the world, not much is known about the ever increasing dangers of industrial disasters. As the process and pace of industrialisation goes on accelerating the world over, with poor countries emulating and vying with their richer counterparts in the race towards greater and yet greater industrialisation, the threat of industrial disasters is ever widening across the board. Major and minor industrial disasters are taking place regularly across the world but these are not so well-known.

Everybody is interested in blanking these off the public gaze, the corporations, governments and the entire network of institutions and people involved in the concerned industries, for their own reasons. In any case, the common people tend to dismiss industrial disasters as no more than accidents or normal hazards associated with any trade or industry.

A few samples of industrial accidents taking considerable toll of human lives across the world are given below:

- In 1942, a coal dust explosion at Honkaiko colliery

- In China left 1572 dead on the spot
- In 1947, a Fertilizer ship explosion off Texas city
- In USA killed 561 persons
- In 1956, 1100 died in a dynamite truck explosion in Call taxi, Columbia.
- In 1975, 433 miners perished in a coal mine disaster in Chasnala colliery in India
- In 1979, an accident in the biological and chemical warfare plant at Novosibirsk in erstwhile Soviet Union took 300 lives.
- In November 1984, natural gas explosion at Pomex plant in Mexico city left at least 452 dead and 4258 injured; 31,000 residents of the area had to be evacuated.

The industrial disaster that dwarfed all others in the scale of devastation occurred at the city of Bhopal in central India in early December 1984. The event which has left many in the city permanently disabled, apart from thousands who were directly consumed by it, was summed by a leading fortnightly, *India Today* dated 31 December, 1984 as follows:

The night of December 2/3, a night that Bhopal and its 800,000 citizens can never forget. A Monday of macabre death, a killer cloud of gas that silently settled on an unsuspecting city and converted a pleasant, mild winter's night into a nightmare of misery, panic, sickness and, for at least 2500 people, babies and children, fathers and mothers, siblings and grandparents, a slow, painful, unnecessary snuffing out of life. That it was the worst ever industrial accident in history, taking an unprecedented and still unaccounted death toll and leaving no fewer than 50,000 affected, was quickly dwarfed by the tidal wave of human suffering that spread quickly across the city like the poison cloud that caused it.

"Methyl isocyanite (MIC) a product that few in Bhopal knew even existed, which Union Carbide, its makers describe in the manuals as 'an extraordinarily hazardous chemical,' a poison against which 'stringent precautions must be observed to eliminate any possibility of human contact', yet it was this lethal substance, a highly volatile chemical that is used by Union Carbide to manufacture pesticide that vaporised silently into Bhopal's night air".

The tragedy was caused by both systems and human failures. The systems that failed were (a) vent gas scrubber, (b) flare tower, (c) water curtain, (d) refrigeration system and (e) spare tank. Even if some of the systems failed, the plant staff could have adopted the laid down measures to render most of the MIC escaping into the air harmless, which they failed to do. As a result, more than a hundred thousand people living in the vicinity of the factory were exposed to MIC in varying degrees. Around sixteen thousand animals perished immediately.

As the poison gas leaked out of the chemical plant, gradually bringing under its sway a 40 square kilometre area, men, women, and children started dying of asphyxiation. The immediate body count put the figure of the dead at 3000, even as more dead bodies were being discovered everyday even a week after the disaster. Even according to the conservative official estimates, no less than one-fourth of the city's population of about eight hundred thousand was affected by the deadly effect of the gas leak. Many were completely blinded, many had their eyesight and hearing partially impaired and still others were maimed one way or the other. The scars of the disaster are still thereon the face of Bhopal in the shape of numerous hapless inhabitants who have become handicapped for life in the prime of their youth. Bhopal has become a symbol of the magnitude and omnious dimensions of industrial disasters the world over.

The range, sweep, scale and frequency of man-made disasters constitute a grim prospect for human well-being in the coming century. It is necessary for social scientists to give serious thought to the problems posed by man-made disasters. By all accounts, there is going to be no let up in the pace of population increase, technological advance and industrialization in the foreseeable future. With the poor and developing countries racing headlong to catch up with the developed ones, there is every possibility of industrialization increasing at a faster pace rather than slowing down, in the process, augmenting the range, ferocity and frequency of disasters. In the event, the only way out is to evolve a suitable strategy to contain and minimize the risks involved.

THE ROLE OF UNDRO

UNDRO is the focal point for disaster management in the UN system (except in those countries where a UN Emergency Unit is established). In relief it provides a framework for coordination of assistance by the UN agencies and helps to coordinate such assistance with that from other sources. In addition, UNDRO has an important role in mobilising external assistance and serving as a clearing house for information concerning disasters. In the area of mitigation, UNDRO promotes long-term measures to reduce disaster-related risks and enhance preparedness in disaster-prone countries. UNDRO is represented at country level on a permanent basis by the resident coordinator/representative. Coordination at headquarters level is often effected by contacts between the Head of Agencies concerned at the beginning of a relief operation, and through frequent ongoing contacts between the relevant focal points. At the country level, coordination is undertaken by the resident coordinator who is also the UNDRO representative. Whenever possible and required, UNDRO supports the resident coordinator by dispatching an UNDRO delegate or emergency assistance team.

UNDRO concentrates on problems related to natural hazards and sudden disasters, but as its mandate covers all kinds of emergencies. UNDRO may also offer its services and advice in situations including droughts, and cases of war and civil conflicts, unless and until the Secretary-General makes other arrangements. Following a disaster, UNDRO, acting on behalf of the Secretary-General, offers its services to the Government of the disaster-stricken state in assessing the need for external relief assistance, and communicating that information to prospective donors and others concerned. Where international assistance is required or requested, UNDRO:

- Helps to identify priority needs on the basis of information from the Government, the resident coordinator/representative, UN-DMT, and other competent bodies.
- Issues international appeals and acts as a clearing house for information on needs and contributions, the assistance extended or planned by all donors, and the progress of relief operations.
- Seeks to mobilise resources and coordinate relief assistance by various UN organisations and agencies, bilateral donors, and inter-and non-governmental organisations and administers funds channelled through it.

Depending on the particular situation after consultations, wherever possible, with the Government or the resident coordinator/representative, UNDRO may: Assign one or more delegates on mission to assist the national authorities in organising the assessment and administering relief operations, and assist the resident coordinator/representative in information management, the local coordination of international relief assistance, and in his reporting responsibilities to UNDRO:

- Provide logistic support to ensure the timely arrival of relief supplies and their prompt delivery to the affected population. This may include organising shared or joint relief flights.

The Coordinator may approve a grant of up to US$ 50,000 per disaster from funds available to UNDRO, subject to certain conditions. In some situations, UNDRO can release supplies from the emergency stockpile it administers in Pisa, Italy.

UNDP-UNDRO Collaboration

UNDP and UNDRO complement each other. UNDP has a wealth of experience in development planning and administration, and well-established field offices. UNDRO has specific knowledge and experience in disaster management, and established contacts with relevant specialist bodies. The fact that the UNDP resident representative also represents UNDRO helps to ensure fruitful cooperation between the organisations.

At the country level UNDP field offices generally administer funds and resources channelled through UNDRO, following normal inter-agency procedures. This includes the local procurement of supplies and services, and the recruitment and appointment of temporary staff.

Coordination: The Resident Coordinator and the UN-DMT

The national Government is ultimately responsible for requesting and coordinating all international assistance. It also approves all programmes and emergency work in the country. However, the UN system stands ready to assist upon request. At the country level, the resident coordinator/representative and the UN Disaster Management Team (UN-DMT) are the essential UN coordinating institutions. Their responsibilities apply to all situations which require significant interventions from more than one UN organisation or agency. At the international level, UNDRO promotes the coordination of responses to particular disaster situations, both within the UN system and in the wider international community, essentially through information-sharing.

Coordination as Used in the Manual, Means

- The intelligent sharing of information and the frank, constructive discussion of issues and possible courses of action.
- Achieving consensus on objectives and an overall strategy.
- The voluntary adoption by those concerned of specific responsibilities and tasks in the context of the agreed objectives and strategy.

Coordination is based on mutual respect for the competencies and agreed responsibilities of each party, and willingness to cooperate in addressing and solving problems in pursuit of a common aim.

ROLE OF THE UN RESIDENT COORDINATOR

The resident coordinator, also representing UNDRO, is both the UN system's team leader at country level, and chairman of the UN-DMT. Following the occurrence of a major disaster, the resident coordinator/representative must be ready to give absolute priority to this coordination role, which also includes helping to ensure the coordination of all international emergency assistance.

Coordination Arrangements for Emergencies

The Secretary-General of the United Nations has appointed an Emergency Relief Coordinator at the level of the Under Secretary-General, who has been entrusted with the responsibility for the coordination of emergency assistance as outlined in General Assembly Resolution 46/182 of 19 December 1991.

The Emergency Relief Coordinator is in charge of the Central Emergency Revolving Fund, which has been established as a cashflow mechanism of US$ 50 million to ensure the rapid and coordinated response of the organisations of the system. He has direct access to the Secretary General in New York and maintains contacts with, and provides leadership to, the field Resident Coordinators.

Disaster Management Responsibilities of the Resident Coordinator

On an ongoing basis, the resident coordinator must:

- Ensure that the UN organisations and agencies active in a disaster-prone country are collectively "prepared" to offer appropriate technical and material assistance as part of an overall international response in the event of a disaster.
- Ensure that the same agencies take account of disaster risks in their long-term development programmes, and provide concerted assistance in relation to disaster mitigation, in consultation with any national IDNDR committee.

In the event of a "multi-sectoral" disaster:

- Bring the various agencies of the UN system together and ensure the provision of prompt, effective, and concerted multi-disciplinary advice and assistance.
- Maintain contact with the government authority responsible for conducting relief operations. Ensure concerted UN assistance to that authority in assessing the situation and the requirements for international assistance.
- Keep UNDRO informed of the situation and needs for international assistance. Provide a clear statement of priority needs for international assistance rapidly

to UNDRO for distribution internationally, and provide similar information to the local representatives of the international community. Update the information continuously to keep it current.

- Recommend that the UN team be reinforced by the appropriate agencies at the country level when necessary.
- Help to secure cooperation and coordination between all international assistance bodies, the government, and other national organisations to ensure proper management of international assistance. In case of a refugee influx or "mono-sectoral" disaster:
- Consult with the local representative of the competent UN organisation or agency (UNHCR or other) to determine what the resident coordinator and UN-DMT should do to support that agency.

The aims of disaster preparedness are to minimise the adverse effects of a hazard through effective precautionary actions, and to ensure timely, appropriate and efficient organisation and delivery of emergency response following the impact of a disaster.

This definition establishes the broad framework for disaster preparedness, but it is worth dwelling on some of the points implicit in the definition "to minimise the adverse effects of a hazard."

Disaster risk reduction is intended to minimise the adverse effects of a hazard by eliminating the vulnerabilities which hazards otherwise would expose and by directly reducing the potential impact of a hazard before it strikes. Disaster preparedness in its starkest form assumes that certain groups of people will nevertheless remain vulnerable, and that preparedness will have to address the consequences of a hazard's impact "through effective precautionary actions."

It is important to note that the term used is "precautionary actions", for all too often the end product of disaster preparedness is seen as a static plan to be devised and then filed until it is needed. Disaster preparedness, to the contrary, must be seen as an active and continuing process. Of course, both plans and strategies are required, but they both must be dynamic ventures, which are frequently reviewed, modified, updated and tested "to ensure timely, appropriate, and efficient organisation and delivery."

Perhaps one of the most difficult aspects of disaster management is that of timing. Timing also impinges upon the concept of disaster preparedness. Speed and timeliness have often been treated synonymously, a major conceptual flaw, pecisions related to timing must consider the relationship between relief inputs and their effects. In some types of disasters, flood, for example, there are certain basics such as shelter and clothing that may be required immediately. In terms of alleviating immediate distress, speed is critical.

However, there are other forms, similarly, appropriate assistance demands careful scrutiny. The issue goes beyond the standard stories of canned pork and high heeled shoes to flooded, Muslim communities. The issue goes to the important and natural link between disaster preparedness, recovery and rehabilitation. Ultimately we need to ask if one of the key objectives of disaster preparedness—the provision of appropriate assistance—is designed merely to ensure the immediate survival of affected communities or, in ensuring immediate survival, to simultaneously pave the way for recovery "efficient organisation and delivery".

Efficient organisation and delivery suggest obvious criteria for effective disaster preparedness. Systematic planning, well executed distribution, clear cut roles and responsibilities are all vital. However, too often disaster situations create conditions of chaos. The best laid plans can mitigate but not eliminate the chaos. To the extent possible, preparedness plans should seek to anticipate the sources of chaos and equally as important should try to anticipate what to do when plans go awry. However, where a criterion of efficiency becomes particularly important is in the context of distribution.

The key here is to ensure that efficiency is measured in terms of the ability to deliver needed assistance to those most vulnerable. All too often in disaster relief situations, food and non-food relief arrives at the scene of a disaster, but no system or structure has been established to ensure that those in greatest need are the beneficiaries. In the final analysis, the most important test of efficiency is that those in need are adequately provided for.

ROLE OF GTZ

Based on the German Federal Government's policy papers on BMZ emergency oriented development aid (1996) and global poverty alleviation (2001)1, GTZ has put together a service package for disaster risk management. It has identified five activity areas for cooperation with partner countries:

- Risk assessment
- Disaster prevention and mitigation
- Disaster preparedness

- Disaster risk management as part of rehabilitation and reconstruction
- Mainstreaming disaster risk management in development cooperation sectors.

In addition to this, two multisectoral strategies are described for supporting measures in disaster risk management. Firstly, we outline ways of raising awareness amongst endangered populations and policymakers as a precondition for sustainable efforts in disaster risk management. Secondly, we discuss the role of local resources for disaster risk management and the practical experience gained. The working concept concludes with a summary of GTZ services for disaster risk management.

To conclude, in an International circuit, it could be some kind of Grass Root Disaster Organisation (GRDO) something like in Thailand or Indonesia or could be a group born intentionally out of volunteerism or could be a designated self-help group formally acknowledged with identified role and having the necessary sensation and skills at the local level. They need to have proficiency in hazards factor in mapping health, mapping emergency planning and must carry out analysis of their own weakness and strength which afflict them. They need to be trained both in communication and in simple skills and they need to have roles specific to the task in a disaster specific situation not forgetting the targets and the strategies for which they work. They need to have a pre-planned coordination, network in advance which may only be formalized during such a situation.

Such advance contingency plans should not be only paper plans but plans arrived at after a long process of participation, negotiation and involvement of the local population who are in the frontline facing the disasters and those who are vulnerable have to also have the major stakes in such planning. In every disaster of any description mentioned above, the communities are basically of two types vulnerable and non-vulnerable and those who are vulnerable have to be informed, pre-educated, galvanised into action and mobilised into a mock-performance in such eventuality while non-vulnerable in terms of location or health status should be made to respond to the vulnerable community in times of distress as a matter of condition reflex.

COMPONENTS OF DISASTER PREPAREDNESS

There are nine major components involved in disaster preparedness which provide a framework upon which a national disaster preparedness strategy can be developed.

Assessing Vulnerability

Fundamental to all aspects of disaster management is information. It is a point that may appear obvious, but it is frequently overlooked. The disaster manager may know that a particular geographic region or community is susceptible to the impacts of sudden or slow-onset hazards. However, in reality, until a decision is made on systematic ways to compile and assess information about disaster vulnerabilities, the manager is and will be working in a void.

Developing and compiling vulnerability assessments is one way of approaching a systematic means of establishing an essential disaster management tool.

Planning

Throughout all the activities designed to promote disaster preparedness, the ultimate objective is to have plans in place that are agreed upon, that are implementable and for which commitment and resources are relatively assured.

The plan itself will have to address other points in this framework.

Institutional Framework

A coordinated disaster preparedness and response system is a prerequisite to any disaster preparedness plan. Each system design will depend upon the traditions and governmental structure of the country under review. However, without ensuring that there is "horizontal coordination" at Central Government levels among ministries and specialised government bodies and "vertical coordination" between central and local authorities, a plan will rapidly disintegrate. This requires a structure for decision-making, inter-ministerial committees to coordinate the plan, focal points within each ministry to be responsible for the plan implementation and communication, as well as regional and community structures to implement the plan at the local level.

Information Systems

The preparedness plan must have an information system. For slow onset disasters this should consist of a formalised data collection process, and early warning system (especially for regions prone to famine), and monitoring system to update the early warning information. For sudden onset disasters a similar system must be in place for prediction, warning, and evacuation communication.

Resource Base

The requirements to meet an emergency situation will clearly depend upon the types of hazards the plan anticipates. Such requirements should be made explicit, and should cover all aspects of disaster relief and recovery implementation. The range of relief requirements is too extensive to put in this module, but this list indicates some of the major requirements:

- Shelter
- Medicines
- Food
- Supplementary food
- Communications systems
- Logistics systems
- Relief workers
- Clearance equipment
- Warning systems.

For most types of rapid onset disasters, a warning system can save many lives.

By giving a vulnerable population adequate notice of an impending disaster, they can either escape the event or take precautions to reduce the dangers.

However, you must assume that functioning communications systems, such as telephones and telexes, may not be available in times of a major disaster. Begin to plan a warning system around that assumption. Consider what type of communications equipment will be needed and sustainable if power lines and receiving stations are destroyed. Preparedness plans should include provisions for access to alternative communication systems among police, military and government networks.

Warning is also critical for slow onset disasters and population displacements. In this case, it is called early warning and has to do with information and its distribution regarding either:

By giving timely notice of an impending world crisis in the supply of food making ready for or preventing forced migrations of people.

Response Mechanisms

The plan's ultimate test is the effectiveness of response to warnings and disaster impacts. At a certain stage in the warning process, various responses will have to be mobilised. The staging of responses becomes an essential factor in designing a preparedness plan.

Public Education and Training

The focus of a disaster preparedness plan should be to anticipate, to the extent possible, the types of requirements needed for action or responses to warnings and a disaster relief operation. The plan should also specify the most effective ways of ensuring that such requirements are met. Yet, the process will only be effective if those who are the ultimate beneficiaries know what to do in times of disasters and know what to expect. For this reason, an essential part of a disaster preparedness plan is the education of those who may be threatened by disaster.

Such education takes many forms, such as: (1) Public education in schools for children and young adults, emphasising what actions should be taken in case of a disaster threat (for example, earthquake tremors); (2) Special training courses, designed for an adult population either specifically or as an extra dimension of ongoing programmes such as Preventive Health Care or Maternal and Child Health programmes; (3) Extension programmes, in which community and village-based extension workers are instructed to provide relevant information and trained for the tasks they should undertake during the event; (4) Public information, through mass media, be they television, radio or the printed word, will never really replace the impact of direct instruction. However, if sensitively designed and presented, mass media may provide a useful supplement to the overall educational process.

Rehearsals

As military manoeuvres cannot fully portray the reality of battle, neither can disaster preparedness rehearsals portray the full dynamics—and potential chaos—of a disaster relief operation. However, that fact should provide no excuse for avoiding the need to rehearse the disaster preparedness plan. Not only will rehearsals re-emphasise points made in separate training programmes, but they will also test the system as a whole and, invariably, reveal gaps that otherwise might be overlooked.

Preparedness for Slow Onset and Sudden Onset Disasters

Preparedness activities for slow onset disasters often vary from those of sudden onset. Slow onset disasters may require more active involvement on the part of planners, especially in terms of monitoring early warning systems, for famine, war, and I civil strife. The remedial response to problems indicated by the early warning (of potential disasters) is an extension of preparedness.

Preparedness for sudden onset disasters include the monitoring of the predictions and warnings of disasters that may occur within a matter of days or hours. The emergency may develop over a very brief time frame and depend on a very different set of procedures and resources than the slow onset emergency.

Preparedness within the United Nations: The UN system at the country level must be able to facilitate and deliver appropriate and coordinated assistance in an emergency. The UN Disaster Management Team (UN-DMT) is the standing inter-agency body for this. The UN-DMT should meet at regular intervals to:

- Review prevention and preparedness arrangements within the country, including the progress of any relevant ongoing development projects.
- Review preparedness arrangements within the UN team of agencies.
- Discuss the analysis and interpretation of data from in-country and external famine early warning systems decide on any specific actions to be taken by members of the group individually and/or collectively.

CHECKLIST OF BASIC INFORMATION REQUIRED BY A UN-DMT

In order to facilitate rapid, appropriate responses to disasters, the following kinds of information should be readily available in advance to all members of the UN-DMT.

If this information is not available, or only partially available, the UN-DMT should compile and maintain it as a team effort, normally in collaboration with national counterparts. The specialised agencies would each address respective areas of concern. The resident coordinator should see that all sectors are covered.

The checklist presented here should be adapted to local circumstances. Special care and attention should be given to information relevant to areas and communities which are particularly vulnerable and disaster-prone.

REVIEW QUESTIONS

Short Answer Type Questions

1. Write a note on IADP.
2. List down the primary objectives of UNDP.

3. What is the need to have a country disaster management team.
4. State the functions of GRDO.
5. Write a note on disaster risk reduction.
6. Differentiate slow onset & sudden onset disaster.
7. Tell us how public education and training is helpful in overcoming a disastrous situation.

Essay Tyes Qusestions

1. Discuss the role of UN in managing complex emergencies.
2. Explain the responsibilities of UN in mitigating the disastrous situation.
3. Elaborately explain the concepts of disaster preparedness.
4. Enumerate the role of GTZ in managing disasters.

CHAPTER 4

DISASTER RISK MANAGEMENT

Disaster risk management is a comparatively new area of social concern and practice. However, it is a very relevant concern for development cooperation given that natural disasters have devastated an increasing number of regions, destroyed investments and set back progress in development. Often, countries victim to the large-scale impacts of earthquakes, tornadoes, typhoons, floods or droughts are barely able to respond and recovering can take years or decades. Following the United Nations initiative for an International Decade for Natural Disaster Reduction (1990-99), this theme has climbed much higher on the international agenda. An increasing number of development cooperation actors are trying to cater for more prevention in their activities. And, the more vulnerable countries of the South are also beginning to make efforts to protect their populations and national economies from future disasters.

What the Risk is all about?

There are many definitions of risk used within public and private sector management circles. A typical definition of risk is "exposure to the chance of loss" or "the degree of probability of such a loss". It is important to distinguish between a problem and a risk. Whereas a risk is the possibility of something going wrong, a problem is something that has gone wrong—a problem is a risk that has materialised.

The link between disasters and development is now apparent to everyone, and disaster risk management is gaining increasing currency as an effective form of investment. But, most developing countries are limited in their ability to effectively integrate a strategic approach to the theme into national policy. It is the poor populations in the disaster areas that are hardest hit by losses and setbacks. Development cooperation supports political, economic, ecological and social development worldwide. It helps improve living conditions and promotes sustainable development. Natural disasters do not just pose a challenge to southern hemisphere countries.

Due to their geographical location developing countries are particularly exposed to extreme natural phenomena. Storms, heavy rains and landslides are more frequent and severe in the subtropical and tropical regions of the South. Hydrometeorological, seismic, volcanic and other natural events pose a permanent ongoing threat to the people living in these regions. The comparatively low level of development, as evident in the fragile infrastructure, the poor building fabric of housing, the vulnerability of productive activities, the low level of political and social organization and the absence of warning systems, makes them more vulnerable to natural disasters. The doubling of the world population since 1950 to more than 6 billion and its impact on settlement patterns and natural resources also makes itself particularly felt in the developing countries. Moreover, the rapid rise in world population has not just caused a drastic increase in the density of settlements; it has also altered their distribution pattern and land use. There is, for example, a growing migratory trend towards valleys and slopes under threat of flooding, landslides and earthquakes, particularly on the outskirts of large and medium-sized conurbations. These are growing too fast for the requisite planning and building regulations to be drafted and supervised. Modernization without the necessary safety precautions (e.g. when building bridges) increases the vulnerability to and risk of adverse impacts resulting from a natural event. Finally, another cause of the increase in natural disasters is the widespread human intervention in the climatic systems and in the equilibrium of fragile ecosystems (forest clearance, soil erosion, single cropping practices).

Natural disasters have direct and indirect effects on developing countries. The poorer population is much harder hit than the middle and upper classes because their vulnerability is far greater. This is due to social, economic and political factors. The poorest people often have nothing left with which to resume their daily battle for survival. It is very difficult for them to recover from the losses they have suffered and many migrate elsewhere in the hope of finding better conditions of life.

Then, the direct losses in productive sectors are followed by indirect impacts. In the largely agrarian economies the production losses lead to the dismissal or unemployment of day labourers. The loss of jobs reduces income and curbs spending power in families that already live under very precarious conditions. This in turn affects trade and transportation as well as other services. Finally, losses can occur in the financial sector and even result in economic collapse if deposits and large amounts of savings are withdrawn. Disasters thus impoverish the population further and increase their vulnerability. A vicious circle of vulnerability to more frequent extreme natural events is established. The international community often provides assistance for reconstruction but this is a huge burden on the economy. Since economic rationale demands that destroyed infrastructure are restored first, little funding is left for years to pursue coherent development strategies. Disasters often have a destabilizing political impact as well given the worsening situation of large sectors of the population in the medium and long term. In the industrialized nations, the damage caused by extreme natural events is also on the increase. This increase may be explained in good part by the higher density of large-scale assets (e.g. infrastructure, industrial plant, technology). Unlike the developing countries, material losses far outweigh human loss. Also, population and governments have the capacity to make good these losses, at least in the medium term. Most are insured and part of the costs of rebuilding and rehabilitation are borne by the insurance firms. Nor does local and national economic stability depend on a few marketable products. This signifies far lower levels of economic vulnerability. The figure below illustrates the different medium-term economic effects of disasters, taking capital formation as a benchmark.

The disaster itself causes disruption to economic development, which is overcompensated at first by the rapid provision of additional capital. After the additional funds for emergency aid and reconstruction have been consumed, the local economy has to cope with the remaining adverse effects on its own.

Disaster Risk Management – Definition

Technical Cooperation defines disaster risk management as a series of actions or programmes, projects and/or measures and instruments expressly aimed at reducing disaster risk in endangered regions, and mitigating the extent of disasters.

Disaster risk management includes risk assessment, disaster prevention and mitigation and disaster preparedness. It is used in the international debate to underscore the current trend of taking a proactive approach to hazards posed by extreme natural phenomena. The intention is a comprehensive reduction in disaster risk accounting for all the factors that contribute to risk (risk management), as opposed to a focus on each individual danger.

Action Needed

As we showed in the previous section, vulnerability to extreme natural events comprises various factors that bear a close relation to the development of a country or region. These provide a number of starting points for bilateral and international development cooperation. In many development cooperation projects and programmes efforts are underway to reduce development constraints and shortcomings. This implicitly translates into lowered vulnerability in developing countries. Nevertheless, as BMZ points out, "*the connections between poverty and vulnerability are quite complex*" and "*not every kind of development effort in areas threatened by disaster qualifies as disaster prevention*".

On the other hand, as the term itself implies, disaster risk management is frequently aimed at finding practical remedies for current problems. There is need here for a wider vision to include the systematic reduction of hazards and vulnerability. This means extending the mandate beyond emergency assistance. "*Assistance in disasters and conflicts and the related preventive measures (development-oriented emergency aid) cannot properly be treated as an isolated field of activity; it must be assimilated into development cooperation as an integral component.*"

Obstacles to Implementation

There are many different reasons why governments are reticent as regards disaster risk management. However, these are compounded by the following difficulties found in mainstreaming disaster risk management in development strategy:

- Preventive measures are seen by government and the private sector as cost factors and not as profitable investments. On the other hand, external aid supplies and reconstruction measures expected in the event of a disaster are mostly cost-free transfers.

- Pure emergency measures taken after disasters are spectacular. And it is easier to make political capital out of them than out of disaster risk management.

- Donors are still more prone to react with reconstruction models rather than with preventive action.

- Expanding infrastructure is often a way of attracting votes during elections. When implementing these measures, however, construction quality standards that are important for disaster risk reduction are often neglected (e.g. streets without drainage systems).

- Uncertainty as to whether an extreme natural event is actually going to occur often deters decision makers from investing scant existing funds in risk-reduction measures. In addition, many disaster risk management technologies are still too costly and sometimes too complicated to be easily applied by poorly equipped and funded organizations and populations.
- Some well-established local political and economic institutions hamper disaster risk management (land law and land distribution, for instance). Reforms meet with strong opposition from all kinds of pressure groups.

From Disaster Relief to Disaster Risk Management

The notion of a continuum of crises and disasters, as coined by the UN, conveys the idea that the phases of emergency aid, rehabilitation, reconstruction and the resumption of development are concurrent but nevertheless interconnected. From this standpoint, they must be viewed as an interactive process. Until a few years ago, disaster relief was a major intervention area whenever sudden events disrupted the functioning of society and overstretched available self-help capabilities. Due to the close link between disasters, development and development cooperation an increasing number of national and international actors are calling for the introduction of disaster prevention measures in development planning, and the establishment of national systems for comprehensive disaster risk management. Mr. Kofi Annan, the Former Secretary General of the United Nations, has also expressly demanded a paradigm shift from the prevalent 'culture of reaction' to a 'culture of prevention'.

The Scope of Disaster Relief and the Factors Involved

The main organizations and institutions involved with disaster relief (humanitarian aid in the phase of emergency assistance and reconstruction) are:

- Friendly governments which proffer their help immediately,
- The various suborganizations of the UN, particularly the UN Office for the Coordination of Humanitarian Affairs (OCHA),
- The European Union (EU) with its specialized ECHO office and
- Non-governmental organizations, such as the well renowned International Federation of Red Cross and Red Crescent Societies (IFRC).

The main responsibility remains, however, with the government and civil society of the affected country. However, developing countries in particular are usually incapable of coping with the magnitude of the financial and technical-organizational tasks. As a rule, state institutions in these countries lack sufficient technical equipment and they do not have the same organizational capabilities as institutions in industrialized countries.

Due to the existence of many national and multilateral institutions as well as the rapid growth in the number of small non-governmental organizations, it is difficult to keep track of all of the actors involved. For this reason it is very difficult to arrive at exact figures as regards the financial scope of disaster relief. Another problem is that the phases of emergency aid, reconstruction and the resumption of development cooperation are often hard to demarcate such that it turns out to be very difficult to exactly allocate costs for each phase. However, it can be clearly established that the share of emergency and disaster relief in total public development cooperation spending by the OECD countries in the 90s was much higher than in the 80s.

The International Path towards Integrated Disaster Risk Management

The United Nations International Decade for Natural Disaster Reduction (IDNDR), which ended in 1999, made a major contribution to raising international community awareness of the need to move from reactive measures towards integrated disaster risk management. The decade was inaugurated in 1989 by the General Assembly of the United Nations with the overall goal of mitigating the adverse consequences of disasters, particularly in developing countries (Resolution 44/236). A secretariat under OCHA was established to coordinate IDNDR activities. The IDNDR initiative also prompted the establishment of national committees for disaster risk management. In Germany the IDNDR committee was appointed in 1989 and renamed German Committee for Disaster Reduction – DKKV (reg. soc.) once the decade expired in 1999. The committee focuses on combining activities in science and practice, innovation development and know-how transfer, social dialogue and raising public awareness, as well as strengthening local disaster preparedness capabilities. GTZ is currently represented on the executive board and in the operative advisory board of the DKKV. In the course of the decade, the early more technical approach of the IDNDR was supplemented with the incorporation of socio-economic factors in the cause-effect matrix of disasters, hazards and vulnerabilities. A major milestone in this process was the United Nations Conference on Natural Disaster Reduction celebrated in Yokohama in 1994. In the Yokohama Declaration, disaster prevention, mitigation, preparedness and relief were specified as the basis for a sustainable development policy. In December 1999 the United Nations General Assembly adopted a resolution (No. 54/219) on actions to be taken following the end of the International Decade for Natural Disaster Reduction. Since then, the issue has been followed up in an International Strategy for Disaster Reduction (ISDR), whose organization (IATF secretariat and task force) is to concentrate on raising political awareness, assisting regional networks and stepping up scientific research. Between 1989 and 1999 other major UN international conferences took place that highlighted the interdependence between disaster risk management and other global challenges facing the international community. Of particular note here are the summits in Rio de Janeiro (1992) and Kyoto (1997) on environment and development. In Rio de Janeiro, Agenda 21 was adopted. With regard to disaster risk management, Agenda 21 points in particular to the threat of sea level changes for densely populated coastal regions, the need to combat drought and desertification and the paramount role of local authorities in revention/preparedness. In September 2002, the World Summit on Sustainable Development (Rio + 10) will take place in Johannesburg. Its aim is to review how sustainable changes have been achieved in the world since the 1992 world summit in Rio.

It is a highly inevitable fact that, Risk management is something that every manager routinely and intuitively does everyday. On a daily basis, he or she analyses a situation and decides what action should be taken, if any, given the uncertainties being faced. This is risk management. In more formal terms, risk management is a systematic approach to setting the best course of action by identifying and acting on risk issues.

Identifying Risks

The first step in developing a risk management strategy is to identify the risks for a programme.

What are some of the things one should keep in mind when identifying risks?

- Obtain a solid understanding of the objectives of the programme and the environment in which it operates;
- Include a brainstorming session to identify the risks;
- Use a risk management framework to conduct brainstorming sessions;
- Consider risks at the operational level and at the strategic or programme level;
- Consider risks in terms of both internal factors (i.e., those risks that might arise due to factors within your organisation) and external factors (i.e., those risks that arise due to factors that are external to or outside your organisation);
- Governance structures;
- Accountability and transparency;

- Policies, procedures and processes;
- Risk management culture; and
- Human resource capacity
  - — Political (e.g., the influence of government bodies);
  - — Economic (e.g., international and national markets);
  - — Social (e.g., demographic and social trends); and,
  - — Technological (e.g., new communications and scientific technologies).

Conducting a Risk Analysis

Once risks have been identified, the risks must be analysed or assessed to identify which risks pose the greatest threat to the programme so that plans to manage and mitigate the risks can be prioritised. One way is to develop a risk analysis framework.

This includes:

How do You Develop a Risk Analysis Framework?

This includes:

a. Definitions for assessing the risk in terms of likelihood and impact.

b. Development of a "risk matrix" to be used to:

   i. score and rank risks; and

   ii. provide management with a means of identifying which risk scores are acceptable.

Obtain a good understanding of the current status of each risk in terms of what factors affect it and what management actions, if any, are currently being taken:

- Assess each risk in terms of "likelihood" and "impact";
- Assign each risk a score based on the risk matrix; and
- Identify which risks, based upon their score, are risks that require development of a plan for further action (i.e., development of a mitigation strategy).

RISK MITIGATION STRATEGIES

Once risks have been assessed, those risks that have been assessed as being unacceptable, or possibly unacceptable (i.e. judgemental boundary), to management, will require development of a risk mitigation strategy.

What is a Risk Mitigation Strategy?

A risk mitigation strategy simply refers to the additional efforts, if any, that must be taken by management to lower the likelihood of the risk occurring and/or to minimise the impact on the programme if the risk did occur. Risk can never be totally eliminated, but risk can be managed and mitigated to lessen the likelihood and or impact of the risk on the programme.

For example, suppose a risk scored "9" during the risk assessment, meaning that "impact" scored "high" and "likelihood" scored "expected".

Since a score of 9 is most likely unacceptable to management, additional efforts will be required to lower the impact and or the likelihood of that risk. If a risk scored "2" during the risk assessment, most likely an acceptable level of risk to management, no further actions would be required in this case.

What Kinds of Information should a Risk Mitigation Strategy Include?

Any risk mitigation strategy should include:

- Roles and responsibilities for developing, implementing and monitoring the strategy;
- Timelines;
- Conditions present in order for risk level to be acceptable;
- Resources required to carry out the planned actions.

Monitoring Risk Assumptions and Risk Areas

Risk assessment is not something that is done once every five years. The environment within which any programme operates is one of continual change. Programme managers must routinely monitor or review the status of risks to determine whether mitigating actions are required. In some cases, the use of risk indicators helps to monitor the status of the risks.

When Might Risk Indicators be Useful for Monitoring the Status of the Risks?

Risk indicators are particularly recommended for either, very large, complex, innovative or risky initiatives where potential benefits could outweigh the additional cost of data collection and analysis.

Example of a Risk Indicator: The identified risk area is internal capacity. The risk indicator is "the amount of overtime."

How Frequently should Risks be Monitored?

The frequency for monitoring risks will vary with the complexity, size and sensitivity of the programme. The roles and responsibilities for ongoing monitoring of the status of each risk should be included as part of the risk management strategy.

Disasters affect millions of people every year. They cause damage to life, property and livelihoods. Some affect large numbers of people over a short period of time, such as the South Asia tsunami in 2004. Other disasters happen over many years, but may kill many more people than sudden events. For example, HIV and AIDS are gradually causing disaster in many places around the world. Every place has the potential to be affected by some type of disaster. Areas that have not experienced disasters before are increasingly likely to find themselves exposed to new ones due to climate change.

There is evidence that the number, severity and negative economic impact of disasters are increasing. This is mainly because more people are living in vulnerable conditions, such as on flood plains, in urban slums or in poor quality housing. Most people affected by disasters live in the poorer countries of the world.

Disasters often reverse development progress. The increase in the number and impact of disasters is one reason why many people predict that the Millennium Development Goals will not be met by 2015.

Many disasters can be avoided, or at least made less destructive, by reducing the risks that people face. Disaster risk reduction has been effective in many countries around the world, by saving lives and protecting livelihoods. Risk reduction makes good economic sense. A relatively small amount of money spent on risk reduction before a disaster happens may save much larger amounts that would need to be spent on humanitarian aid and reconstruction after the disaster. A study of a community-based project to reduce the risk of flooding in India found that the benefits of the projects were four times higher than the cost of the project. A similar project to reduce the risk of drought and flooding produced thirteen times more benefits than the cost of the projection.

The most effective way to reduce disaster risk is to work with local people to identify and analyse their vulnerabilities and capacities, and to develop and implement an action plan.

PARTICIPATORY ASSESSMENT OF DISASTER RISK (PADR)

The PADR process should involve the active participation of local people. It is an empowering process, as people begin to understand the reasons for their vulnerability, and identify their own capacities. These capacities then become the focus of action planning. The action plan looks at how capacities can be developed and used to overcome some of the vulnerabilities. Some activities can be carried out locally to reduce risk, while others may require external support or involve advocacy at district, national or international levels.

In order to increase ownership and sustainability of the action planning, it is best if Participatory Assessment of Disaster Risk is carried out where local people have identified a need to reduce disaster risk. A development organisation that has worked in the area for some time could provide a field worker to work through the PADR process with local people. At all times, the staff member must ensure that ownership remains with local people. The development organisation should only facilitate.

Natural disasters are caused not only by hazard events but also by the degree of exposure and vulnerability of society. High-risk areas are candidates for increased attention to, and investment in, disaster risk identification, reduction and transfer plans are underway to further identify disaster risk levels and factors on national and sub-national scales in high-risk countries to create evidence for improved risk management decision-making.

Disaster risk management based on identification of disaster risks offers a preferable alternative to the current overreliance on emergency management as a means of dealing with disasters.

One of the key challenges in promoting a shift from disaster management to risk management is to make the risk factors that cause disasters more visible. Prior to disasters these causal factors may be hidden. Only after a disaster occurs does it become crystal clear the extent to which latent risk factors were present. Unfortunately by then it is too late to prevent losses.

Identifying where and when conditions of hazardousness and vulnerability are present creates the potential for acting before disasters occur, to reduce the risks.

Risks can also be transferred away from exposed populations and assets, through insurance, contingency funds, catastrophe bonds and other financial mechanisms.

In the past several years, a concerted effort has been mounted by international agencies seeking to promote a shift from emergency to risk management to create an evidence base on global disaster risk. Examples include Reducing Disaster Risk: A Challenge for Development (UNDP 2004), Natural Disaster Hotspots: A Global Risk Analysis (Dilley et al. 2005) and System of Indicators for Disaster Risk Management: Programme for Latin America and the Caribbean (Cardona, 2005; IDEA, 2005).

For the first time, there is complete global coverage of information on risk levels and specific factors that cause disasters associated with most major natural hazards. These global and regional reports complement risk analyses undertaken at national and local scales. This type of evidence allows the factors that cause disasters to be addressed through the development process. Since many of the most meaningful risk management decisions are made at the national-to-local levels, it is particularly important to strengthen the evidence base for disaster risk management at these scales.

The intent is to suggest a common framework for cooperation among scientists, practitioners and decision-makers, with a special focus on building capacity at the national level in high risk areas.

This report by UNDP, released in 2004, assesses disaster-related mortality risks associated with cyclones, floods and earthquakes. Countries are the unit of analysis. The report identifies the relative contributions of hazard exposure and vulnerability factors to mortality risk and analyses how these can be reduced or exacerbated through the development process.

The analysis is based on a Disaster Risk Index, developed by the United Nations Environment Programme, that measures relative vulnerability to the above hazards. Relative vulnerability is measured as the number of people killed in a country due to a particular natural hazard compared to the number of people exposed. Countries that suffer a higher loss of life than others who are equally exposed have a higher relative vulnerability to the hazard in question.

Countries with relatively high vulnerability to earthquakes, for example, include the Islamic Republic of Iran, Turkey, India, Italy, Algeria, and Mexico. Countries with relatively low vulnerability include Japan, Costa Rica and the United States of America.

Disaster Risk Hotspots

The Disaster Risk Hotspots project, a collaboration between Columbia University, the World Bank and a host of partner organisations, assessed global risks of disaster-related mortality and economic losses associated with cyclones, drought, earthquakes, floods, landslides and volcanoes (Dilley et al. 2005). Mortality and economic loss risks for each hazard were assessed for each 5x5 km cell on the earth's surface, excluding those with small populations and/or low agricultural production. The project identified relative risk levels for each hazard and all hazards together. Risks were calculated based on the hazard exposure of people and GDP in each grid cell, weighted by historical loss rates for each hazard — stratified by region and country wealth status — as a means of representing vulnerability. The report emphasises the theory, data, methods, results and applications of the analysis.

Disaster-related mortality risks associated with hydro-meteorological hazards are highest across the subtropical zones, with drought related mortality risks being highest in semi-arid regions of Africa. Mortality risks associated with geophysical hazards are highest along plate boundaries, around the Pacific rim and across southern Asia. Some countries such as the Philippines and Indonesia are at high risk from all three types of hazards. In general mortality risks tend to be highest in developing or middle income countries.

The project also evaluated total economic loss risks, which, compared to mortality risks are more concentrated in wealthier countries. Large areas of Europe, North America and Southern and Eastern Asia are hotspots with respect to total economic loss risks. Large areas of the caucuses region are at relative high risk from all three types of hazards.

When risks are evaluated for economic losses in proportion to GDP per unit area, the largest risk burden shifts back to the developing world. Coastal zones and large areas of Africa and Central Asia are at relatively highest risk by this measure.

Loss and Risk Identification Priorities: Opportunities for Cooperation: The first focuses on loss assessment and loss information, the second on improving the evidence on disaster risks and the third on systematically enhancing the knowledge, experience and tools for loss and risk identification.

Information on Disaster Losses: Data and Applications

Information on disaster losses plays a crucial role in disaster and risk management.

Considerable value-added can be obtained by organizing the collection and use of this information to serve multiple purposes. The first area of use is disaster management. Secondly, over time, data on accumulated losses can be captured in loss databases containing essential information on each disaster. This information on accumulated losses and the costs of relief, recovery and reconstruction document the impact of disasters on development. The third area in which loss data is a crucial input is the assessment of risks of future disasters. Risk information is vital for contingency planning and disaster preparedness as well as for prioritising measures to reduce losses over time.

When a disaster occurs, the response can be divided into three phases: relief, recovery and reconstruction. Each phase is supported by assessment information that supports key decisions in each domain. In the relief phase, assessment data includes how many people were killed, injured or displaced, and their degree of access to basic requirements — water, food, shelter and medical care. This information is used to estimate needs for relief supplies.

Recovery involves the initial restoration of the functioning of the economy, government and society. Damage and loss data, combined with an analysis of political, livelihood and social systems, supports recovery planning. Data on the economic value of damages and losses is used as the basis for estimating the financial requirements for reconstruction and for reconstruction planning. More work needs to be done to integrate data collection, compilation and analysis in support of decision-making in each of these phases.

They document the cost of disasters to development and the allocation of these costs across economic sectors and socio-economic classes. The disaster history of a country or region also provides information concerning the risks of future disasters.

Loss trends provide important indicators for monitoring the successfulness of disaster reduction efforts. Although such databases exist, they are not well integrated and capacity is needed in disaster-prone countries to collect and maintain this type of data on a sustained basis.

One crucial convention for building and maintaining disaster databases is the Global disaster IDEntifier, or GLIDE. The GLIDE was conceived by the Asian Disaster Reduction Centre, in Kobe Japan. It consists of a unique number for each disaster, incorporating a two-letter hazard code, a unique sequence number and geolocation codes based in ISO standards. The location codes are hierarchically formatted to allow data to be desegregated or aggregated regionally, nationally or subnationally.

Use of the GLIDE allows historical events to be unambiguously identified. This facilitates verifying data on a single event across multiple sources, linking hazard event data to disaster data, and referencing reports, evaluations and other material about the disaster. The GLIDE creates the potential for a global, multi-tiered, decentralised tracking system for disaster losses, in which data on losses, hazards and other information from multiple sources can be virtually linked.

Accumulated information on historical losses is a crucial input for understanding disaster risk patterns. While historical losses may not completely reflect future losses, information on historical losses is vital for corroborating results of risk analyses based on hazard exposure and vulnerability. Risk information supports decisions related to setting risk reduction priorities and measures, the design of risk transfer schemes, and disaster preparedness. One particular preparedness activity is contingency planning.

Identification of high risk areas creates the possibility of developing scenarios of likely future disasters. Such scenarios can be used to refine response roles and responsibilities, pre-locate resources and work out logistics in advance of potential disasters. Contingency plans lead to more effective, quicker response.

Risk information allows contingency planning and preparedness efforts to be more systematically prioritised. The potential for such prioritisation based on new evidence of disaster risk patterns has not been fully explored, however.

Regularly Updated Risk Information at Multiple Scales

Many crucial risk management decisions are made at the national and local levels. It is, therefore, crucial to begin to systematically develop more in-depth information on risk levels and risk factors at larger scales to inform risk management efforts. Much work has been done at larger spatial scales, but many high-risk areas remain inadequately served with evidence concerning the causal factors of disasters. Much could also be done to compile risk information at larger scales more systematically, to begin to evaluate methods and results and contribute to development of a global knowledge base on risk patterns and risk identification good practices. Information on global and regional risk patterns described above provides a basis for focusing efforts in areas where risks of disasters are highest.

On National Level

Areas experiencing frequent disasters and known to be at high risk are prime candidates for comprehensive risk management planning in order to reduce risks and losses. An adequate evidence base on which to make risk management decisions is crucial in order to get maximum benefit from available resources. Coverage of these high risk areas with risk identification analyses is uneven. Greater focus on these areas, using rigorous methods and high-resolution data at national and subnational scales, would yield improvement. Compiling and evaluating existing analyses would provide an invaluable foundation for this effort and constitutes an important next step.

For many reasons it is important that local institutions have the primary responsibility for generating and maintaining risk assessment products. These include the need to incorporate local knowledge, sustainability, ownership, maintenance and cost. Having the ability to generate, maintain and apply risk information at national and subnational scales may require infusions of financial and technical resources, however. Therefore a system that can routinely provide this type of support is needed if high-quality risk information is to become widely available for risk management decision-support in high risk areas.

As one moves from smaller to larger spatial scales, from the global to the community level, scientific rigour must be increasingly complemented by stakeholder participation. In parallel with, and in support of, the promotion of science-based risk identification in high risk countries, there is a need to continue to advance work on risk identification globally. One area of work is to systematise technical support for risk assessment "downscaling" at the national level. This includes development and application of methods, collaboration with local experts on specific aspects of risk identification analysis, and development of a toolkit for risk identification. The toolkit would be initiated by compiling methods, lessons learned and best practices from existing risk assessment literature and practice. As new results are obtained, new methods, results, lessons learned and good practices would be compiled and added to the tool kit.

Improvements can also be made in existing global products. Areas for improvement include better global data on hazards, exposure and vulnerability and better methods for integrating these data to assess risks. Given the importance of floods and droughts globally, improving the global data on these hazards is particularly important. The recent Indian Ocean tsunami underscores the need for a better characterisation of risks associated with that hazard in coastal areas as well.

Cross-scale Integration

One means of supporting the process of compiling and enhancing risk information at multiple scales is to create a global risk information platform in which data at multiple scales can be integrated. The higher the risks, the most important it is to have higher resolution. An integrated risk information system could support the regular release of global report on the state of disaster risk. The report could regularly update the status of risk globally, with chapter submitted by countries focusing on particular high risk area; Routinely generating such a report would be facilitated by having a GIS-based, web accessible platform into which data and results at different scales could be incorporated. As risk patterns change, or new data and results become available revised results could be generated and interpreted for priority setting and decision-making. In the interim the risk information platform would support development and integration of new data sets and ongoing revision of results.

A later phase could begin to incorporate dynamic risk assessment and predictions - ongoing recalculation of risk based on such things as current storm tracks, cumulative and projected rainfall anomalies, volcanic activity etc. Hydro meteorological hazard probabilities in particular vary seasonal by and inter-annually in ways that are increasingly well understood.

The setting of standards is also important. The credibility of loss and risk information as a basis for decision-making and resource allocation depends on scientifically rigorous theory data and methods. As the demand for these products grows it is critical that the ability to supply them keeps pace.

Risk Management Decision Support

The investment required to realise the above vision would only be justified to the extent that it has a material impact or the reduction of disaster losses. By this standard, the effective use of loss and risk information to reduce losses constitute; another evaluation factor in addition to the technical quality of loss and risk assessment work. A number of criteria affect the likelihood of loss and risk information contributing to the overall goal of loss and risk reduction.

In high risk areas, there should be a broad-based commitment to risk management, particularly within the government, but also including civil society, research institutions and the private sector. Involvement of these stakeholders in the process of identifying risks is key to developing analyses that support real-world decisions by real-world agents.

Since many disaster prone countries are also poor, it helps if there is a strong commitment to risk management by the international community as well. Agencies that have key roles to play in this regard include the United Nations system, bilateral donors, international finance institutions, and non-governmental organisations. Risk and loss information can help raise the visibility of disaster risks among these constituencies and encourage them to work together to develop and act upon a common set of evidence based risk management priorities. Increasingly the private sector is participating in the development of innovative ways to transfer as well as reduce risks.

Requirements for achieving high quality loss and risk assessment results include national and/or local technical capacity, adequate and accessible data, and inter-institutional cooperation. Scientific work at national and local scales with insufficient engagement by local experts is unlikely to contribute to achieving reduced losses over the longer term.

Finally, the biggest payoffs will be in the highest risk areas, where disasters are virtually guaranteed to continue to occur until measures are taken to reduce and transfer the risks. Such areas warrant the time, effort and resources necessary to mobilise comprehensive, address the root causes of disasters, rather than the consequences. Reduction of recurrent losses in disaster-prone areas would increase the potential for secure, sustainable development.

Standards and Norms for Assessing Disaster Losses

Continuum of Humanitarian/Relief and Development Phase: How can a needs assessment methodology best address the continuum from relief, through transitional recovery to longer term development? Risk Mitigation Needs: Assessment should take into account the causes of the disaster, focus on identifying underlying risks and vulnerabilities which magnify impacts of hazards and identify which risk reduction measures will be effective in recovery strategies and programmes in the specific context.

- **Absorptive Capacity:** To what extent and how should the needs assessment evaluate absorptive capacity? Related to this is the need to assess institutional capacity, major institutional gaps and prioritisation of institutional support efforts.

- **Participation of Civil Society and NGOs.** What should be the role of NGOs and civil society in the needs assessment process? How to manage the trade-offs between the need for speed and the need to build ownership from stakeholders in the NGO community and in civil society organisations that will have an interest in how needs are defined and assessed and are likely to have a role in the reconstruction phase.

Disaster Needs Assessment Standing Capacity for Governments

- Government Ownership: How can the needs assessment exercise build government ownership from the start and assist in the capacity building effort? How and to which extend should government counterparts participate in needs assessment missions and subsequent follow up?
- Data, Indicators and Monitoring: How could/should a needs assessment methodology address the unavailability and/or inaccuracy of relevant data and likely difficulties in defining realistic and meaningful indicators and monitoring benchmarks?
- Conclusion: Develop a predisaster recovery planning, capacity development programme in high risk countries, targeting high risk local governments and statistical agencies.

Responding to Natural Disasters: Helping Children and Families

Natural disasters can be especially traumatic for children and youth. Experiencing a dangerous or violent flood, storm, or earthquake is frightening even for adults, and the devastation to the familiar environment (i.e., home and community) can be long lasting and distressing. Often an entire community is impacted, further undermining a child's sense of security and normalcy. These factors present a variety of unique issues and coping challenges, including issues associated with specific types of natural disasters, the need to relocate when home and/or community have been destroyed, the role of the family in lessening or exacerbating the trauma, emotional reactions, and coping techniques.

Children look to the significant adults in their lives for guidance on how to manage their reactions after the immediate threat is over. Schools can help play an important role in this process by providing a stable, familiar environment. Through the support of caring adults school personnel can help children return to normal activities and routines (to the extent possible), and provide an opportunity to transform a frightening event into a learning experience.

Immediate response efforts should emphasise teaching effective coping strategies, fostering supportive relationships, and helping children understand the disaster event. Collaboration between the school crisis response team and an assortment of community, state, and federal organisations and agencies is necessary to respond to the many needs of children, families, and communities following a natural disaster. Healing in the aftermath of a natural disaster takes time; however, advanced preparation and immediate response will facilitate subsequent coping and healing.

ISSUES ASSOCIATED WITH SPECIFIC DISASTERS

Hurricanes: Usually hurricanes are predicted days to weeks in advance, giving communities time to prepare. These predictions give families time to gather supplies and prepare. At the same time, however, these activities may generate fear and anxiety. Although communities can be made aware of potential danger, there is always uncertainty about the exact location of where the hurricane will impact. When a hurricane strikes, victims experience intense thunder, rain, lightning, and wind. Consequently, startle reactions to sounds may be acute in the months that follow.

Among a few children subsequent storms may trigger panic reactions. Immediate reactions to hurricanes can include emotional and physical exhaustion. In some instances, children may experience survivor guilt (e.g., that they were not harmed, while others were killed or injured). Research indicates that greater symptomatology in children is associated with more frightening experiences during the storm and with greater levels of damage to their homes.

Earthquakes: Aftershocks differentiate earthquakes from other natural disasters. Since there is no clearly defined endpoint, the disruptions caused by continued tremors may increase psychological distress. Unlike other natural disasters (e.g., hurricanes and certain types of floods), earthquakes occur with virtually no warning. This fact limits the ability of disaster victims to make the psychological adjustments that can facilitate coping. This relative lack of predictability also significantly lessens feelings of controllability.

While one can climb to higher ground during a flood, or install storm shutters before a hurricane, there is usually no advance warning or immediate preparation with earthquakes. Survivors may have to cope with reminders of the destruction (e.g., sounds of explosions and the rumbling of aftershocks; smells of toxic fumes and smoke; and tastes of soot, rubber, and smoke).

Tornadoes: Like earthquakes, tornadoes can bring mass destruction in a matter of minutes and individuals typically have little time to prepare. Confusion and frustration often follow. Similar to a hurricane, people experience sensations during tornadoes that may generate coping challenges. It can be difficult to cope with the sights and smells of destruction. Given the capricious nature of tornadoes, survivor guilt has been observed to be an especially common coping challenge. For instance, some children may express guilt that they still have a house to live in while their friend next door does not. In addition, a study following a tornado that caused considerable damage and loss of life revealed significant associations between children's disturbances and having been in the impact zone, been injured, and having experienced the death of relatives.

Floods: These events are one of the most common natural disasters. Flash floods are the most dangerous as they occur without warning; move at intense speeds; and can tear out trees, destroy roads and bridges, and wreck buildings. In cases of dam failure, the water can be especially destructive. Research has reported that many children who survive a destructive flood experience psychological distress. The two most significant predictors of impairment are the degree of disaster exposure and perceptions of family reactions. Sensations that may generate coping challenges include desolation of the landscape, the smell of sludge and sodden property, coldness and wetness and vast amounts of mud. Most floods do not recede overnight, and many residents have to wait days or weeks before they can begin the cleanup.

Finally, it is important to acknowledge that although natural disasters may last for only a short period, survivors can be involved with the disaster aftermath for months or even years. In attempts to reconstruct their lives following such a natural disaster, families are often required to deal with multiple people and agencies (e.g., insurance adjusters, contractors, electricians, roofers, the Red Cross, the Federal Emergency Management Agency (FEMA), and the Salvation Army).

Possible Reactions of Children and Youth to Natural Disasters: Most children will be able to cope over time with the help of parents and other caring adults. However, some children may be at risk of more extreme reactions.

The severity of children's reactions will depend on their specific risk factors. These include exposure to the actual event, personal injury or loss of a loved one, dislocation from their home or community, level of parental support, the level of physical destruction, and pre-existing risks, such as a previous traumatic experience or mental illness. Symptoms may differ depending on age but can include:

- ***Pre-schoolers:*** Thumb sucking, bedwetting, clinging to parents, sleep disturbances, loss of appetite, fear of the dark, regression in behaviour and withdrawal from friends and routines.
- ***Elementary School Children:*** Irritability, aggressiveness, clinginess, nightmares, school avoidance, poor concentration and withdrawal from activities and friends.
- ***Adolescents:*** Sleeping and eating disturbances, agitation, increase in conflicts, physical complaints, delinquent behaviour and poor concentration.

A minority of children may be at risk of post-traumatic stress disorder (PTSD). Symptoms can include those listed above, exhibited over an extended period of time. Other symptoms may include re-experiencing the disaster during play and/or dreams; anticipating or feeling that the disaster is happening again; avoiding reminders of the disaster; general numbness to emotional topics; and increased arousal symptoms such as inability to concentrate and startle reactions. Although rare, some adolescents may also be at increased risk of suicide if they suffer from serious mental health problems like PTSD or depression. Students who exhibit these symptoms should be referred for appropriate mental health evaluation and intervention.

Immediately Following a Natural Disaster: Information for School Crisis Teams

Identify Children and Youth Who are High Risk and Plan Interventions: Risk factors are outlined in the above section on children's reactions. Interventions may include individual counselling, small group counselling, or family therapy. From group crisis interventions, and by maintaining close contact with teachers and parents, the school crisis response team can determine which students need supportive crisis intervention and counselling services. A mechanism also needs to be in place for self-referral and parental-referral of students.

Support Teacshers and Other School Staff: Provide staff members with information on the symptoms of children's stress reactions and guidance on how to handle class discussions and answer children's question. As indicated, offer to help conduct a group discussion.

Reinforce that teachers should pay attention to their own needs and not feel compelled to do anything they are not comfortable doing. Suggest that administrators provide time for staff to share their feelings and reactions on a voluntary basis as well as help staff develop support groups. In addition, teachers who had property damage or personal injury to themselves or family members will need leave time to attend to their needs.

Engage in Post-disaster Activities that Facilitate Healing: La Greca and colleagues have developed a manual for professionals working with elementary school children following a natural disaster. Activities in this manual emphasise three key components supported by the empirical literature:

(a) exposure to discussion of disaster-related events,

(b) promotion of positive coping and problem-solving skills, and

(c) strengthening of children's friendship and peer support. Specifically:

Important Influences

Relocation: The frequent need for disaster survivors to relocate creates unique crisis problems. For example, it may contribute to the social, environmental and psychological stress experienced by disaster survivors. Research suggests that relocation is associated with higher levels of ecological stress, crowding, isolation, and social disruption.

Parent's Reactions and Family Support: Parents' adjustment is an important factor in children's adjustment and the adjustment of the child in turn contributes to the overall adjustment of the family. Altered family functions, separation from parents after natural disaster and ongoing maternal preoccupation with the trauma are more predictive of trauma symptomatology in children than is the level of exposure. Thus, parents' reactions and family support following a natural disaster are important considerations in helping children's cope.

Emotional Reactivity: Preliminary findings suggest that children who tend to be anxious are those most likely to develop post-trauma symptomatology following a natural disaster. Research suggests that children who had a pre-existing anxiety disorder prior to a natural disaster are at greater risk of developing PTSD symptoms.

Coping Style: It is important to examine children's coping following a natural disaster because coping responses appear to influence the process of adapting to traumatic events. Research suggests that the use of blame and anger as a way of coping may create more distress for children following disasters.

Long-term Effects

Research suggests that long-term difficulties following a natural disaster (e.g., PTSD), are most likely to be seem among children who experienced any of the following:

- Had threats to their physical safety.
- Thought they might die during the disaster.
- Report that they were very upset during the disaster.
- Lost their belongings or house as a result of the disaster.
- Had to relocate in the aftermath.
- Attended schools following the disaster that had multiple schedule changes, double sessions or a lot of disruptions.

Consequently, crisis response team members need to identify students who experience these risk factors and closely monitor their status. These students may require long-term coping assistance.

World Conference on Disaster Reduction

The World Conference on Disaster Reduction (WCDR) is a milestone event to increase the profile of disaster risk reduction in development planning and practice. The Conference will provide a unique opportunity to promote a strategic and systematic approach at the national level to address vulnerabilities and to reduce risk to natural hazards.

Commitment to the reduction of disasters has been growing although actual materialisation is still slow. Human and economic losses due to natural disasters continue to rise and remain as a major obstacle to sustainable development and achievement of the Millennium Development Goals (MDGs). New risks are emerging. The WCDR is expected to guide and motivate governments and their policy makers to pay more attention to such vital issues, identifying practical ways to incorporate risk reduction measures into action to reduce poverty.

The Conference will build on the findings of the review of the implementation of the Yokohama Strategy and Plan of Action of 1994, aiming at:

- Assessing achievements and identifying good practices;
- Defining the remaining challenges, critical needs and opportunities in disaster reduction initiatives worldwide and examining emerging issues; and,
- Developing a set of objectives and areas of action for disaster risk reduction to implement the objectives of the Johannesburg Plan of Implementation for Sustainable Development, as essential conditions to achieve the relevant Millennium Development Goals (MDGs).

COMMUNICABLE DISEASES FOLLOWING NATURAL DISASTERS

Risk Assessment and Priority Interventions: Natural disasters are catastrophic events with atmospheric, geologic and hydrologic origins. They include earthquakes, volcanic eruptions, landslides, tsunamis, floods and drought. Natural disasters can have rapid or slow onset and serious health, social and economic consequences. During the past two decades, natural disasters have killed millions of people, adversely affecting the lives of at least one billion more people and resulting in substantial economic damage. Developing countries are disproportionately affected because of their lack of resources, infrastructure and disaster preparedness systems.

The potential impact of communicable diseases is often presumed to be very high in the chaos that follows natural disasters. Increases in endemic diseases and the risk of outbreaks, however, are dependent upon many factors that must be systematically evaluated with a comprehensive risk assessment. This allows the prioritisation of interventions to reduce the impact of communicable diseases post-disaster.

The Communicable Diseases Working Group on Emergencies (CD-WGE) at WHO/ HQ has developed this document to describe the communicable disease risks in populations affected by natural disasters. It is hoped that this document, by detailing the priority measures that are necessary to reduce the impact of communicable diseases following natural disasters, will help to protect the health of disaster-affected populations.

Assessing the Risk of Communicable Diseases

Communicable Diseases Associated with Natural Disasters: The sudden presence of large numbers of dead bodies in disaster-affected areas can heighten expectations of disease outbreaks, despite the fact that dead bodies do not pose a risk of outbreaks following natural disasters. Rather, the risk of outbreaks is associated with the size, health status and living conditions of the population displaced by the natural disaster. Crowding, inadequate water and sanitation and poor access to health services, often characteristic of sudden population displacement, increase the risk of communicable disease transmission.

Although the overall risk of communicable disease outbreaks is lower than often perceived, the risk of transmission of certain endemic and epidemic-prone diseases can increase following natural disasters.

Waterborne Diseases: Diarrheal disease outbreaks can/occur following contamination of drinking water and have been reported following flooding and related displacement. An outbreak of diarrheal disease post flooding in Bangladesh in 2004 involved more than 17,000 cases, with the isolation of Vibrio cholerae and enterotoxigenic Escherichia coli. A large (>16,000 cases) cholera epidemic in West Bengal in 1998 was attributed to preceding floods, and floods in Mozambique in January-March 2000 led to an increase in the incidence of diarrhoea. The risk of diarrheal disease outbreaks following natural disasters is higher in developing than in developed countries.

In Aceh Province, Indonesia, a rapid health assessment performed in the town of Calang two weeks after the December 2004 tsunami found that 100 per cent of the survivors drank from unprotected wells and that 85 per cent of residents reported diarrhoea in the previous two weeks. In Muzaffarabad, Pakistan, following the 2005 earthquake, an outbreak of acute watery diarrhoea occurred in an unplanned, poorly-equipped camp of 1800 persons. The outbreak involved over 750 cases, mostly adults, and was controlled following the provision of adequate water and sanitation facilities. In the United States, diarrheal illness was noted following hurricanes Allison and Katrina and Norovirus, Salmonella and toxigenic and non-toxigenic cholerae were confirmed among Katrina evacuees.

Hepatitis A and E are also transmitted by the faecal-oral route, in association with lack of access to safe water and sanitation. Hepatitis A is endemic in most developing countries and children are exposed and develop immunity at an early age. As a result, the risk of large outbreaks is usually low in these settings. In endemic areas, hepatitis E outbreaks frequently follow heavy rains and floods; it is generally a mild, self-limited illness, but in pregnant women case-fatality rates can be up to 25 per cent. Clusters of both hepatitis A and hepatitis E were noted in Aceh following the December 2004 tsunami.

Leptospirosis is a zoonotic bacterial disease that is transmitted through contact of the skin and mucous membranes with water, damp vegetation or mud contaminated with rodent urine. Infected rodents shed large amounts of leptospires in their urine. Flooding facilitates the spread of the organism due to the proliferation of rodents and the proximity of rodents to humans on shared high ground. Outbreaks of leptospirosis occurred in Taiwan, China, associated with Typhoon Nali in 2001 and following flooding in Mumbai, India, in 2000.

Diseases Associated with Crowding: Measles and the risk of transmission in the disaster-affected population is dependent on the baseline vaccination coverage rates among the affected population and in particular among children aged <15 years. Crowded living conditions, as is common among people displaced by natural disasters, facilitate transmission and necessitate even higher immunisation coverage levels to prevent outbreaks. A measles outbreak in the Philippines in 1991 among people displaced by the eruption of Mt. Pinatubo involved more than 18,000 cases. In Aceh following the tsunami, a cluster of measles involving 35 cases occurred in Aceh Utara district and continuing sporadic cases were common despite mass vaccination campaigns. Sporadic cases and clusters of measles (>400 clinical cases in the six months following the earthquake) also occurred in Pakistan following the 2005 South Asia earthquake.

Meningitis caused by Neisseria meningitis is transmitted from person to person, particularly in situations of crowding. Cases and deaths from meningitis among those displaced in Aceh and Pakistan have been documented. Prompt response with antibiotic prophylaxis, as occurred in Aceh and Pakistan, can interrupt transmission.

Acute respiratory infections (ARI) are a major cause of morbidity and mortality among displaced populations, particularly in children aged <5 years. Lack of access to health services and to antibiotics for treatment further increases the risk of death from ARI. Risk factors among displaced persons include crowding, exposure to indoor cooking and poor nutrition. The reported incidence of ARI increased four-fold in Nicaragua in the 30 days following Hurricane Mitch in 1998 and ARI accounted for the highest number of cases and deaths among those displaced by the tsunami in Aceh in 2004 and by the 2005 earthquake in Pakistan.

Vector-borne Diseases: Natural disasters, particularly meteorological events such as cyclones, hurricanes and flooding, can affect vector breeding sites and vector-borne disease transmission.

While initial flooding may wash away existing mosquito breeding sites, standing-water caused by heavy rainfall or overflow of rivers can create new breeding sites. This can result (with typically some weeks delay) in an increase of the vector population and potential for disease transmission, depending on the local mosquito vector species and its preferred habitat. The crowding of infected and susceptible hosts, a weakened public health infrastructure and interruptions of ongoing control programmes are all risk factors for vector-borne disease transmission.

Malaria outbreaks in the wake of flooding are a well-known phenomena. An earthquake in Costa Rica's Atlantic Region in 1991 was associated with changes in habitat that were beneficial for breeding and preceded an extreme rise in malaria cases. Additionally, periodic flooding linked to El Nino-Southern Oscillation has been associated with malaria epidemics in the dry coastal region of northern Peru.

Dengue transmission is influenced by meteorological conditions including rainfall and humidity and often exhibits strong seasonality. However, transmission is not directly associated with flooding. Such events may coincide with periods of high transmission risk and be exacerbated by increased availability of vector breeding sites — mostly artificial containers — caused by disruption of basic water supply and solid waste disposal services.

The risk of vector-borne disease outbreaks can be influenced by other complicating factors, such as changes in human behaviour (increased exposure to mosquitoes while sleeping outside, movement from non-endemic to endemic areas, a pause in disease control activities, overcrowding), or changes in the habitat which promote mosquito breeding (landslide deforestation, river damming and re-routing).

Other Diseases Associated with Natural Disasters: Tetanus is not transmitted from person to person, but is caused by a toxin released by the anaerobic tetanus bacillus Clostridium tetani. Contaminated wounds, particularly in populations where routine vaccination coverage levels are low, are associated with morbidity and mortality from tetanus. A cluster of 106 cases of tetanus, including 20 deaths, occurred in Aceh and peaked 2Vi weeks following the tsunami. Cases were also reported in Pakistan following the 2005 earthquake.

An unusual outbreak of coccidiomycosis occurred following the January 1994 southern California earthquake. The infection is not transmitted from person to person, but is caused by the fungus Coccidioides immitis, which is found in soil in certain semi-arid areas of North and South America. This outbreak was associated with exposure to increased levels of airborne dust subsequent to landslides in the aftermath of the earthquake.

Disaster-related Disruptions: Power cuts related to disasters may disrupt water treatment and supply plants, thereby increasing the risk of waterborne diseases. Lack of power may also affect proper functioning of health facilities, including preservation of the cold chain. An increase in diarrheal incidence in New York City followed a massive power outage in the United States in 2003. Investigation of the outbreak revealed an association with the consumption of meat and seafood after the onset of the power outage, when refrigeration fails.

Dead Bodies and the Risk of Communicable Diseases

Deaths associated with natural disasters are overwhelmingly caused by blunt trauma, crush-related injuries or drowning. The sudden presence of large numbers of dead bodies in the disaster-affected area can fuel fears of outbreaks. There is no evidence that dead bodies pose a risk of epidemics following natural disasters.

When death is directly due to the natural disaster, human remains do not pose a risk for outbreaks; the source of infection is more likely to be the survivors than those killed by the natural disaster. Even when death is directly due to communicable diseases, pathogenic organisms do not survive long in the human body following death.

Dead bodies pose health risks only in a few situations requiring specific precautions, such as deaths from cholera or haemorrhagic fevers.

Management of Dead Bodies

The mass management of dead bodies is often based on the false belief that they represent an epidemic hazard if not buried or burned immediately.

- Burial is preferable to cremation in mass casualty situations.
- Every effort should be made to identify the bodies.
- Mass burial should be avoided if at all possible.
- Families should have the opportunity and access to materials, to conduct culturally appropriate funerals and burials according to social custom.
- Where existing facilities such as graveyards or crematoria are inadequate, alternative locations or facilities should be provided. For workers routinely handling dead bodies.
- Ensure universal precautions for blood and body fluids.
- Ensure use and correct disposal of gloves.
- Use body bags if available.
- Wash hands with soap after handling dead bodies and before eating.
- Disinfect vehicles and equipment.
- Dead bodies do not need disinfection before disposal (except in case of cholera, shigellosis, or haemorrhagic fever).
- The bottom of any grave must be at least 1.5 m above the water table, with a 0.7 m unsaturated zone.

Prevention of Communicable Diseases Following Natural Disasters

The following priority measures are critical to reduce the impact of communicable diseases after natural disasters:

Safe Water, Sanitation, Site Planning: Ensuring uninterrupted provision of safe drinking-water is the most important preventive measure to be implemented following a natural disaster.

Chlorine is widely available, inexpensive, easily used and effective against nearly all waterborne pathogens. Settlement planning must provide for adequate access for water and sanitation needs and meet the minimum space requirements per person, in accordance with international guidelines.

Primary Health-care Services: Access to primary care is critical to prevention, early diagnosis and treatment of a wide range of diseases, as well as providing an entry point for secondary and tertiary care. The immediate impact of communicable diseases can be mitigated with the following interventions:

- Ensure early diagnosis and treatment of diarrheal diseases and ARI, particularly in those aged <5 years.
- Ensure early diagnosis and treatment for malaria in endemic areas (within 24 hours of onset of fever, using artemisinin-based combination therapy ACT for falciparum malaria).
- Ensure the availability and application of treatment protocols for the main communicable disease threats.
- Ensure proper wound cleaning and care. Tetanus toxoid with or without tetanus immunoglobulin, as appropriate, should accompany wound treatment post-disaster.
- Ensure availability of drugs included in the interagency emergency health kit, e.g. oral rehydration salts for management of diarrheal diseases, antibiotics etc.
- Distribute health education messages, including:
  - — Encouraging good hygienic practices;
  - — Promoting safe food preparation techniques;
  - — Ensuring boiling or chlorination of water;
  - — Encouraging early treatment seeking behaviour in case of fever;
  - — Encouraging use of insecticide-treated mosquito nets as a personal protection measure in malaria-endemic areas.
- Vector control interventions adapted to the local context and disease epidemiology.

  Surveillance/Early Warning System: Rapid detection of cases of epidemic-prone diseases is essential to ensure rapid control. A surveillance/early warning system should be quickly established to detect outbreaks and monitor priority endemic diseases.

- Priority diseases to be included in the surveillance system should be based on a systematic communicable disease risk assessment. In some situations, the threats may include rare diseases such as viral haemorrhagic fevers, plague or tularaemia. A comprehensive communicable disease risk assessment by WHO can identify and prioritise these threats.

- Ensure health-care workers are trained to detect priority diseases and that prompt reporting to lead health agency occurs.
- Ensure sampling and transport materials for investigation and appropriate stockpiles are readily available for rapid response to outbreaks, e.g. cholera kits, in areas where cholera is considered a risk.

Immunisation:

- Mass measles immunisation together with vitamin A supplementation are immediate health priorities following natural disasters in areas with inadequate coverage levels. Where baseline coverage rates among those aged <15 years are below 90 per cent, mass measles immunisation should be implemented as soon as possible. The priority age groups are 6 months to 5 years, and up to 15 years if resources allow.
- Current typhoid vaccines are not recommended for mass immunisation campaigns to prevent typhoid disease. Typhoid vaccination in conjunction with other preventive measures may be useful to control typhoid outbreaks, depending on local circumstances.
- Hepatitis A vaccine is generally not recommended to prevent outbreaks in the disaster area.
- The cost of the cholera vaccine and the logistic difficulties involved with the administration, have prohibited its widespread use. Although helpful in specific circumstances, it should not be viewed as a replacement for the provision of adequate water and sanitation. The usefulness of the cholera vaccine, relative to other public health priorities, has not been evaluated in disaster-affected areas.

Prevention of Malaria and Dengue

- Specific preventive interventions for malaria must be based on an informed assessment of the local situation, including on the prevalent parasite species and the main vectors.
- An increase in mosquito numbers may be delayed following flooding, allowing time for implementation of preventive measures such as indoor residual spraying of insecticides, or the retreatment/distribution of insecticide-treated

nets preferably Long Lasting Insecticidal Nets (LLIN) in areas where their use is well-known and accepted.

- Early detection of a possible malaria outbreak can be enhanced by monitoring weekly case numbers must be part of the surveillance/early warning system. Periodic laboratory confirmation of rapid test-positive fever cases is recommended to track the slide/test positivity rate.
- Treatment with artemisinin-based combination (ACT) therapy should be provided free of charge to the user in disaster-affected areas with falciparum malaria. An active search for fever cases may be necessary to reduce mortality.

Disaster Preparedness Plans and Control Self-Communicable Diseases: Although disaster-related deaths are overwhelmingly caused by the initial traumatic impact of the event, disaster preparedness plans should consider the health needs of the surviving disaster-affected populations. The health impacts associated with the sudden crowding together of large numbers of survivors, often with inadequate access to safe water and sanitation facilities, will require planning for both therapeutic and preventive interventions, such as rehydration materials, antibiotics and measles vaccination materials.

Disaster response teams should be aware of and have access to the latest updated guidelines for communicable disease prevention and control, such as the WHO field manual on Communicable disease control in emergencies and the Sphere project's Humanitarian charter and minimum standards in disaster response.

The risk of outbreaks following natural disasters, though often incorrectly connected to the presence of dead bodies, is closely related to the size, health status and living conditions of the displaced population. The risk of transmission of endemic communicable diseases, such as ARI and diarrheal diseases, is increased in displaced populations due to associated crowding, inadequate water and sanitation and poor access to health care. Improved detection and response to communicable diseases is important in order to monitor the incidence of diseases, to document their impact and to help to better quantify the risk of outbreaks following natural disasters.

While natural disasters cannot be avoided, there are ways to improve safety, minimise loss and injury and increase public awareness of the risks involved. One of the most effective ways to lessen the impact of natural disasters on people and property is through risk assessment and mitigation — the topic of this study. Conducted over a four-year period (1999-2003), the study is a thorough risk and loss assessment of potential earthquakes in the NY-NJ-CT region. This study documents the scale and extent of damage and disruption that may result if earthquakes of various magnitudes occurred in this area. In short, it addresses the first step in risk reduction: to identify potential problems. It focuses on the vulnerability of the building stock; future studies will deal with the inventory, fragilities, and losses from lifeline infrastructure systems, such as transportation, communication, water, liquid waste, and energy.

RISK REDUCTION

The number of people affected by natural disasters in poor countries is growing annually. Jeggle pinpoints a major economic and political dilemma contributing to the global insufficiency of positive risk reduction action. The hesitation to which Jeggle refers is a persistent enemy of the ongoing endeavour to create a preventive culture in which risk reduction is 'normalised' or accepted as a fact of life. In the words of Ressler (United Nations Children's Fund (UNICEF)), we should be saying to governments and others:

You need to do much more than you are doing to reduce risks. Why should any children look like this if they are malnourished, or crushed, or flooded? We should be saying 'Why? How can you accept this?'

Yet the number of people affected by disasters continues to rise and the attitude of many towards such events remains one of detachment and resigned despondency.

Evidence of a lack of a preventive culture can be found in countries of low, medium and high human development. Donors and governments appear to succumb to a sense of the inevitability of extreme events and so adopt an apathetic approach to reducing disaster risks. For instance, following the floods of 2002 in central Europe, the EU re-established the Solidarity Fund — a reserve of 1 billion Euros only to be used after a disaster event has occurred. Jeggle observes this is tantamount to saying, 'These resources and assets are not worth our attention until after they are lost and then we will spend 1 billion Euros to help the communities and the countries recover.

Integrating risk reduction into development planning is — key to creating a culture of prevention. Risk reduction, by name at least, is usually undertaken by relief departments within agencies whose primary concern is with managing disasters.

Consequently, their natural focus is on the 'preparedness' (or 'preparing to respond') aspect of the subject more than the purposefully preventive 'mitigation' aspect. This raises a further problem as highlighted by Pisano (International Strategy for Disaster Reduction (ISDR)), that risk reduction is merely'.. .the study of the last disaster'. He continued, 'If we rely on this, I am afraid we will have to kill half the world's population before we put sizeable prevention in place.'

Clearly, much more needs to be done if 'sizeable prevention' is to be achieved, so as to cut the unacceptably high death toll and destruction of lives and property caused by disasters. Consequently, this report explains how the interlinked key issues of 'knowledge', 'ownership' and 'competition' are hindering the creation of a preventive culture among donors and its recommendations are underpinned by the need for all those in a position to reduce risks (governments, NGOs, etc. as well as donors) to adopt a more practical outlook. Ramon (European Commission Humanitarian Office Disaster Preparedness (DIPECHO)) stated: Lots of people talk about disaster risk reduction but there is nothing concrete. No one is saying this is what I suggest for this type of situation ... We need practical solutions that are not too expensive and are appropriate for communities.

Faced with serious levels of disaster risk, the IADB, in its March 2002 Action Plan,12 emphasised the need to build a culture of prevention as well as reduce the vulnerability of the poor and mainstream risk reduction in all Bank operations. Such an approach is not unusual and is echoed in many other institutions and organisations. It is argued in this report, however, that the method adopted by the IADB, with its development of a practical checklist to aid development professionals in their assessment, analysis and subsequent reduction of risks, is a positive contribution to disaster risk reduction as it may help bridge the gap between rhetoric and practice.

It would of course be easy to criticise the IADB's method of expanding a preventive culture with cries of over-simplicity, lack of contextual analysis and an overly aggressive or unrealistic imposition on development sectors. However, against the reality of rapidly increasing community vulnerability to natural disasters and following discussions with several institutions and risk reduction experts, we believe that the urgency of the problem requires rapid and concrete action to change institutional responses, even if the checklist approach may be open to improvement.

Another factor contributing to the lack of knowledge of, and confusion over, disaster risk reduction is that it is very broad in its scope (Aysan of the United Nations Development Programme (UNDP) referred to it as 'nebulous'). This point is echoed in the British Red Cross study NGO Natural Disaster Mitigation and Preparedness Projects.

REVIEW QUESTIONS

Short Answer Type Questions

1. Differentiate a problem and a risk.
2. Define disaster risk management.
3. State any two obstacles in mainstreaming disaster risk management.
4. What do you understand by the term integrated disaster risk management.
5. List down the steps involved in conducting a risk analysis.
6. Describe how one can monitor risk assumptions and risk areas.
7. Expand PADR and note down its functions.
8. Tell us how information on disaster losses is highly helpful in managing a disaster risk.
9. What does cross-cultural integration is all about.
10. What is meant by RMDS and state its importance?
11. What is the need to have a standards and norms for assessing disaster loss?
12. List down some of the major objectives of World Conference on disaster risk reduction.
13. Name the steps involved in risk management process.
14. Name the four major categories in potential risk treatment.
15. Differentiate risk avoidance and risk reduction.
16. Differentiate risk retention and risk transfer.
17. Define cost overrun.
18. What critical event chains are?
19. List down the benefits of operational risk management.
20. Write a note on social risks.

Essay Type Questions

1. Elaborate the international path towards integrated disaster risk management.
2. Explain the importance of risk mitigation strategies in detail.
3. Explain the advantages that one can derive out of regularly updating the risk information at multiple scales.
4. Critically analyze all the issues associated various disasters.

5. Elucidate the risk imposed by the communicable diseases and suggest some ways to overcome the same.
6. Eloborately explain what are all the areas to be focused in controlling the risk.
7. Explain the concept of enterprise risk management in detail and explain how it is applied to a project management.
8. Enumerate the role of internal audit in ERM.
9. Explain the operational risk management and elucidate how it is categorized.

CHAPTER 5

THE RELIEF AND REHABILITATION

THE REHABILITATION

Anthropology the Science of Man in its totality has to deal with disaster management at the start of the new millennium and has to equip itself with management skills.

In tribal India and also in other parts of the world, we frequently find drought, flood, epidemic, mysterious diseases leading to de-population, migration and other allied problems. The concept of tribe has drawn wide range of attention varying from anthropologists, administrators, policy makers, historians, members of judiciary, politicians, journalists, members of international bodies like UNESCO, Human Rights Commission, UNO, etc. But here we are using the term strictly in Anthropological terminology.

The elements constituting the tribe may or may not be coordinated by formal or centralised political power, ideally the term 'tribe' implies large elements of solidarity based on strongly shared primary sentiments. Such solidarity becomes contractual in nature as the tribal organisation become more formally organised.

Empowerment means putting the external force in an individual, tribe, caste, country, etc., to make him powerful. It is a process. It cannot be done in a day. It takes place systematically and scientifically. It is an experiment. If the chemical substances are mixed in proper order, then it is bound to be successful otherwise it will fail. Here comes the role of anthropologists and bureaucratic experts who have sufficient knowledge of social administration inputs like chemical substance. He knows in which or what cultural/social system ; how much typological variant chemical substances are required.

The various forms of power act and interact on each other so significantly, that if the study of power was confined to a single aspect, such as, political, economic or social power, much would be lost in the understanding of the overall dynamics of the system.

Empowerment can be cultural, ethnic, educational, economic, political, health related, etc. It can be of many more types depending upon the requirement and suitability of the target group for whom the whole exercise of 'developmental planning' is done. Now comes the question of empowering the tribals. Here we are using the term tribals strictly in anthropological terminology. For some, it may correspond to ethnic group or racial group but we will include them to the extent they fall within our term of reference. It is true that differential development has taken place at the global level among the tribes. Therefore, the necessity of this Commission has arisen in order to integrate them through the process of an empowerment which is the emerging need of 21st century of anthropology.

RELIEF WORK

The term disaster may be defined as an unexpected happening causing a huge loss of life and property. It may be both natural as well as man-made in the sense that in some parts of the country, floods are coming due to the construction of check dams and embankments on the rivers.

Disaster may come in the forms of earthquakes, cyclones, floods, drought, fire, etc., and ruin the life and property of the people. Anthropology is mainly concerned with how to prevent, predict and mitigate major disasters. So far, scientific and technological development the prevention of earthquakes, cyclones, floods, droughts, fires, etc. may be prevented and predicted to some extent, but there is no doubt that proper planning and effective management can reduce the effects and hazards of disasters, since it is not the earthquake itself but the defective buildings which cause loss of life and property.

To prevent disaster, there should be pre-planning of all the, available resources, communication facilities, manpower, etc. Experience has shown that before starting the rescue work administration has to clean the roads and bridges which are badly damaged. For this not only an inventory of local resource should be prepared but also bypasses and alternative routes should be identified in the plan itself.

It is the poorest who suffer the most, but all of us are caught up in the same syndrome. Humankind inherit but one earth, which they conspire against while destroying the gifts of nature by reducing the water-table, deforestation and pollution to name a few, which results in climatic changes and consequences measured in terms of human suffering which are likely to be acute.

The common view of disaster is due for a radical change. Though triggered of by natural events such as floods and earthquakes, disasters are increasingly man-made. Some disasters (floods, droughts, famines) are caused more by environmental and resource mismanagement than by too much or too little rainfall. The impact of other disasters which are triggered by acts of nature (earthquake, volcano, hurricane) are magnified by unwise human actions. Disasters are social and political events which can be and often are prevented. In the Third World, where the poor are forced to over use their land and live on dangerous grounds, disasters are taking a rising toll. By emphasising mitigation instead of development, current disaster relief is often inadequate to the task it sets itself.

We can only tackle the root causes if disaster prevention and response are designed so as to incorporate both developmental and environmental strategies. We must get at the root causes and reverse the trends of increasing poverty and environmental degradation before it is too late. A sustainable ecosystem must be our aim, as one in which the global family can live in balanced harmony with the whole of nature. The rural poor, who are the principal victims of the three elements which between them make up the major part of the Third World disasters — deforestations, soil erosion and desertification should be central to the work of all disaster agencies. All the trends emphasise that ignorance and grinding poverty accelerate the onslaught of disasters and exacerbate the cruel impact they have, particularly on vulnerable groups of people. The poor, the handicapped, the infant and the aged are the first to lose their basic right to food, shelter and health. They need and deserve our help.

The social development of people and their communities in disaster prone areas has been grossly ignored by governments and agencies alike. Such appalling human conditions can best be fought through the weapons of self-reliance, literacy, preventive health care and equitable pricing structures for rural food producers, that is, helping people to respond to their own basic needs, within their environment.

Disasters are not unforeseen events and the technology now exists to identify the hazards that threaten a community and to estimate the areas and the settlements that will be affected. In most places and segments of society where calamities are occurring, the natural events are about as certain as anything within a person's lifetime.

The very essence of disaster mitigation is long-term planning, while the very essence of Third World poverty is the struggle of day-to-day existence. The local people are more concerned with their children's education or lack of it, their health and the scarcity of medicine in the dispensaries and the difficulties of selling their crops at a decent price, which relates to the problems of access to markets in the accessible terrain. So vulnerability to natural hazards has to be recognised within the cultural and economic context of poverty and deprivation. And as with our own society, long-term logical action is frequently overwhelmed by short-term expediency.

Effective disaster mitigation and prevention depends on long-term planning for development towards a more sustainable and less vulnerable society. Some relief agencies are embarking on new types of community based disaster prevention programmes. Improved self-reliance in respect of food and fuel, access to land, employment, better health and nutrition, family planning and education are important components of disaster prevention. Disaster prevention and the elimination of poverty are closely linked as are poverty and environmental degradation. Many relief agencies are beginning to complement their emergency aid with their development programmes and are now working towards gaining knowledge, experience, training personnel and public backing to initiate new ideas into practice, in order to understand and minimise the problems of disasters.

Spread of AIDS: A Man-made Disaster

The anthropology of disaster management deals with both natural disaster as well as disaster created by man. Prevalence of AIDS in Tribal India is an example of recent disaster created by man.

Perhaps the most worrying aspect is the growing evidence in India of what HIV experts call "transmission chains" by which the virus percolates insidiously through social substrata and afflicts low risk individuals like housewives and children.

Life of the Indian HIV victim ends the moments he tests positive. Illiteracy, social taboos and retrograde customs are just some of the barriers that confront those infected and those working to prevent the spread of the disease. At the beginning of the new millennium, India is projected to suffer one of the world's most rapid expansions of the HIV pandemic.

REHABILITATION AND DISPLACEMENT PERSPECTIVE OF DISASTER

An anthropologist who is quite often turned into a social doctor looks at the problems of displacement and rehabilitation. Anthropological, psychological issues which are natural outcomes of displacement resulting in rehabilitation because of which the development projects are the subject matter of disaster management.

It discusses anthropo-psychological consequences on the people affected by these projects and attempts to provide a basic framework to understand its anthropological perspective. It presents basic guidelines, action strategies for effective implementation of projects with a view to minimise advise anthropo-psychological effects on displaced population. It is also presumed that this will help those who are the key participants in planning and implementation of disaster projects.

Current Status of Displacement and Development

Development is an ongoing process which leads to commissioning of various kinds of development projects such as: Construction of new irrigation dams, establishing new factories, mines, road construction, railways and many other projects related to infrastructural growth leading to regional/ national economic development. This often necessitates the government to acquire land which leads to 'involuntary displacement' of people from the original home land.

It uproots people from their original land and creates psycho-sociological stress leading to many dysfunctional consequences. More often, both social and economic benefits of such developmental projects are not shared equally by displaced population.

The problem of displacement is normally related to economic aspects but truly speaking, it has more of psycho-sociological implications. Though the meagre economic compensation provides temporary relief to evacuees, but it leads to many psycho-sociological and cultural problem of serious nature.

Displaced Population

The Report of the Commissioner for Scheduled Castes and Scheduled Tribes (1990), points out that when the land is acquired and under the present law, only its property form is considered vital. Questions concerning the very survival of the displaced persons are settled on this basis.

Even those, who are identified, are very inadequately compensated. Lack of accurate data on such crucial issues, such as this, is itself an indication of both the Central and State Governments degree of concern for the rehabilitation of oustees (Viegas, 1987). This current status of displacement is leading to an alarming situation. How to sustain the historical right which the oustee has been deprived of, is an important issue today.

Rehabilitation and Development

Rehabilitation is more often understood as economic rather than a psycho-sociological phenomenon resulting from displacement. It is normally perceived as a 'planned change effort'. In a strict sense, it implies that, while there is a change the overall effects of the change is to restore the situation to its original condition. In other words, change or no change (Franks, 1991). Though rehabilitation is sought for development but its nature is quite different from other developmental processes. All developmental efforts imply planned change to improve existing conditions, whereas rehabilitation is designed to restore the status quo. This makes it imperative to understand the term rehabilitation in a much wider perspective, and its components which make it different from other developmental processes.

Components of Rehabilitation

Rehabilitation can be described as having the following components:

(i) Antecedent conditions: Displacement and rehabilitation of people are required when certain 'antecedent conditions' exist in the situation. For example, National long-term interest for socio-economic development of the country leading to commissioning of various developmental projects; National calamities, such as, war and political turmoil; Natural disasters, such as, floods, earthquakes, drought and also man-made disasters.

(ii) Cognitive state of the individuals involved, i.e., their perception and awareness of the situation, such as:

- Fears and apprehensions about the possible problems to be faced by the affected people.
- Fears and apprehensions about their acceptability by the host population.
- Fears and apprehensions about fulfilment of government promises with respect to providing facilities.
- Attitudes about various 'developmental projects' and about 'government'.

(iii) Affective state of the individuals involved in the situation: Perception of a situation may affect the people in a variety of ways such as, developing anxieties, psychological tension, stress and hostility.

(iv) Manifest behaviour: Psychological effects manifest themselves in variety of behavioural patterns. These range from passive resistance to active resistance, overt aggression and finally agreeing for displacement under stress leading to many other dysfunctional behaviour patterns resulting in poor mental health.

(v) Rehabilitation: Displacement leading to rehabilitation of people through various rehabilitation programmes such as: Allotment of land: houses, monetary compensation, occupation and many other facilities required for resettlement.

(vi) Further demands by people from government: Any rehabilitation results in an aftermath which manifests itself in further demands by people from government.

Compensation Package

Inadequate or inappropriate compensation package also results in psychological tension / stress among the oustees. It has been reported that adequate or inappropriate compensation packages to the oustees have also resulted in lot of psychological stress for the people. The illiterates found it difficult to utilise the compensation amount appropriately. This has led to social evils like alcoholism, gambling and prostitution (Advani, 1990).

Impact at Group Level

Displacement also results in disintegration of family, other social groups and occupational groups. Evidence from Augucha Mines of Hindustan Zinc Ltd., at Bhilwara, Rajasthan suggests that providing occupation to one representative of each evacuee's family by HZL, helped families, but created family tension resulting in breaking of joint family system and difficulties in getting match in their own community for their children (Advani, 1990).

All these psycho-sociological factors discussed above, result in psychological tensions, stress, hostility, sometimes leading to trauma. These get manifested in variety of dysfunctional behaviours leading to mental ill health and sometimes to mental sickness.

MANAGEMENT OF DISPLACEMENT AND REHABILITATION PROCESS

In order to achieve the efficacy of various objectives of resettlement and rehabilitation projects, minimising the adverse effects of displacement must form the primary focus. The success of these projects depends upon, how effectively the displacement is managed and the various rehabilitation programmes are perceived, as appropriate and adequate sources of gratification of needs by the affected population. This makes it imperative to plan, design and implement strategies as 'preparedness measures' and 'rehabilitation programmes', to cope with negative aspects of displacement, at the appropriate stages of the rehabilitation process.

Need for a 'National Policy'

Recognising the adverse impact on human beings, the sufferings and hardships caused by involuntary settlement, the World Bank policy states as its first requirement, that "whenever feasible, the involuntary resettlement must be avoided or minimised and alternative developmental solutions must be explored" (Cemea, 1988). Notwithstanding this policy, there have been cases, when projects have been designed and approved without examining such possible alternatives.

Lack of provision of psycho-sociological consideration in the Land Acquisition Law 1994 and also Land Acquisition Amendment Act 1984, further weakens the implementation of the Bank policy. Though rehabilitation has normally been envisaged as a planned change effort, evidences suggest that implementation of each project, called for an ad hoc policy of its own. The Bank policy can be made effective only, if a well-defined national policy is designed.

Introducing of psycho-sociological perspective in the Land Acquisition Law will also greatly enhance the efficacy of bank policy. Therefore, the need for a well-defined national policy is a first prerequisite for effective implementation of resettlement and rehabilitation projects.

Appropriate preparedness measures needed to be designed at this stage are as follows:

Preparedness Measures: Preparedness measures must focus around issues like:

(i) Prepare individuals psychologically to agree for displacement without much resistance.

(ii) Dissemination of timely information about displacement.

(iii) Minimising adverse impact on people.

Conscious efforts at all levels are required to formulate motivational strategies, around perceived potential fears and threats by the people.

Operational Interventions

Detailed Microlevel Planning: Detailed planning in advance, before the onset of displacement, should necessarily form an integral part of the process. The government must procure the data regarding the following aspects about the population to be displaced.

Data Needed Regarding Displaced Population

(i) Correct estimate of land to be acquired,

(ii) Number of households/families to be displaced,

(iii) Housing pattern of the area,

(iv) Population structure of the place: adults, males, females, children and old people,

(v) Caste structure of the area,

(vi) Educational profile of the people,

(vii) Professional skills available with the people,

(viii) Aptitudes and potentials available with the people,

(ix) Correct estimate of movable and immovable property with the people,

(x) Schools, hospitals, temples, transport and other facilities available to the people in the area.

(xi) Attitude of the host population to know acceptability of the displaced population. The services of research organisations and other agencies can be of immense help in this regard.

All this data will provide the guidelines to decide the nature of compensation package and facilities to be offered to the people. It will also enable the government to design appropriate communication strategy to create a desirable impact over the people in generating positive outlook about displacement.

Communication Strategy: Communication strategy should have the following objectives:

(a) Developing awareness among individuals about need for displacement.

(b) Providing knowledge about the rehabilitation package and its commitment benefits to people.

(c) Preparing individuals psychologically to cope with the unwanted psychological stress.

(d) Preparing host population for accepting the displaced people.

PRIORITIES AND OPPORTUNITIES IN REHABILITATION AND RECONSTRUCTION

The disaster occurred because the society was vulnerable to the impact of the hazard concerned. Rehabilitation and reconstruction must, therefore, not be seen as a process of simply restoring what existed previously. The need is rather to develop strategies and modalities to reconstitute services and renovate or replace essential structures such that vulnerability is reduced. These strategies must include long-term development policies and plans which take account of the current situation including any basic changes resulting from the disaster.

The disaster may, in fact, have created new opportunities for development by changing the environment and the point of departure, both in terms of physical structures and/or social patterns and attitudes. It will certainly have heightened awareness concerning disaster risks and both the local populations and national authorities are likely to be especially receptive to proposals for risk reduction and preparedness measures. Such opportunities must be recognised and seized in the planning of rehabilitation and reconstruction projects, as well as in the formulation of new, long-term development programmes.

Assistance to rehabilitation and reconstruction must, therefore, be planned on the basis of a thorough assessment and appraisal of the technical and social issues involved. While planning of such assistance cannot be unduly rushed, it must be accomplished as expeditiously as possible. There are two reasons for this:

- Certain rehabilitation and reconstruction measures, if organised rapidly enough, can shorten the period for which emergency relief assistance is needed and eliminate the need to invest resources in temporary measures.
- The "window of opportunity" may be short for the incorporation of risk reduction measures in reconstruction (of housing, for instance) or for new development initiatives (especially social aspects).

Seasonal factors must be considered and may determine the needed timetable for reconstruction, for example, the replacement of emergency shelter or the rehabilitation of irrigation systems in time for the next crop. The aim is to promote and assist recovery. Assistance during the post-disaster phase must be planned and implemented with this clearly in mind.

Damaged structures and services which are essential to the society must be repaired or replaced, duly protected against future risks. At the same time, and no less important, ways must be found to help people recover, particularly those people who have the least resources to call on.

As noted earlier, "the majority of people affected are the poor." For the poor, disasters represent lost property, jobs and economic opportunity. In real terms that can represent an enormous economic setback. Therefore, reconstruction assistance should be designed to:

- Relieve economic constraints and reduce the cost of reconstruction.
- Inject capital into the community.
- Create employment opportunities.
- Support and strengthen existing economic enterprises.

Timely and imaginative planning is, therefore, required to dovetail rehabilitation and reconstruction with short-term "relief" measures and to make the most effective use of external financial resources, materials and technical assistance in achieving development gains while satisfying humanitarian needs.

The Danger of Planning and Conducting Reconstruction in Haste: Post-disaster programmes, even reconstruction programmes, are often planned and carried out in haste. The rush may occur because of the reconstruction planners' perceived need to return the community to "normal" as soon as possible or because of time constraints on donor funding. Thus the sort of careful planning and community involvement necessary for development planning is often overlooked. Without such planning, these programmes may infringe on longer-term development efforts or delay their implementation. Reconstruction programmes that are ill-planned and merely return communities to the status quo may leave them almost as vulnerable again to a future disaster, while at the same time creating a sense of complacency because something has been seen to have been done.

THE MITIGATION

Mitigation is one of the positive links between disasters and development. Agencies, communities and individuals can use their development resources to reduce the risk of hazards through mitigation projects. They can also ensure that their other development initiatives contain components that mitigate against future disaster. In its broadest usage, mitigation has become a collective term used to encompass all actions taken prior to the occurrence of a disaster (pre-disaster measures). This includes long-term risk reduction and preparedness measures. Many individuals and institutions, however, apply a narrower definition to mitigation.

They use mitigation to mean actions taken to reduce both human suffering and property loss resulting from extreme natural phenomena. The concept of mitigation accepts the fact that some hazard event may occur but tries to lessen the impact by improving the community's ability to absorb the impact with minimum damage or disruptive effect. More simply stated, for this group, mitigation is risk reduction.

Mitigation applies to a wide range of activities and protection measures that might be instigated: from the physical, like constructing stronger buildings or agricultural diversification, to the procedural, like standard techniques for incorporating hazard assessment in land-use planning. In the 1990s, a major effort is underway to encourage the implementation of disaster mitigation techniques in development projects around the world. The General Assembly of the United Nations adopted the decade of the 1990s as the International Decade for Natural Disaster Reduction. The aim is to make a significant reduction in the losses of life and material damage caused by disasters by the end of the decade.

Disaster have, until recently, been seen in much the same way as disease was in the early 19th century: unpredictable, unlucky and part of the everyday risk of living. Concentrations of people and rising population levels across the globe are increasing the risk of disasters and multiplying the consequences of natural hazards when they occur. However, the "epidemiology" of disaster — the systematic science of what happens in a disaster shows that disasters are largely preventable. There are many ways to reduce the impact of a disaster and to mitigate the effects of a possible hazard, accident, or conflict. Just like the fight against disease, the fight against disasters has to be fought by everyone together.

It must involve public and private sector investment, changes in social attitudes and improvements in the practices of individuals. Governments can use public investment to improve their countries' infrastructure and to promote a physical environment where a disaster is less likely to occur. Individuals must also learn how to act to protect themselves.

Just as public health depends on personal hygiene, so public protection depends on personal safety.

The type of cooking stove an individual uses and their awareness that a sudden earthquake could tip it over is more important in reducing the risk of a disastrous fire than having the community maintain a large fire brigade. The type of house individuals build and where they consider a suitable place to live affects the potential for disaster in a community more than large engineering projects to reduce flood risk, or landslide stabilisation efforts or sophisticated typhoon warning systems.

Saving Life and Reducing Economic Disruption: The worst effects of any disaster are the deaths and injuries caused to the population. The scale of disasters and the number of people they are capable of killing is the primary justification for mitigation. Understanding the way that people are killed and injured in disasters is a prerequisite for reducing casualties.

Targeting Mitigation Where it has Most Effect: Understanding how the occurrence of a natural hazard of an accident turns into a disaster enables us to forecast likely situations where a disaster is possible. For example, some buildings (elements) are more vulnerable to earthquakes (hazard) than others. Identifying these elements most at risk, can indicate priorities for mitigation.

Actions to Reduce Risk

- **Reduce the Hazard or Reduce Vulnerability:** Protection against the threats of disaster can be achieved by modifying or removing the causes of the threat, (reducing the hazard) or by reducing the effects of the threat if it occurs (reducing the vulnerability of elements affected).

  For most types of natural disasters, it is impossible to prevent the actual event from occurring. The focus of mitigation policies against these hazards is primarily on reducing the vulnerability of elements that are likely to be affected. Obviously, some natural hazards can be reduced. The construction of levees along a riverbank is an example of risk reduction.

- **Tools, Powers and Budgets:** It is evident that risk reduction is complex and needs to be built up through a range of activities happening together. Governments, for example, can employ a wide range of tools and use their powers in many ways to influence the safety of the community. Legislative powers, administrative functions, spending and project initiation are all part of the tools they can employ to bring about change. Powers of persuasion are sometimes classified into two types: passive and active. Another power of persuasion is diplomacy, perhaps the most useful tool to mitigate against warfare or civil conflict.

The Menu of Mitigation Actions

The range of techniques that an authority might consider in order to assemble an appropriate package for disaster mitigation can be classified into:

- Engineering
- Spatial planning

- Economic
- Management and institutionalisation
- Societal
- Conflict reduction.

Engineering: Engineering measures are those that result in stronger individual structures that are more resistant to hazards. This is sometimes referred to as "hardening" facilities against hazard forces. Building codes are critical defensive measures for achieving stronger engineered structures. Training techniques to teach builders the practicalities of disaster resistant construction are now well understood and form part of the menu of mitigation actions available to the disaster planner.

Spatial Planning: Many hazards are localised with their likely effects confined to specific known areas. For example floods affect flood plains, and landslides affect steep soft slopes. The effects can be greatly reduced if it is possible to avoid having hazardous areas used for settlements or as sites for important structures. Urban planning needs to integrate awareness of natural disaster risk mitigation into the normal procedures of planning a city.

For populations displaced by hazards or conflict, opportunities to reduce their risk include the identification of safe zones for resettlement in areas with adequate security and resources to support displaced persons.

Economic: Economic development is key to disaster mitigation. A strong economy is the best protection against a future disaster. A strong economy means more money to spend on stronger buildings, safer sites and larger financial reserves to cope with future losses.

Management and Institutionalisation of Disaster Mitigation: Disaster mitigation also requires certain organisational and procedural measures. The time scale over which a significant reduction can be achieved in the potential impact of a disaster is medium and long term. Changes in location planning, upgrading structures and changes in the characteristics of building stock are process that take decades. The objectives and policies that guide the mitigation processes have to be sustained over a number of years. They have to survive the changes in political administration that are likely to happen within that time, the changes in budgetary priorities and policies on other matters. The institutionalisation of disaster mitigation means the acceptance of a consensus of opinion that efforts to reduce disaster risk are of continual importance.

Societal: Education, training and the development of professional expertise are necessary components of institutionalising disaster mitigation. The mitigation of disasters will only come about when there is a consensus that it is desirable. In many places, the individual hazards that threaten do not result in disasters, me steps that people can take to protect themselves are not known and the mandate of the community to have itself protected is not forthcoming. Mitigation planning should aim to develop a disaster "safety culture," one in which the general public is fully aware of potential hazards, chooses to protect itself as fully as possible and can readily support protective efforts made on its behalf.

Conflict Reduction: In the disasters and emergencies created by conflict, mitigation must include conflict reduction. Measures at conflict reduction must start with identifying and addressing the root causes of the conflict. Although negotiation will often be the primary tool of conflict reduction, the issues may arise over such causes as land tenure, employment, access to resources and intolerance of ethnic or religious differences. These issues need to be anticipated through a form of early warning and defused before conflict erupts.

Classification of Mitigation Measures

Developing a mitigation strategy should include a structure to facilitate decision making. The following series of questions suggests such a structure. What risk is being reduced? To what level should the risk be reduced?

What criteria are used to reduce the risk?

Who decides what the criteria are?

What is the political process to implement the measure?

Mitigation measures may be classified in several ways.

Active and Passive: For active measures, authorities promote desired actions by offering incentives. For passive measures, authorities prevent undesired actions by using controls and penalties.

Structural and Non-structural: Structural mitigation involves physical measures taken to reduce risk by erecting structures (such as dams). Non-structural measures are policies and practices of development whose implementation reduces the risks to development.

Short-term and Long-term: Short-term measures are those which dare taken rapidly and which have a short life or usefulness such as sand bag reinforcements of a dyke. Long-term measures may include a process that is itself long in implementation, consider an extended timeframe, and change public attitudes through education.

Restrictive and Incentive: Restrictive measures result in practices that promote safety by making some actions or development unlawful or prohibitively expensive. Incentive measures provide financial, legal or other advantages to promote activities which are also beneficial in terms of mitigation.

Sectoral-based Activities: Sectoral-based activities start from the vantage point of a sector, such as agriculture, and ask: "within this sector, what can be done to reduce risk?" A response might be to introduce hazard resistant crops, or to diversify cropping patterns.

Timing for Mitigation

The risk reduction measures of mitigation are often placed in the pre-disaster time frame. In fact, the most opportune time to implement mitigation is in the period after a disaster. Public awareness of the problems posed by hazards is high and the political will to act may also be at its peak. This period probably will not last for more than two to three years before other development priorities take precedence.

Disaster Mitigation as a Development Theme

Hazards are a part of the natural and human-made environment. Exposure to hazards and the risks of disastrous consequences must be considered in all development planning. They must certainly be considered by UNDP at an early stage of programme and project formulation and design.

An awareness of the relationship between disasters and development must be maintained in the UNDP country programme and project cycles. The needs and options for litigation must be specifically addressed in:

- The continuing dialogue between UNDP, other UN agencies, the Government, and aid donors.
- **The Country Programme Cycle:** In the preparation of the UNDP Advisory Note and the Administrator's Note, and in the country programme document, review and evaluation processes.
- **The Project Cycle:** In project identification, design and formulation, approval (PAC/A.C), implementation (PPER, TPR) and evaluation. It is essential that government bodies responsible for development priorities and planning be fully aware of the impact of natural and man-made hazards on societies and economies. This itself may require certain institution-building initiatives during both the preparation and the implementation of the country programme.

The UN-DMT should review the priorities and possibilities for international assistance, especially in cases where technical assistance is anticipated in different sectors and different UN organisations or agencies and expected to be involved or provide financing.

PEOPLE'S PARTICIPATION

"What is needed for construction are three things; *money, technical skills and the understanding of people in the community,* most important is the latter."

Therefore, it is required that we must train and educate the community on pre and post-disastrous situations. Community is required to be better informed through awareness and education programmes. At the same time, the community should also work closely with local bodies, NGOs, etc. The community volunteers can play an important role as they are flexible and that official authorities are not.

People's participation should be the core managing technique in designing as well as implementation of communication strategy. All castes, different occupational groups, local leaders and other influential people who are key participants in day-to-day functioning of the affected area, should be represented in the rehabilitation process. Resettlement and rehabilitation plans about site for resettlement of people, housing pattern, compensation packages and other facilities should be drawn in consultation with the core participative group. People's involvement would enable the government to elicit commitment and would make the displacement less uncomfortable for people.

Procuring all this data from the people before the onset of displacement can provide a glimpse of government's sincere intentions and efforts of rehabilitating the people after displacement. This will have a positive impact on people and would considerably reduce the adverse affects of displacement.

What we can do?

(1) Can train communities from grass root level to professional and administrators level;

(2) Can adopt villages, townships and cities to demonstrate healthy, safe and environment friendly lifestyle, and

(3) Can extend our hand to fund rehabilitation programmes under schemes of the Government.

What We Need to Do?

(1) Need to set up a techno-legal regime by enacting laws for enforcement of provisions for disaster resistance techniques including by-laws on use of building codes;

(2) Prepare vulnerability atlas in place;

(3) Need to disseminate message of preparedness through training workshops and research and design efforts;

(4) Prepare disaster and community action plans;

(5) Involve community for the purposes of planning to development action plans;

(6) Introduce regulations for disaster prone areas;

(7) Need for urban and regional planners to work closely with engineers and architects; and

(8) Need to carry out resource inventories in conflict prone zones. Because, people have been made to evacuate from their land forcefully and have been made to experience psychological shocks, undergo trauma, more often resulting in mental illness.

TRAINING OF PROFESSIONALS

Capacity building for the technical/professional persons is very material. This should also include refresher courses. Communication channels and warnings are the most vital issues. Local authorities are required to establish the communication system for warning, evacuation and relief measures, etc. Local authorities are required to assist in management of post-disaster audits and can also reveal facts or weakness in present procedures.

Last but not the least, resources including trained people should be organised and deployed where they will have the greatest effect. They should also prepare a list containing Do's and Don'ts for the information of general public. These lists should be displayed in all the local schools, offices, libraries, etc. They should also undertake mock exercises to make people aware the steps to be taken in case of any such exigency.

District Planning Cell can be Made More Active

Lastly, as per the 74th Amendment to the Constitution, the district planning committees are required to be constituted, wherein a plan can be formulated keeping in view both the preparedness, i.e. pre-disaster and post-disaster aspects, to meet the exigencies at the time of emergency. The Government should hand over the regional planning aspect as formulated under the 12th Schedule to Panchayati Raj Institutions (PRIs) in view of 73rd and 74th Constitutional Amendment. Funds required for rehabilitation for giving assistance to the victims of natural disasters, i.e. flood, cyclone and earthquake should be at the disposal of district planning committees. PRIs should contribute towards rehabilitation efforts of disaster victims through:

(1) Financial assistance in the form of loans;

(2) Training of local artisans and supervisors in appropriate technologies;

(3) By giving technical advice for disaster resistance, construction and repair through pamphlets indicating do's and don'ts in vernacular languages;

(4) Establishment of building centres for production of cost effective building materials besides dissemination of information on appropriate technologies;

(5) Construction of demonstration units using disaster resistant technologies;

(6) Providing consultancy service for appropriate house design for rehabilitation of disaster victims;

(7) To prepare by-laws through necessary legislation ensuring that the designs incorporate the provisions for required safety measures which are safe enough to resist natural disasters, to which that region is prone;

(8) Invoke unsafe buildings clause to make mandatory in existing deficient houses in case of natural calamity; and

(9) Local bodies to pass the plans for new buildings only if the required provisions have been met with.

Building Safety into System

The Centre has taken an initiative to enact a model law for regulating the activities of developers, builders and architects, which would be seen by the septic as a weak attempt to reign in the construction industry, which is amongst the least regulated industries in India today. It is, however, a step that should be welcomed, coming as it does in the wake of the Bhuj earthquake, which exposed the hollowness of the tall claims of structural integrity of high-rise buildings. A major problem with the construction business is corruption and the builder- architect-contractor nexus that has eaten into its very foundation. A builder selects an architect not only for his ability to design safe and aesthetic buildings, but also for getting the building plans "approved". The contractor typically cuts corners because he is under pressure to do the quickest and the cheapest job.

Conclusion

The population which is more often displaced by the developmental projects usually belong to lower strata of society, such as Scheduled Castes and Scheduled Tribes who are more affected as compared to other displaced population. Therefore, as a part of socio-economic development, `the Rehabilitation Programme must concern with safeguarding the interests of minority, the affected population, and minimising the negative impacts of relocations.

In spite of intentions of the government to provide a comfortable rehabilitation to the affected population, no attention has been paid to the psycho-sociological consequences associated with the process. Though rehabilitation projects are often viewed as a planned change effort with developmental objectives, they are rarely implemented in a manner to achieve those objectives.

"The immediate humanitarian needs are an absolute priority. But what has happened in the towns and cities in Turkey is an important symbol of how devastation, caused by natural disaster, is compounded by the unchecked process of urbanisation. The international community has to make a global effort to ensure that our cities are better governed. The best way to minimise the destruction caused by natural disasters is to ensure that local authorities are trained and equipped to enforce appropriate construction laws. That is essential if we are to secure a safe future for ordinary citizens everywhere." As the trend towards urbanisation is accelerating, the suffering and devastation by natural disasters including earthquake has been worsening.

It can be done by way of management processes, training programmes, new building techniques, new understandings of how we interact with our environment. The post-disaster activities are as follows:

(1) Rescue;

(2) Release;

(3) Repair;

(4) Rehabilitation;

(5) Reconstruction; and

(6) Renewals.

The immediate post-disaster activities can be formulated by giving assistance to the people who have suffered a great loss by way of rescue, evacuation and provision of shelter: in shelters already built or by constructing temporary shelters if permanent are not available. Assistance can also be given by moving people to a safer place and by providing them basic amenities for example water, sanitation, food, health care, etc., and at the same time, protecting them from diseases and epidemics.

The Chief Ministers of various states should indeed take up the recommendation of incorporating the norms suggested by the National Building Code and Bureau of Indian Standards in municipal by-laws and zoning regulations. While Mr. Jagmohan, Minister for Urban Development, GOI, says that the new law would be enacted and enforced in Delhi, other states would be well advised to follow suit.

The State of Maharashtra has already formulated its State Disaster Mitigation Plan. The other states are following the lead and are in the process of formulating such plans, which will help in identifying remedial measures suited for the region well in advance to avoid taking hasty decisions in panic. As disasters increase, it becomes clear that neither governments nor local communities can themselves continue to assume the rising costs of compensating the citizens for the losses incurred. The only affordable solution lies in mitigation and prevention. Shared information is the beginning of prevention and partnership is crucial for successful application of disaster prevention practices.

REVIEW QUESTIONS

Short Answer Type Questions

1. Define Anthropology.
2. Tell us how one can be empowered to contribute towards relief work.
3. List down the components of rehabilitation.
4. Write a note on detailed moving planning.
5. Name the actions to be taken to reduce risk mitigation.
6. List down the menu of mitigation actions.
7. On what basis mitigation measures can be classified.

Essay Type Questions

1. Enumerate the displacement perspective of a disaster.
2. Explain the components of rehabilitation in detail.
3. Discuss the need for having a 'National Policy' towards managing displacement and rehabilitation.
4. Enumerate the importance of people's participation in the relief & rehabilitation measures.

CHAPTER 6

DISASTER RECOVERY: BUSINESS CONTINUITY PLANNING

EMERGENCY MANAGEMENT

Emergency management (or disaster management) is the discipline dealing of with and avoiding risks. It is a discipline that involves preparing, supporting and rebuilding society when natural or human-made disasters occur. In general, any Emergency management is the continuous process by which all individuals, groups, and communities manage hazards in an effort to avoid or ameliorate the impact of disasters resulting from the hazards. Actions taken depend in part on perceptions of risk of those exposed. Effective emergency management relies on thorough integration of emergency plans at all levels of government and non-government involvement. Activities at each level (individual, group, community) affect the other levels. It is common to place the responsibility for governmental emergency management with the institutions for civil defence or within the conventional structure of the emergency services. In the private sector, emergency management is sometimes referred to as business continuity management.

Business Continuity Planning (BCP) is an interdisciplinary peer mentoring methodology used to create and validate a practiced logistical plan for how an organisation will recover and restore partially or completely interrupted critical function(s) within a predetermined time after a disaster or extended disruption. The logistical plan is called a Business Continuity Plan.

In plain language, BCP is how an organisation prepares for future incidents that could jeopardise the organisation's core mission and its long-term health. Incidents include local incidents like building fires, regional incidents like earthquakes, or national incidents like pandemic illnesses.

BCP may be a part of an organisational learning effort that helps reduce operational risk associated with lax information management controls. This process may be integrated with improving information security and corporate reputation risk management practices.

A completed BCP cycle results in a formal printed manual available for reference before, during, and after disruptions have occurred. Its purpose is to reduce adverse stakeholder impacts determined by both the disruption's scope (who and what it affects) and duration (how bad, implications last for hours, months, etc.). Measurable Business Impact Analysis (BIA) "zones" (areas in which hazards and threats reside) include civil, economic, natural, technical, secondary and subsequent.

Prior to January 1, 2000, governments anticipated computer failures, called the Y2 K problem, in important public utility infrastructures like banking, power, telecommunication, health and financial industries. Since 1983, regulatory agencies like the American Bankers Association and Banking Administration Institute (BAI) required their supporting members to exercise operational continuity practices (later supported by more formal BCP manuals) that protect the public interest. Newer regulations were often based on formalised standards defined under ISO/IEC 17799 or BS 7799.

Both regulatory and global business focus on BCP arguably waned after the problem-free Y2K rollover. Some believe this lax attitude ended September 11th 2001, when simultaneous terrorist attacks devastated downtown New York City and changed the 'worst case scenario' paradigm for business continuity planning.

BCP methodology is scalable for an organisation of any size and complexity. Even though the methodology has roots in regulated industries, any type of organisation may create a BCP manual, and arguably every organisation should have one in order to ensure the organisation's longevity. Evidence that firms do not invest enough time and resources into BCP preparations are evident in disaster survival statistics. Fires permanently close 44 per cent of the business affected. In the 1993 World Trade Centre bombing, 150 businesses out of 350 affected failed to survive the event. Conversely, the firms affected by the Sept. 11 attacks with well-developed and tested BCP manuals were back in business within days.

A BCP manual for a small organisation may be simply a printed manual stored safely away from the primary work location, containing the names, addresses, and phone numbers for crisis management staff, general staff members, clients, and vendors along with the location of the off-site data backup storage media, copies of insurance contracts, and other critical materials necessary for organisational survival. At its most complex, a BCP manual may outline a secondary work site, technical requirements and readiness, regulatory reporting requirements, work recovery measures, the means to re-establish physical records, the means to establish a new supply chain, or the means to establish new production centres. Firms should ensure that their BCP manual is realistic and easy to use during a crisis. As such, BCP sits along side crisis management and disaster recovery planning and is a part of an organisation's overall risk management.

The development of a BCP manual can have five main phases:

1. Analysis
2. Solution design
3. Implementation
4. Testing and organisation acceptance
5. Maintenance.

The above list is not exhaustive. There are a number of other considerations that could be included in your own plan/manual: Risk Identification Matrix — Roles and Responsibilities (ensuring names are left out but titles are included, e.g. HR Manager). Identification of top risks and mitigating strategies. Considerations for resource reallocation, e.g. skills matrix for larger organisations.

Much of the BCP material on the internet is sponsored by consultancies who offer fee-based services for BCP solution development, however, basic tutorials are freely available on the internet for properly motivated organisations.

Analysis

The analysis phase in the development of a BCP manual consists of an impact analysis threat analysis and impact scenarios with the resulting BCP plan requirement documentation.

Impact Analysis

An impact analysis results in the differentiation between critical and non-critical organisation functions. A function may be considered critical if the implications for stakeholders of damage to the organisation resulting are regarded as unacceptable. Perceptions of the acceptability of disruption may be modified by the cost of establishing and maintaining appropriate business or technical recovery solutions. A function may also be considered critical if dictated by law. Next, the impact analysis results in the recovery requirements for each critical function. Recovery requirements consist of the following information:

- The time frame in which the critical function must be resumed after the disaster;
- The business requirements for recovery of the critical function, and/or;
- The technical requirements for recovery of the critical function.

Threat Analysis: After defining recovery requirements, documenting potential threats is recommended to detail a specific disaster's unique recovery steps. Some common threats include the following:

- Disease
- Earthquake
- Fire
- Flood
- Cyber attack
- Bribery
- Hurricane
- Utility outage
- Terrorism.

All threats in the examples above share a common impact: the potential of damage to organisational infrastructure — except one (disease). The impact of diseases can be regarded as purely human and may be alleviated with technical and business solutions.

However, if the humans behind these recovery plans are also affected by the disease, then the process can fall down. During the 2002-2003 SARS outbreak, some organisations grouped staff into separate teams, and rotated the teams between the primary and secondary work sites, with a rotation frequency equal to the incubation period of the disease.

The organisations also banned face-to-face contact between opposing team members during business and non-business hours. With such a split, organisations increased their resiliency against the threat of government-ordered quarantine measures if one person in a team contracted or was exposed to the disease. Damage from flooding also has a unique characteristic. If an office environment is flooded with non-salinated and contamination-free water (e.g., in the event of a pipe burst), equipment can be thoroughly dried and may still be functional.

Definition of Impact Scenarios

After defining potential threats, documenting the impact scenarios that form the basis of the business recovery plan is recommended. In general, planning for the most wide-reaching disaster or disturbance is preferable to planning for a smaller scale problem, as almost all smaller scale problems are partial elements of larger disasters. A typical impact scenario like 'Building Loss' will most likely encompass all critical business functions and the worst poiential outcome from any potential threat. A business continuity plan may also document additional impact scenarios if an organisation has more than one building. Other more specific impact scenarios—for example a scenario for the temporary or permanent loss of a specific floor in a building—may also be documented.

Recovery Requirement Documentation

After the completion of the analysis phase, the business and technical plan requirements are documented in order to commence the implementation phase. A good asset management programme can be of great assistance here and allow for quick identification of available and re-allocatable resources. For an office-based, IT intensive business, the plan requirements may cover the following elements which may be classed as ICE (In Case of Emergency) Data:

- The numbers and types of disks, whether dedicated or shared, required outside of the primary business location in the secondary location.
- The individuals involved in the recovery effort along with their contact and technical details.
- The applications and application data required from the secondary location desks for critical business functions.
- The manual work around solutions.
- The maximum outage allowed for the applications.
- The peripheral requirements like printers, copier, fax machine, calculators, paper, pens, etc.

- Other business environments, such as production, distribution, warehousing, etc. will need to cover these elements, but are likely to have additional issues to manage following a disruptive event.

Solution Design

The goal of the solution design phase is to identify the most cost effective disaster recovery solution that meets two main requirements from the impact analysis stage. For IT applications, this is commonly expressed as:

1. The minimum application and application data requirements.
2. The time frame in which the minimum application and application data must be available.

Disaster recovery plans may also be required outside the IT applications domain, for example in preservation of information in hard copy format, or restoration of embedded technology in process plant. This BCP phase overlaps with disaster recovery planning methodology. The solution phase determines:

- The crisis management command structure.
- The location of a secondary work site (where necessary).
- Telecommunication architecture between primary and secondary work sites.
- Data replication methodology between primary and secondary work sites.
- The application and software required at the secondary work site, and
- The type of physical data requirements at the secondary work site.

Implementation

The implementation phase, quite simply, is the execution of the design elements identified in the solution design phase. Work package testing may take place during the implementation of the solution, however, work package testing does not take the place of organisational testing.

Testing and Organisational Acceptance

The purpose of testing is to achieve organisational acceptance that the business continuity solution satisfies the organisation's recovery requirements. Plans may fail to meet expectations due to insufficient or inaccurate recovery requirements, solution design flaws, or solution implementation errors. Testing may include:

- Crisis command team call-out testing.
- Technical swing test from primary to secondary work locations.
- Technical swing test from secondary to primary work locations.
- Application test.
- Business process test.

At minimum, testing is generally conducted on a biannual or annual schedule. Problems identified in the initial testing phase may be rolled up into the maintenance phase and retested during the next test cycle.

Maintenance

Maintenance of a BCP manual is broken down into three periodic activities. The first activity is the confirmation of information in the manual, roll out to ALL staff for awareness and specific training for individuals who's roles are identified as critical in response and recovery. The second activity is the testing and verification of technical solutions established for recovery operations. The third activity is the testing and verification of documented organisation recovery procedures. A biannual or annual maintenance cycle is typical.

Information Update and Testing

All organisations change over time, therefore, a BCP manual must change to stay relevant to the organisation. Once data accuracy is verified, normally a call tree test is conducted to evaluate the notification plan's efficiency as well as the accuracy of the contact data. Some types of changes that should be identified and updated in the manual include:

- Staffing changes,
- Staffing persona,
- Changes to important clients and their contact details,
- Changes to important vendors/suppliers and their contact details,
- Departmental changes like new, closed or fundamentally changed departments.

Testing and Verification of Technical Solutions

As a part of ongoing maintenance, any specialised technical deployments must be checked for functionality. Some checks include:

- Virus definition distribution,
- Application security and service patch distribution,
- Hardware operability check,
- Application operability check,
- Data verification.

Testing and verification of organisation recovery procedures as work processes change over time, the previously documented organisational recovery procedures may no longer be suitable.

Some checks include:

- Are all work processes for critical functions documented?
- Have the systems used in the execution of critical functions changed?
- Are the documented work checklists meaningful and accurate for staff?
- Do the documented work process recovery tasks and supporting disaster recovery infrastructure allow staff to recover within the predetermined recovery time objective?

Treatment of Test Failures

There is a direct relationship between the test and maintenance phases and the impact phase. When establishing a BCP manual and recovery infrastructure from scratch, issues found during the testing phase often must be reintroduced to the analysis phase.

Disaster Recovery: Definition

Disaster recovery is the process of regaining access to the data, hardware and software necessary to resume critical business operations after a natural or human-induced disaster. A disaster recovery plan (DRP) should also include plans for coping with the unexpected or sudden loss of key personnel the focus of which is data protection. DRP is part of a larger process known as Business Continuity Planning (BCP).

Business Data Protection

With the rise in information technology and the reliance on business-critical data, the landscape has changed in recent years in favour of protecting irreplaceable data. This is especially evident in information technology, with most large computer systems backing up digital information to limit data loss and to aid data recovery.

It is believed that some of the companies spend up to 25 per cent of their budgets on disaster recovery planning; this is intended to avoid larger losses. Of companies that had a major loss of computerised records, 43 per cent never reopen, 51 per cent close within two years and only 6 per cent will survive long-term.

The current data protection market is characterised by:

- Rapidly changing customer needs that are driven by data growth, regulatory issues and the growing importance to access data quickly by retaining it online.
- An ever-shrinking time frame for backing up data, which is burdening conventional tape backup technologies.

As the disaster recovery market continues to undergo significant structural changes, the shift presents opportunities for next-generation startup companies that specialise in business continuity planning and off-site data protection such as Recall, Switch Communications, Symagio, NetMass, SunGard Availability Services, and CyGem.

Events that Necessitate Disaster Recovery

There are many different risks that can negatively impact the normal operations of an organisation. A risk assessment should be performed to determine what constitutes a disaster and which risks a specific company is most susceptible to, including:

- Natural disasters
- Fire
- Power failure
- Terrorist attacks
- Organised or deliberate disruptions
- Theft

- System and/or equipment failures
- Human error
- Computer viruses
- Legal issues
- Worker strikes
- Testing

Preventions Against Data Loss

- Backups sent off-site in regular intervals.
  - — Includes software as well as all data information, to facilitate recovery
- Create an insurance copy on Microfilm or similar and store the records off-site.
  - — Use a remote backup facility if possible to minimise data loss.
- Storage Area Networks (SANs) over multiple sites are a recent development (since 2003) which make data immediately available without the need to recover or synchronise it.
- Surge Protectors—to minimise the effect of power surges on delicate electronic equipment.
- Uninterruptible Power Supply (UPS) and/or Backup Generator.
- Fire Preventions—more alarms, accessible extinguishers
- Anti-virus software and other security measures.

Disaster Recovery Planning

Disaster recovery planning falls into the realm of Business Continuity Planning, as well as Risk management.

The planning process consists of the following steps:

- **Assess Business Impact and Risk:** This should include an assessment of the business unit's function and, preferably, a business impact analysis (BIA). The purpose of the assessment is to determine the business unit's relative contribution to the larger organisation (monetary and functional).

- **Develop a Disaster Recovery Framework:** Data should be categorised by importance. Two measures of importance are used, RTO and RPO. Recovery Time Objective (RTO) is the acceptable amount of time between the disaster and the post-disaster resumption of function (how long can we wait to restore data?). Recovery Point Objective (RPO) is the acceptable data roll-back (how current does the data have to be?).
- **Adjust Information Systems to Make Disaster Recover/ Easier:** This includes consolidating servers and data, perhaps with a Storage Area Network or other archival storage method.

  A good plan takes into account many different factors. The most important are:
- **Communication**
  - **Personnel:** Notify all key personnel of the problem and assign them tasks focused towards the recovery plan.
  - **Customers:** Notifying clients about the problem minimises panic.
- **Recall Backups:** If backup tapes are taken off-site, these need to be recalled. If using remote backup services, a network connection to the remote backup location (or the Internet) will be required.
- **Facilities:** Having backup hot sites or cold sites for larger companies. Mobile recovery facilities are also available from many suppliers.
- **Prepare Your Employees:** During a disaster, employees are required to work longer, more stressful hours, and a support system should be in place to alleviate some of the stress. Prepare them ahead of time to ensure that work runs smoothly.
- **Business Information:** Backups should be stored in a completely separate location from the company.

Disaster Recovery and Business Continuity Auditing

Disaster recovery and business continuity refers to an organisation's ability to recover from a disaster and/or unexpected event and resume or continue operations. Organisations should have a plan in place (usually referred to as a "Disaster Recovery Plan", or "Business Continuity Plan") that outlines how this will be accomplished.

When conducting an audit of a disaster recovery plan several factors should be considered. These are described below.

Written Disaster Recovery Plan with Continual Updating

To be effective the plan must be written, must be understandable and must be accessible to those who need it they need it. Because of the constant changes that occur in the modern business environment, a plan should be updated frequently to deal with new and existing threats as they develop. The auditor needs to determine if procedures stated in the plan to achieve these ends are actually used in practice.

This can be accomplished through:

- Direct observation of procedures.
- Examination of the disaster recovery plan.
- Inquiries of personnel.
- Testing of processes for reasonableness and validity.

Designated Hot Site or Cold Site

A hot/cold site is a location that an organisation can move to after a disaster if the current facility is unusable. The difference between the two is that a hot site is fully equipped to resume operations while a cold site does not have that capability. There is also what is referred to as a warm site which has the capability to resume some, but not all operations. The decision a company makes when determining what type of site to establish depends on a cost-benefit analysis and the needs of the individual organisation. The plan should also spell out how relocation to a new facility is to be conducted. A company should have occasional tests and conduct trials to verify the viability and effectiveness of the plan and to determine if any deficiencies exist and how they can be dealt with. An audit of a company Disaster Recovery Plan should primarily look into the probability that operations of the organisation can be sustained at the level that is assumed in the plan, as well as the ability of the entity to actually establish operations at the site.

The auditor should:

- Examine and test the procedures involved.
- Conduct outside research relating to disaster recovery.
- Determine reasonable standards relating to implementation.
- Tour, examine and research the outside facility.

Ability to Recover Data and Systems

The continual backing up of data and systems can help minimise the impact of threats. Even so, the plan should also include information on how best to recover any data that has not been copied.

Controls and protections should fin place to ensure that data is not damaged, altered, brayed during this process. Information technology exports procedures need to be identified that can accomplish this endeavour. Vendor manuals can also assist in determining how best to proceed.

Both Manual and Automated Procedures in Place

Procedures in place to accomplish the needed objectives should take into account the possibility of power failures or other situations in which technology cannot be utilised.

The plan should indicate what procedures to be used in this situation and should also include information on storage of flashlights and candles, as well as additional safety procedures in case of gas leaks, fires or other phenomena. Trial runs should be conducted to test the procedures' effectiveness and viability.

The auditor should:

- Examine and test procedures for reasonableness.
- Make inquiries on personnel.
- Conduct outside research.

Contractual agreements with external agencies/companies: The plan needs to take into account the extent of its responsibilities to other entities and their ability to make those commitments in lieu of a major event. Are their clauses in contracts that minimise against any legal liability for lack of performance in the event of disaster or any other unusual circumstance? Agreements pertaining to establishing support and assisting with recovery for the entity should also be outlined.

The auditor should:

- Examine the reasonableness of the plan.
- Determine whether it takes all factors into account.
- Verify the contracts and agreements through documentation and outside research.

In conducting the audit, the individual or team should make use of various other procedures and processes to achieve the objectives of the audit. These objectives should be clearly stated in the audit plan. Certification to the British Standard on Business Continuity BS 25999 is available from BSI.

Pay-Store

Pay-Store is a UK-based organisation committed to reducing customer information (data, documents, images or video) storage costs while increasing levels of data security by analysis of current information storage processes and techniques, followed by deployment of practical and achievable efficiency improvements. Pay-Store's solutions and services are appropriate for medium to large organisations with short and long term information storage and access requirements. Pay-Store's solutions are available either as in-house or remotely managed services. Furthermore, the solutions can include in-built Business Continuity and Compliance Management facilities whereby end-users have instant access to their organisation's key data, e.g. in the event of a disaster. This approach may also be utilised to share relevant documents/date across an organisation and/or with your remote business partners in the most cost-effective way.

Backup Site

A backup site is a location where a business can easily relocate following a disaster, such as fire, flood, or terrorist threat. This is an integral part of the disaster recovery plan of a business.

A backup site can be another location operated by the business, or contracted via a company that specialises in disaster recovery services. In some cases, a business will have an agreement with a second business to operate a joint disaster recovery facility.

A Disaster Recovery Centre is a backup facility used in case of a disaster. Disaster recovery in Information Technology is the ability of an infrastructure to restart operations after a disaster. Disaster recovery is used both in the context of data loss prevention and data recovery.

There are three types of backup sites, including cold sites, warm sites, and hot sites. The differences between the types are determined by the costs and effort required to implement each.

Cold Sites

A cold site is the most inexpensive type of backup site for a business to operate. It does not include backed up copies of data and information from the original location of the business, nor does it include hardware already set up. The lack of hardware contributes to the minimal startup costs of the cold site, but requires additional time following the disaster to have the operation running at a capacity close to that prior to the disaster.

Warm Sites

A warm site is a location where the business can relocate to after the disaster that is already stocked with computer hardware similar to that of the original site, but does not contain backed up copies of data and information.

Hot Sites

A hot site is a duplicate of the original site of the business, with full computer systems as well as near-complete backups of user data.

Following a disaster, the hot site exists so that the business can relocate with minimal losses to normal operations. Ideally, a hot site will be up and running within a matter of hours. This type of backup site is the most expensive to operate. Hot sites are popular with stock exchanges and other financial institutions who may need to evacuate due to potential bomb threats and must resume normal operations as soon as possible.

IT Service Continuity

IT Service Continuity is a specific form of business continuity planning. It is the process of assessing and managing risks associated with information technology (IT) departments. It involves the evaluation of values, threats, risks, vulnerabilities and development of countermeasures to ensure continuation the event of a disaster.

NC4

NC4 (National Centre for Crisis and Continuity Coordination) is an El Segundo, California based company of provides real-time notification to business and government on significant incidents as they occur.

During Hurricane Katrina the Centre provided real time ratifications on over 40 specific incidents in the Gulf region before the storm had moved inland. The Centre provides situational awareness to businesses and governments across the country, which improves the country's readiness posture.

NC4 produces E Team Incident management software which is a complete emergency management and EOC operations software package. E Team is in wide use around the world.

Off-site Data Protection

Off-site Data Protection is the strategy of sending business critical data to an off-site location as part of an IT Disaster Recovery Plan.

Data is usually transported off-site using removable storage media such as magnetic tape, but can also be sent off-site electronically via a remote backup service. Sending data off-site electronically is also known as Electronic Vaulting (or E-Vaulting).

Although some organisations manage and store their own off-site backups, many chose to have their backups managed and stored by third parties who specialise in the commercial protection of off-site data.

Data Vaults

The storage of off-site data is also known as vaulting as backups are stored in purpose built vaults. There are generally no standards for type of building that contains a vault. Generally commercial vaults fit into 3 three categories:

- **Underground Vaults:** These are often converted disused cold war military or communications facilities, or disused mines.
- Free-standing dedicated vaults.
- **Insulated Chambers Sharing Facilities:** These are often implemented within existing record centre buildings.

Statutory Obligations

Data Protection Statutes are usually non-prescriptive in how data is to be protected, but they are increasingly requiring the active protection of data.

Statutes which mandate the protection of data are:

- Health Insurance Portability and Accountability Act
- Sarbanes-Oxley

- Basel II
- Gramm-Leach-Bliley
- Data Protection Act 1998
- Foreign Corrupt Practices Act ("FCPA") — The FCPA of 1977.

Point Objectives

The Recovery Point Objective (RPO) describes a point in time to which data must be restored in order to be acceptable to the owner(s) of the processes supported by that data.

This is often thought of as the time between the last available backup and the time a disruption could potentially occur. The RPO is established based on tolerance for loss of data or re-entering of data. The RPO in conjunction with the Recovery Time Objective (RTO) is the basis on which data protection strategy is developed.

Time Objectives

The recovery time objective (RTO) is the boundary of time and service level within which a business process must be accomplished to avoid unacceptable consequences associated with a break in continuity.

In accepted Business Continuity Planning methodology the RTO is established during the Business Impact Analysis (BIA) by the owner of a process (usually in conjunction with the Business Continuity planner). The RTOs are then presented to senior management for acceptance.

It should be noted that the RTO attaches to the business process and not the resources required to support the process.

Backup Service

A remote, online, or managed backup service is a service that provides users with an online system for backing up and storing computer files. Managed backup providers are companies that provide this type of service.

Online backup systems are typically built around a client software programme that runs on a schedule, typically once a day. This programme collects, compresses, encrypts and transfers the data to the remote backup service provider's servers. Other types of product are also available in the market, such as remote continuous data protection (CDP).

REVIEW QUESTIONS

Short Answer Type Questions

1. What is meant by Emergency management?
2. Define Business Continuity Planning.
3. Name the five phases in the development of BCP manual.
4. Differentiate impact analysis over threat analysis.
5. Define disaster recovery.
6. Tell us how one can protect the business data.
7. Name some of the available preventive measures against data loss.
8. List down the steps involved in disaster recovery planning.
9. Differentiate hot site over cold site.
10. Write a note on NC4.
11. What do you understand by the term data vaults
12. List down the importance of Recovery Time Objective (RTO).

Essay Type Questions

1. Explain the scope and applicability of BCP in detail.
2. Explain the process of Disaster Recovery Planning (DRP) in detail.
3. Bring out the importance of IT service continuity.

CHAPTER 7

ROLE OF NGOs IN MANAGING DISASTER

It is virtually impossible to prevent occurrence of most Natural Disasters, but it is possible to minimise or mitigate their damage effects. Mitigation measures aim to reduce the Vulnerability of the System [e.g. by improving and enforcing building codes, etc.]. Disaster prevention implies complete elimination of damages from a hazard, but it is not realistic in most hazards, [e.g. Relocating a population from a flood plain or from beach front]. Medical casualty could be drastically reduced by improving the structural quality of houses, schools, public or private buildings. Also ensuring the safety of health facilities, public health services, water supply, sewerage system, etc., mitigation complements the disaster preparedness and disaster response activities.

A specialised unit within the National Health Disaster Management Programme by the name Non-Governmental Organizations (NGOs) should coordinate the works of experts in the field of:

- Health, Public Policy and Public Health
- Hospital Administration
- Water Systems
- Engineering and Architecture
- Planning, Education, etc.

The Mitigation Programme will direct the following activities:

1. Identify areas exposed to natural hazards and determine the vulnerability of key health facilities and water systems.
2. Coordinate the work of multi-disciplinary teams in designing and developing building codes and protect the water distribution from damages.
3. Hospitals must remain operational to attend to disaster victims.
4. Include disaster mitigation measures in the planning and development of new facilities.
5. Identify priority hospitals and critical health facilities that complies with current building codes and standards.
6. Ensure that mitigation measures are taken into account in a facility's maintenance plans.
7. Inform, sensitise and train those personnels who are involved in planning, administration, operation, maintenance and use of facilities about disaster mitigation.
8. Promote the inclusion of disaster mitigation in the curricula of professional training institutes.

TECHNICAL HEALTH PROGRAMMES

- Treatment of casualties.
- Identification and disposal of bodies.
- Epidemiological surveillance and disease control.
- Basic sanitation and sanitary engineering.
- Health management in shelters or temporary settlements.
- Training health personnel and the public.
- Logistical resources and support.
- Simulation exercises/mock exercises

1. Desktop simulation exercises [war games]
2. Field exercises
3. Drills designed to impart skills.

Epidemiologic Surveillance and Disease Control

Natural disasters may increase the risk of preventable diseases due to adverse changes in the following areas:

- Population density.
- Population displacement.
- Disruption and contamination of water supply and sanitation services.
- Disruption of public health programmes.
- Ecological changes that favour breeding of vectors.
- Displacement of domestic and wild animals.
- Provision of emergency food, water and shelter in disaster situation.

The principles of preventing and controlling communicable diseases after a disaster are to:

- Implement as soon as possible all public health measures to reduce the risk of disease transmission.
- Organise a reliable disease reporting system to identify outbreaks and to promptly initiate control measures.
- Investigate all reports of disease outbreaks rapidly. Early clarification of the situation may prevent unnecessary dispersion of scarce resources and disruption of normal progress.

Environmental Health Management

Post disaster environmental health measures can be divided into two priorities:

1. Ensuring that there are adequate amounts of safe drinking water, basic sanitation facilities, disposal of excreta, waste water and solid wastes and adequate shelter.
2. Providing food protection measures, establishing or continuing vector control measures and promoting personal hygiene:

- Water Supply
  - — Alternate water sources
  - — Mass distribution of disinfectants
- Food Safety
- Basic Sanitation and Personal Hygiene
- Solid Waste Management
- Vector Control
- Burial of the Dead
- Public Information and the Media.

EVALUATION

In the case of disaster management, the Evaluator will be looking at the "actual" verses the "desired" on two levels, i.e. the overall outcome of disaster management efforts and the impact of each discrete category of relief efforts (Provision of food, shelter, management of communications, etc.)

A critical step in the management of any disaster relief is the setting of objectives, which specify the intended outcome of the relief. The general objectives of the disaster management will be the elimination of unnecessary morbidity, mortality and economic loss directly and indirectly attributable to mismanagement of disaster relief.

The comparison of the "actual" with "desired" is the first critical step of evaluation. If the objectives were met, those who have participated in the relief have demonstrated that they have accomplished what they set out to do. On the other hand, if the objectives were not met, it is desirable for those conducting the evaluation to continue with the evaluation process, identify the reasons for the discrepancy and suggest corrective action. Simulated Disaster Preparedness Operations should be undertaken to test the various components before actual need arise.

Evaluation of the Health Disaster Management Programme

- Evaluation of the preparedness programme.
- Evaluation of the mitigation measures.
- Evaluation of the training.

PREVENTION OF DISASTERS

Existing knowledge that might reduce the undesirable effects of disasters is often not applied.

- Hurricane/Tornado/Cyclone warning systems.
- Legislation preventing building in the flood prone areas.
- Requirement of protective cellars/shelters in disaster prone areas.
- A Seismic housing code for earthquake-prone area.
- Strict procedural code followed to prevent Nuclear, Toxicological and Chemical disasters.
- Early warning systems, and Disaster preparedness which will help to minimise morbidity, mortality and economic loss.

Disasters have resulted in significant morbidity, mortality and economic loss. Public health is concerned with two objectives in disaster management:

- The elimination of the preventable consequences of the disaster.
- The prevention of losses due to disaster mis-management.

Appropriate disaster relief follows a specific pattern

- Gathering information on the situation,
- Analysis of this information,
- Developing and implementing an appropriate response. This pattern occurs at various levels,
- Immediate assessment,
- Short-term assessment,
- Ongoing assessment.

Through study of the past disasters, their effects and their relief efforts [what has been effective and what have been mismanaged] better plans are now available for effective disaster management as well as for the reduction of preventable losses.

- The disaster proneness varies widely from State to State.
- The country will have to pay more attention towards creating public awareness and preparedness in respect of people living in known disaster prone areas.

- Special training is required to the medical, paramedical, voluntary workers in the relief and rescue work.
- Any disaster is an emergency situation and the health sector alone cannot tackle it in isolation.
- It must have coordination with the local community, civil defence, army, police, fire brigade and with various governmental and non-governmental bodies including voluntary organisations like Red Cross.

DISASTER PROBLEMS

From the outset it is worth reminding ourselves that disasters and emergencies are all too often regarded as aberrant events, divorced from "normal life." In reality, however, the opposite is true. Disasters and emergencies are fundamental reflections of normal life. They are consequences of the ways societies structure themselves, economically and socially; the ways that societies and states interact; and the ways that relationships between the decision-makers are sustained. Hence a flood or an earthquake is not a disaster in and of itself.

The disaster stems from the fact that certain communities or groups are forced to settle in areas susceptible to the impact of a raging river or a volcanic eruption. It is essential to make a distinction between hazards and disasters and to recognise that the effect of the former upon the latter is essentially a measure of the society's vulnerability.

Vulnerability is seen as the progression of three stages:

1. **Underlying Causes:** A deep-rooted set of factors within a society that together form and maintain vulnerability.
2. **Dynamic Pressures:** A translating process that channels the effects of a negative cause into unsafe conditions; this process may be due to a lack of basic services or provision or it may result from a series of macro-forces.
3. **Unsafe Conditions:** The vulnerable context where people and property are exposed to the risk of disaster; the fragile physical environment is one element; other factors include an unstable economy and low income levels.

CAUSAL FACTORS OF DISASTERS

The magnitude of each disaster, measured in deaths, damage, or costs for a given developing country increases with the increased marginalisation of the population.

This is caused by a high birthrate, problems of land tenure and economic opportunity, and the lack or misallocation of resources to meet the basic human needs of an expanding population. As the population increases, the best land in both rural and urban areas is taken up and those seeking land for farming or housing are forced to accept inadequate land. These offer less productivity and a smaller measure of physical or economic safety.

Poverty

The most important single influence on the impact of a disaster is poverty. All other factors could be lessened if the affected population were not also limited by poverty. Virtually all disaster studies show that the wealthiest of the population either survive the disaster unaffected or are able to recover quickly. Across the broad spectrum of disasters, poverty generally makes people vulnerable to the impact of hazards.

Poverty explains why people in urban areas are forced to live on hills that are prone to landslides, or why people settle near volcanos or rivers that invariably flood their banks. Poverty explains why droughts claim poor peasant farmers as victims and rarely the wealthy and why famines more other than not are the result of a lack of purchasing power to buy food rather than an absence of food. Increasingly, poverty also explains why many people are forced to move from their homes to other parts of their countries or even across borders to survive. Such crisis-induced migration poses considerable challenges both in terms of immediate assistance to the displaced and of longer-term development.

Rapid Urbanisation

Rapid population growth and migration are related to the major phenomenon of rapid urbanisation. This process is also accelerated in developing countries. It is characterised by the rural poor or civilians in an area of conflict moving to metropolitan areas in search of economic opportunities and security. These massive numbers of urban poor increasingly find fewer options for availability of safe and desirable places to build their houses. Here again, competition for scare resources, an inevitable consequence of rapid urbanisation, can lead to human-made disasters.

Many landslides or flooding disasters are closely linked to rapid and unchecked urbanisation which forces low-income families to settle on the slopes of steep hillsides or ravines, or along the banks of flood-prone rivers. Many earthquake victims in urban areas have been impoverished families whose sites have failed rather than their houses, usually through landslides onto the house or out from under it.

Transitions in Cultural Practices

Many of the inevitable changes that occur in all societies lead to an increase in the societies' vulnerability to disasters. Obviously, all societies are constantly changing and in a continual state of transition. These transitions are often extremely disruptive and uneven, leaving gaps in social coping mechanisms and technology. These transitions include nomadic populations that become sedentary rural people who move to urban areas and both rural and urban people who move from one economic level to another. More broadly, these examples are typical of a shift from non-industrialised to industrialising societies.

One example of the impact of these transitions is the introduction of new construction materials and building designs in a society that is accustomed to traditional materials and designs. This often results in new materials being used incorrectly. In disaster prone areas, inadequate new construction techniques may lead to houses that cannot withstand earthquakes or wind storms.

Compounding this problem is the new community where the disaster survivors find themselves may not have a social support system or network to assist in the relief and recovery from the disaster. The traditional coping mechanisms may not exist in the new setting and the population becomes increasingly dependent on outside interveners to help in this process.

Conflicting as well as transitional cultural practices can also lead to civil conflict, for example, as a result of communal violence triggered by religious differences.

Environmental Degradation

Many disasters are either caused or exacerbated by environmental degradation. Deforestation leads to rapid rain run off, which contributes to flooding. The destruction of mangrove swamps decreases a coast line's ability to resist tropical winds and storm surges.

Lack of Awareness and Information

Disasters can also happen because people vulnerable to them simply didn't know how to get out of harm's way or to take protective measures. This ignorance may not necessarily be a function of poverty, but a lack of awareness of what measures can be taken to build safe structures on safe locations. Perhaps some people did not know about safe evacuation routes and procedures.

Other populations may not know where to turn for assistance in times of acute distress. Nevertheless, this point should not be taken as a justification for ignoring the coping mechanisms of the majority of people affected by disasters. In most disaster-prone societies, there is a wealth of understanding about disaster threats and responses. This understanding should be incorporated into any efforts to provide external assistance.

Phases of a Disaster

Disasters can be viewed as a series of phases on a time continuum. Identifying and understanding these phases helps to describe disaster related needs and to conceptualise appropriate disaster management activities.

DISASTER AND DEVELOPMENT

For a long time the cause and effect relationship between disasters and social and economic development was ignored. Ministries of Planning and Finance and other development planners did not concern themselves with disasters. At best, development planners hoped that disasters would not occur and, if they did, were most effectively handled by relief from donor countries and relief organisations. Development programmes were not assessed in the context of disasters, neither from the effect of the disaster on the development programmes nor from the point of whether the development programmes increased either the likelihood of a disaster or increased the potential damaging effects of a disaster.

Disasters were seen in the context of emergency response — not as a part of long-term development programming. When a disaster did occur, the response was directed to emergency needs and cleaning up. Communities under disaster distress were seen as unlikely places to institute development. The post-disaster environment was seen as too turbulent to promote institutional changes aimed at promoting long-term development.

The growing body of knowledge on the relationships between disasters and development indicates four basic themes. The themes may be as follows:

1. Disasters set back development programming destroying years of development initiatives.
    - Infrastructure improvement, e.g. transport and utility systems are destroyed by a flood.

2. Rebuilding after a disaster provides significant opportunities to initiate development programmes.
   - A self-help housing programme to rebuild housing destroyed by an earthquake teaches new skills, strengthens community pride and leadership and retains development dollars that otherwise would be exported to large construction companies.
3. Development programmes can increase an area's susceptibility to disasters.
   - A major increase in livestock development leads to overgrazing, which contributes to desertification and increases vulnerability to famine.
4. Development programmes can be designed to decrease the susceptibility to disasters and their negative consequences.
   - Housing projects constructed under building codes designed to withstand high winds result in less destruction during the next tropical storm.

Decision-makers who ignore these relationships between disasters and development do a disservice to the people who place their trust in them. Increasingly, around the world, forward thinking Ministries of Planning and Finance with the support of United Nations and Non-Governmental Organisation (NGO) officials are assessing development projects in the context of disaster mitigation and are designing disaster recovery programmes with long-term development needs in mind.

Disruption of Development by Disasters

Disasters can seriously disrupt development initiatives in several ways, including:

- Loss of resources.
- Interruption of programmes.
- Impact on investment climate.
- Impact on the non-formal sector.
- Political destabilisation.

Loss of Resources: Development resources are lost when a disaster wipes out the products of investment — it shortens the life of development investments. The disasters affect development through:

- Impact on capital stock and inventory.

- Loss of production and provision of services due to disruption and increased cost of goods and services.
- The secondary effects of the disaster include inflation, balance of payment problems, increase in fiscal expenditure, decreases in monetary reserves.
- Other indirect losses, for example: the impact on a country's debt position could be mat as the debt service burden increases, the country has less resources available to invest in productive enterprises.
- The outcome of these losses of resources include: loss of economic growth, delays to development programmes, cancellation of programmes and disincentives to new investment.
- There may also be a shift in skilled human resources towards high visibility recovery activity — a diversion from long-term to short-term needs.

Interruption of Programmes: Disasters interrupt ongoing programmes and divert resources from originally planned uses.

Impact on Investment Climate: Disasters, especially when they have occurred repeatedly within a short period of time, have a negative impact on the incentive for further investment. Investors need a climate of stability and certainty to be encouraged to risk their money.

The disaster further clouds the investment picture when it has caused loss of employment, thereby depressing market demand and resulting in a stagnation which limits overall growth.

Impact on Non-formal Sector: Disasters have special negative impacts on the non-formal sector where approximate costs of disasters are often underestimated. Disasters depress the non-formal economy through the direct costs of lost equipment and housing (which often also serves as business sites). The indirect costs of disasters include lost employment and lost income. Sometimes the importation of relief items creates disincentives to producers.

Political Destabilisation: The stress to a country caused by a disaster often results in the destabilisation of the government. This may occur for several reasons. For example, the government may have mismanaged the disaster relief and recovery, leading to discontent on the part of affected communities. Or the survivors may have had unmet expectation which, for whatever reason, translate into some form of protest. The government could also become the scapegoat for problems beyond its control, again leading to its possible downfall. In fact, it is very common for a government to collapse or be overthrown within two or three years of a major disaster.

Development may Cause Disasters

The side effects of well-meaning development efforts sometimes have disastrous consequences. Development projects implemented without taking into account existing environmental hazards may increase vulnerability to natural disasters.

For example, projects designed to increase employment opportunities, and thus income, usually attract additional population growth. Low-income people may then have to seek housing in areas previously avoided, on hillsides or in floodplains. The costs of relief assistance after a landslide or flood can easily outweigh the benefits to the economy of more jobs. Similarly, development projects may lead to negative political consequences that increase the vulnerability to civil conflict.

Some types of development projects commence without fully assessing their impact on the environment. This can occur even in programmes resulting from a disaster, such as reconstruction projects that increase demand for wood to fortify houses. The resulting deforestation can then bring increased vulnerability to mudslides and possibly long-term environmental changes.

Development projects may even consciously force a choice between reducing disaster vulnerability and economic vulnerability. A project's design may require a trade-off between the two and force a decision between the lesser of two evils.

Development Opportunities Afforded by Disasters

Despite an increasing disaster awareness in the international community and the recognition of the importance of developing coherent plans for relief activities, it often takes the actual or imminent occurrence of a large-scale destructive event to stimulate individual governments to think about a developmental approach.

Thus, a disaster can serve as a catalyst for introducing mitigation activities. Few development workers realise the opportunities that disasters can provide in the development field. Disasters often create a political and economic atmosphere wherein extensive changes can be made more rapidly than under normal circumstances. For example, in the aftermath of a disaster, there may be major opportunities to execute land reform programmes, to improve the overall housing stock, to create new jobs and job skills and to expand and modernise the economic base of the community-opportunities that would not otherwise be possible. The collective will to take action is an advantage that should not be wasted.

Disasters can also highlight high-risk areas where action must be taken before another disaster strikes. The realisation of vulnerability can motivate policy-makers and the public to participate in mitigation activities. Disasters may also serve to highlight the fact that the country is seriously underdeveloped.

They can thus bring in funding and the attention of donor communities to apply to long-term development needs.

Natural Hazards

In earlier, the discussion about disasters and emergencies resulting from natural and human-made hazards has been developed in general terms. However, each hazard has its own characteristics. To understand the significance and implications of a particular type of disaster we must have a basic understanding about the nature, causes and effects of each hazard type.

The list of hazard types is very long. Many occur infrequently or impact a very small population. Other hazards, such as severe snowstorms, often occur in areas that are prepared to deal with them and seldom become disasters. However, from the perspective of a disaster victim it is not particularly useful to distinguish between minor and major disasters. Some disasters are now of limited interest to the international community. These include avalanches, fog, frost, hail, lightning, snowstorms and tornadoes. The international interest is less for these hazards because their impacts affect relatively few people and the countries in which they normally occur have sufficient resources and systems in place to respond without external assistance.

Typical Post-disaster Needs

Different types of disasters have characteristic effects while retaining unique aspects. Risk reduction and preparedness measures, and emergency and post-disaster response can all be facilitated by some “rules of thumb” — as outlined in this section — but must also be tailored to the specificity of local conditions.

Remember

(a) Where different types of disaster occur in combination — e.g. floods accompanying tropical storms — the combined effects must be considered; and where one disaster leads to another (for example a famine leading to civil strife) the compound effects must be anticipated.

(b) The severity of the actual impact on the society depends on human and organisation factors as well as natural and topographical ones.

Socio-political Forces

Increasingly throughout many parts of the world one type of hazard can trigger a disaster which in turn triggers another hazard and subsequent disaster. For example, a drought may lead to a famine which in turn leads to a civil conflict that results in the mass displacement of people. A flood may force people to seek refuge across an international border where conflicts ensue between refugees and local communities.

Such compound hazards and disasters need not happen sequentially; they can also occur simultaneously. Thus, people caught between contending forces in a civil war find that in the midst of a major drought they have no means either to grow food or to receive outside assistance.

In a growing number of countries, complex disasters are also becoming more evident. Essentially a complex disaster is a form of a human-made emergency in which the cause of the emergency as well as the assistance to the afflicted are bound by intense levels of political considerations. The single most prevalent political condition of a complex emergency is civil conflict, resulting in a collapse of political authority in all or part of a country. In such cases, at least one of three situations arise:

1. The government's ability to assist the disaster-afflicted becomes severely constrained.
2. The government becomes extremely suspicious of or uninterested in afflicted people who have fled from non-government to government held areas.
3. The government or opposition groups actually create or compound a disaster through actions that generate refugees and the mass displacement of people.

In fact, many affected people live in areas outside of government control. They are often the persons who are most in need and they are often the most difficult to reach with aid.

The disaster becomes "complex" because either the collapse or diffusion of political control makes assistance highly problematic. Solutions ultimately depend upon agreements with all parties involved in the conflict to permit assistance to be provided to recognise civilian non-combatants. These solutions may be agreements that are seen essentially as compromising fundamental aspects of sovereignty for what have been labelled as "new mechanisms of humanitarian assistance" (for example, corridors of tranquillity).

An acute example of a situation illustrating the characteristics of both compound and complex emergencies is the Horn of Africa. For the past several years the situation in the Horn of Africa has been characterised by internal conflicts in Ethiopia, Sudan, and Somalia. These conflicts have been exacerbated by recurrent droughts and have resulted in famines on a massive scale and the flight of large numbers of people across national borders. After years of drought in some parts of the region, by 1991 food shortages were widespread.

Under all the above mentioned, the relief measures are brought in place with an overwhelming helping hand rendered the NGOs and their immense contribution in terms of physical as well as mental aspects.

REVIEW QUESTIONS

Short Answer Type Questions

1. Who the NGOs are? State their roles and responsibility in the society.
2. Name some of the activities taken care by the NGOs towards disaster mitigation.
3. List down a few technical health problems initiated by the NGOs.
4. Why it is necessary to evaluate the disaster mitigation activities.
5. Name the casual factors of disasters.
6. Tell us how disasters disrupt the development initiatives.
7. In contrast, radical phase of development paved the way for disaster – Justify.
8. State some of immediate post-disaster needs.

Essay Type Questions

1. Critically analyze the strenuous efforts taken by the NGOs in conducting a health disaster management programmes.
2. Explain how socio-political factors contributing to meet the requirements of a post-dsaster, alongside with the helping hand rendered by the NGOs.

CHAPTER 8

SOCIAL AND PSYCHOLOGICAL DIMENSIONS OF DISASTER

INTRODUCTION

Anxiety or tension is our body's way of telling us that something is going wrong and we need to correct it. It is an absolutely essential signal, necessary for our survival and well being. If primitive humans did not have food, the anxious anticipation of hunger motivated them to find food. If a worker hasn't been productive yet today, the fear of criticism from a supervisor or co-worker helps him/her get busy. If I am driving a little too fast on a rainy night on tires with 70,000 miles on them, my concern about safety slows me down. These are valid reasons for feeling that action is needed to avoid trouble. Isn't it wonderful that we have a built-in automatic warning system? Yes, except when the system goes awry. Sometimes the expectation of trouble or danger is wrong; we exaggerate the problems or become tense for no good reason. At other times, the warning is accurate but nothing can be done and we fret needlessly about our inability to change the situation. Sometimes, we have this stress alarm going off, but we don't know what is wrong. In each of these cases, we are psychologically and bodily all tensed up to run or fight an enemy, but the real enemy (the creator of the scary situation) is us.

Obviously, a major problem is telling the difference between realistic, helpful tensions, fears, or worries and unrealistic, unhealthy nervousness. This is because we all *could* start fretting about some possibly stressful event at almost any time. Risks are all around us. Thus, unrealistic worries are over-reactions to a tolerable situation or a prolonged over-reaction to a threatening situation that cannot be avoided. But how can you be sure a situation won't cause trouble? You can't. How can you be sure you won't handle the problem any better if you worried about it a lot more? You can't be. However, we can learn to recognize *extreme* over-reactions, e.g. being terrified while flying or obsessing for hours about an insoluble problem. But a little worry about crashing while flying is realistic and some thought is necessary to know that you can't do much about a problem. So, how much time should you devote to a particular problem? There isn't an exact answer; that's why some of us let anxiety overwhelm us. Instead of an over-reaction, some people under-react to a risk. They dismiss or deny it. They never get serious at work or prepare for a "bad spell;" they die on rain-soaked highways. Maybe they are unaware of the danger; maybe they just prefer to not think about it; maybe the situation is so threatening that they are scared witless, and shove awareness of the problem out of their mind. Both over-reactors and under-reactors to a threat are poorly prepared to deal with it. Both need to learn to react differently. This chapter deals more with over-reactors than with under-reactors.

Everyone has Some Anxiety

The complexity, confusion, and commonness of anxiety is reflected in the many words in the English language for anticipated troubles: tension, feeling on edge, up-tight, hassled, nervous, jittery, jumpy, wound up, scared, terrified, insecure, pressured, alarmed, anxious, worried, dreading what might happen, uncertain, vulnerable, apprehensive, edgy, troubled and many more. Anxiety is one of the most common symptoms seen in a psychologist's or psychiatrist's office. The broadest definitions of stress include the entire complex sequence of events: (1) the event that requires some change (external or mental; real or imaginary), (2) internal processes (perception, Interpretation of the event, learning, adaptation, or coping mechanisms), (3) emotional reactions (our feelings) and (4) other behavioural-bodily reactions (nervousness, sweating, stumbling over words, high blood pressure and all the medical conditions mentioned below). In a more limited usage, *stress* is the upsetting situation and *strain* is the mental and physical reactions. However, most of us use the term stress loosely for both the threatening situation and the anxious reaction. Stress may refer to meeting any "demand" made of us, even good, reasonable, enjoyable ones. Thus, the experienced jogger meets the demands of running five miles and thoroughly enjoys it. A person given a promotion is delighted even though it means more responsibility and work. Doing well in school involves the stress of learning what you need to know to get high grades on tests. No one could work and raise a family without stress. How could anyone strive for a high, competitive goal or make sacrifices in order to live according to his/her values without experiencing stress?

And, surely, stress is part of self-discovery growth and using all of one's potential, because these efforts open us up to failure when we find our limitations. Even the most wonderful events of life — loves, friendships, family, sex, travels, holidays—add stress because these situations require us to cope and adapt. So, some writers speak of "good" stress and "bad" stress. We all have both.

In everyday speech, however, we usually find other words, rather than anxiety or fear, for the hard work, uncertainty and tension associated with doing a good job at work, in school, or in our relationships. We may say, "it's a hard job but he/she is handling it," rather than "his/her job is making him/her highly anxious." When we use the phrase "he is anxious" or "insecure" or "she is nervous" or "jumpy," we usually mean things aren't going well, the person is close to loosing control or threatened with failure. Therefore, words which imply the amount of anxiety and stress being experienced become a commonly accepted index — a barometer — of how well we are coping. Indeed, very high anxiety is an aspect of most psychological breakdowns or disorders. So, the stress-related words mentioned above usually communicate to others that we are having serious difficulty handling some situation.

What other emotions and/or terms are closely related to stress?

Fears are when you feel **scared in specific situations**. Some are fears of real dangers; a fear of speeding or fighting or driving while drunk is healthy. Other fears, also called *phobias*, are not realistic; phobias of heights, flying, bugs, enclosed places, open spaces, or of speaking to groups are all over-reactions to the actual risks involved. *Panic reactions* are sudden, overwhelming fear reactions, often without an obvious external cause, usually involving rapid breathing, heart palpitations, fear of dying and a frantic attempt to get to safety. *Anxiety* is an unpleasant **tension state, something like fear, in certain circumstances but not associated with a specific stimulus**, perhaps not with an external event at all. One might be generally anxious at work, meeting people, taking a class, or in many other situations; yet, no specific aspect of those situations is the identifiable source of the fear. Because stress, fears, and anxiety are so unpleasant, you might be tempted to seek total relaxation in undemanding situations. Actually, the leisurely, effortless lifestyle is not possible or even desirable for most of us. As I have already made clear, if you seek to do your best, to do new things, to stretch your capabilities, you will be challenged and stressed. Many of us are good students, good workers, or good religious folks partly because we are scared not to be. Many outstanding athletes, students, managers, scholars, professionals, and others obtain part of their drive by overcompensating for feelings of inadequacy. As we have mentioned, the forewarnings of trouble help us cope and achieve. Thus, tension must, in many ways, be valued and welcomed. Psychologists don't yet know which achievements could have been accomplished without stress (demands from the environment and upon oneself), perhaps almost none. Thus, it seems likely that the better adjusted among us are constantly both reducing some of their unneeded anxieties and increasing other beneficial anxieties. It is a skilful, cogent person who can orchestrate his/her life into a pleasant *and* productive symphony of high and low stresses.

Thus far, psychology has focused mostly on lowering high anxiety for good reason: it is a serious and fairly common problem. The diagnosis of Generalized Anxiety Disorder (GAD) is a chronic, debilitating condition consisting of excessive worry, disruptive anxiety, and distressful tension that has lasted for at least 6 months and maybe for years. It is the second most common psychiatric disorder (after depression); about 5% of the world's population suffers this disorder. Even in developed countries, however, less than 20% of sufferers get proper treatment. It is treatable, but many MDs have trouble diagnosing it and are uncertain how to treat it. GAD frequently results in sleeplessness, irritability, poor concentration and fearful hyper-vigilance. There may be a variety of other symptoms including fatigue, muscle tension, sweating, heart palpitations, stomach trouble, diarrhea and others.

As we will see later, anxiety and depression are frequently and closely associated. Intense anxiety is also a part of or connected with many burdensome psychological or physiological conditions and psychiatric disorders. For instance, some aspect of anxiety accompanies *neurotic* disorders, including *somatoform or somatization or conversion* (a physical problem with a psychological cause), *psychogenic pain*, *hypochondriasis* (fear and excessive complaints of bodily disease), *dissociative reactions* (amnesia, sleepwalking, multiple personality), *factitious conditions* (faking an illness), *obsessive compulsive* disorders, *phobias* and other disorders. See an abnormal psychology text for a detailed description of these disorders. Some of these problems are dealt with in the last section of this chapter.

Theories Explaining Stress and Anxiety

Each person's stress-level is not just the result of the problems that have accidentally occurred in their lives recently. It is more complicated than that for one thing we are surely, to some extent, in control of how many and what kind of problems come along. More importantly, as individuals we respond to a problem or stressor very differently. Examples: being dumped crushes some of us while others are happily dating someone else in a week or so. Being fired makes some of us feel very incompetent while others are certain they can get a better job. Having a handicap makes some of us think we were meant to be inferior while others become obsessed with becoming superior and do. Our theories must explain these enormously different reactions to stresses.

There are several relevant theories and each one has something to teach us about self-help, the main theories that reviews the explanations of fear and anxiety are: ***constitutional, learning-behavioural, cognitive-humanistic, and psychoanalytic.***

New Research about Fears, Panic, and Anxiety

Behaviours associated with anxiety, e.g. panic reactions, phobias and worries, are paradoxical since these behaviours, although unpleasant, keep on occurring over and over, perhaps for months or years. Being by their very nature unwanted, distressing, self-punishing acts or experiences, why don't those behaviours gradually go away extinguish? Why don't people just stop or escape the behaviours? If you were hurting yourself by holding your hand near a stove burner, you'd stop. Why don't you stop getting uselessly scared or worried? The usual answer given by psychologists is that the panic, compulsion, phobia or worry may be a useful warning that something is wrong or they actually *reduce* our level of anxiety or stress in some way. That "relief" is powerful enough, we must assume, that it overrides the unpleasantness of the act or experience, such as compulsion, fear, or worry.

Psychologists are gradually learning more about the creation of intense physiological stresses (more so in some people than in others) that require rather extreme ("neurotic") acts/feelings, such as intense fears or compulsions, to lessen the tension or disease. Apparently, something in an individual's history makes him/her more prone to use an excessive (and neurotic) tension-reduction method, such as a compulsion, prolonged worry, or a repeated obsession that becomes a part of a disorder. First of all, it is obvious that anxiety disorders are not easily stopped. Indeed, they often become chronic, presumably because they produce some pay off, some benefit, such as worry or fretting may help us feel we have done our best to deal with a scary situation. It might surprise you how common anxiety disorders are. For reasons we don't clearly understand, certain kinds of anxiety disorders, such as panic attacks and phobia of insects or small animals, occur much more often in women than in men. Perhaps the new research summarized below will provide some hints as to why these disorders develop more often in women. These gender differences start early — by age 6, girls are twice as likely to feel anxious as boys or, at least, they admit feeling anxious.

Research in the last decade or so (much of this information is taken from Barlow, 2000) has shown that anxiety reactions are not just simple conditioned responses (like Little Albert's learned fear reaction to the rat), not just some chemical imbalance (like a physician might have us believe), and not just some cognitive misjudgment of the danger involved (as the Cognitive therapist would tell you).

Emotions, in general, have apparently evolved over eons to help us survive, partly by helping us to be mindful of dangers and to help us communicate with others. Likewise, some emotion-based symptoms seem to be inherited from recent ancestors. However, although feeling stress is the nature of our species, emotional responses can certainly be modified by an individual's life experiences and by the species evolution. For instance, some (but not all) **fear** responses have apparently evolved to enable us to instantly respond (fight or flee) to an immediate danger; the nerve impulses tend to go straight from the eye or ear to our primitive emotional brain, then to the muscles, bypassing the thoughts ("cognition") in the brain's cortex. Most people's fear of snakes is like this.

In contrast with the instant reaction of many fears and panic, **anxiety** is usually quite cognitive, i.e. how we see a situation determines how we feel about it. Barlow says anxiety results from perceiving one's self as helpless and feeling unable to cope with an anticipated danger or problem. A fear of public speaking might be an example — you aren't going to be physically hurt but your pride and self-esteem may be damaged. Anxiety, thus, involves constant tension — vigilance, expecting trouble, and sensing, perhaps wrongly, that we will be unable to handle a possible danger. He suggests a better term might be "anxious apprehension." Anxiety is future oriented cognition, e.g. "I will mess things up in the future because that is what I have done in the past." (Note: depression tends to be a past-oriented disorder, "because of my past losses or guilt, I feel bad.") It is important to realize that you may not be aware of the specific trigger or cue that sets off the "danger alert." Also, one may not have specific notions about exactly how he/she will be inadequate in coping with the problem. In the more extreme cases, all these directs us to have some expectations of disasters and failures to cope may become chronic and intense, interfering with effective coping by the brain. The panicking brain no longer effectively thinks of solutions; concentration is lost. Human emotions are not simple. Several things are happening when we are anxious, unreasonably afraid, or excessively scared: primitive alarms are being set off inappropriately, previous trauma has conditioned us to over-respond and our estimate of the true risks involved has gotten confused. Of course, it is sometimes necessary and healthy to respond to true threats with fight, flight, or freeze responses. But what happens when real threats are actually present but quite unlikely to happen? Some of us mis-calculate and become *overly* fearful and panicky. As the anxiety becomes intense, we often try to handle it in a couple of ways: (1) we avoid the frightening situation (avoiding it may be self-defeating or lead to rituals/

compulsions and denial) or (2) we uselessly and excessively worry (which ironically often produces more anxiety, not less) and our body tightens. Both worry and body tension are central features of a Generalized Anxiety Disorder (GAD). As the result of research, fear reactions are now seen by psychologists as quite different from anxiety responses, although they may feel similar. In the past, fear and anxiety were usually seen as a very similar physiological response, except that fear was set off by a specific triggering external situation and anxiety was a persistent autonomic response to a vague general external situation or to an unknown internal trigger. Today, however, fear and panic reactions are thought to result largely from primitive animal reflexes to danger, i.e. the old fight, flight, or freeze responses that have helped us and our primitive animal ancestors survive for millions of years. Panic is, in part, like an automated fear reaction, except we don't usually understand what sets off a panic attack. Panic attacks have a cognitive aspect too. Barlow, while explaining panic attacks, has described "false alarms" that contribute to major panic reactions. Panic disorders — the feeling of impending doom — seem to be a complex result of (a) primitive innate biological alarm reactions (emotionality) which generally evolved over eons but also "run in families," (b) our learned psychological coping mechanisms (such as learning that a panic attack gets the attention of others or gets us back to a safe place), and (c) the life stresses we are experiencing (such as a concern that one might lose his job or a lover might leave). Panic may be complex but it is not an uncommon experience — between 10% and 15% of Americans have reported a panic reaction within the last year. So, while the primitive, automatic response may be the crux of fears or panic, they often also have a cognitive part too.

In the 1980s, the general concept of neurotic disorders was discarded and replaced with more specific labels, such as anxiety, mood, somatoform and other disorders. Yet, central to all these disorders is negative affect (fear, sadness, disappointment); the same medicines work on all or most of them; the same behavioural treatments work with most of them; the disorders tend to increase or are relieved together. So, now Barlow argues that **anxiety and depression have so many of the same features** that both disorders need to be studied and understood together (back to a broad, general neurotic label?). He maintains that anxiety and depression both result from (1) genetic contributions (about ⅓ to ½ of the total causes; commonly, families are seen as nervous, tense, high strung), (2) early childhood experiences, like rejection or abuse, that sensitize us to certain adolescent or adult stresses, and (3) psychological vulnerabilities or personality tendencies that direct certain individuals toward a specific disorder, like social anxiety, panic disorder, phobias, obsessions or compulsions, suspiciousness, aggressiveness and irritability, unhappiness, pessimism, disorganization and impulsivity and many others. Of course, each of these specific disorders has unique characteristics, but they have a similar basic underlying emotion, namely, strong negative and tense feelings.

In Barlow's (2001) new experimentally-based book, the crux of anxiety is described as being an anticipation of trouble and **feeling unable to control** events in one's life. This suggests that one's sense of self-control (or Bandura's self-efficacy) is of vital importance. Note that "normal" people often believe they have more control over events than they really have (an exaggerated sense of mastery to quell our fears?). Many experiments with animals deprived of control have immediately produced agitation and intense tension. Also, psychological experiments studying the much later impact of early experiences, like animals allowed to control their food and water supply vs. animals having plenty to eat and drink but no control, have demonstrated marked and complex influences on the adult animal's behaviour (less emotionality, fewer fears, less stress hormones, different brain organization, more adventurous exploratory behaviour). An interesting and surprising contrast is that early *physical* trauma did *not* produce as much adult emotionality in animals (there is some reason to doubt that this holes true in humans). Apparently, gaining a sense of mastery or learning one is able to handle problems early in life, e.g. in monkeys who get good mothering and social support when young, seems to protect the adult from serious anxiety. So, learn your self-help lessons well.

Okay, now we are getting to the crux of this book — self-control and self-confidence. But how does a sense of control develop in humans? Barlow (2000) points out two characteristics of parenting that develop a child's sense of control. **Attentive parents**, who promptly respond to the young child's needs, wishes, cries, etc., build a sense of safety and an "I-can-get-things-done" expectation. Likewise, encouraging parents, who are **less over-protective** and let the child explore and handle situations in his/her own way, foster more independence, more security, and more self-confidence in the child. **Parental overcontrol** does the opposite, leading to less of a sense of self-control in the child (more of an "externalizer"— see chapter 8), to seeing the world as a more dangerous place requiring constant vigilance and help from others, and to feeling more anxiety and depression, perhaps throughout life (unless some self-changes are made or intervention is provided later in life). Thus, in addition to the genes, the learned sense of mastery or self-control determines, in large part, the amount of stress, anxiety or tension we feel. However, there is at least one more important factor — beginning to think of some situation or condition as particularly dangerous. Although fears are generally based on primitive automatic emotional reactions, more intense panic and specific fears occur when we feel particularly vulnerable — open to being seriously hurt. Some of this vulnerability may be genetic tendencies but much is probably learned, often at an early age. How are these dangers, these ***"Wow, that scares the hell out of me!"*** reactions, learned? Sometimes, we see the actual results of a real danger — a heart attack, an auto accident, someone going crazy — and we vividly imagine that might happen to us.

Examples: Panic attacks often are exacerbated by the scary thoughts that the tightness in my chest and high anxiety means I'm dying from a heart attack, going to faint, going crazy, etc. Such thoughts greatly increase the panic. Sometimes, we are given specific instructions by others to expect danger, e.g. some social phobics have been told that interacting with others can be disastrous — "they will think you are stupid or weird," "you can't trust them," "you'll make a fool of yourself," etc. Sometimes, we have started to think in a certain way (the source may be totally unknown — a TV, movie, book, or just our own fantasy as a child) that implies some situation is dangerous. Examples of this might be: "Oh, what I just said sounded really selfish... dumb... critical... " which grows into "I'm going to mess up when I talk to them," "I'm not good at socializing," "I can't think of anything to say," or "I get really uptight and start to sweat when I try to talk to someone." We can create, in effect, our own dangers, and may be especially prone to do that if we are given certain genes and childhood experiences. Unfortunately, as a self-helper you cannot un-do many of the early origins of your anxieties — your genes, your traumatizing childhood experiences, or the mistaken but frightening ideas you developed as a child. **What you can do now** is (1) learn the skills that will help you cope, (2) armed with those coping techniques, expose yourself to the scary situations to learn that they will not result in a catastrophe, and (3) work diligently to test out your anxiety producing ideas and correct your false beliefs that make your life less happy or unproductive. The rest of this chapter will help you learn useful self-change methods for coping with fears and for developing a realistic sense of mastery.

How to Cope with Stress, Anxiety, and Fears

After determining the nature and seriousness of the stressful situation you are in, your next task is to decide what you can do about it. Do you need professional help? If not, how well can you handle the threatening or challenging situation you face? Your answer to this question — your ability to cope — determines, along with your assessment of the importance and severity of the problem, how anxious or scared you will be. This is where your skills, knowledge, practice, experience, optimism, courage, etc. come into play — where they pay off for you. This is where you pit all your self-help ability against the threatening forces created by your situation. Your level of anxiety will indicate the outcome of this battle: if you develop and carry out a good battle plan, you should hold the anxiety to a moderate level (assuming the stresses are controllable). If you feel helpless, deny or run away, or, worse yet, blame yourself for the problems, you will have a high level of distress in the long run (Kleinke, 1991).

Several studies have evaluated the effectiveness of ordinary methods of dealing with stressful situations (Billings & Moos, 1981; Lazarus & Folkman, 1984; Carver, Scheier & Weintraub, 1989). The most effective methods of untrained people were: take responsibility for planning a way to cope, take rational composed action and avoid rash impulsive reactions, seek advice and support, look for something to "get out of it," i.e. to learn from difficult situations, express feelings privately but not publicly, stay confident, and use humour. The poorest responses to stress were: being hostile and confrontive, publicly venting strong feelings, self-blaming, indecisiveness, ignoring or denying or downplaying the problem hoping it will go away, keeping feelings to self or suppressing emotions, giving up trying, and escaping by watching TV, working, eating, smoking, or drinking a lot. In short, people who handle difficult situations well are (1) quick to take responsibility for handling the problems that come along, (2) confident of their ability to deal with life's challenges, (3) actually able to assess the situation accurately, get help as needed and devise a good plan, after considering many alternative approaches, and (4) effective in carrying out the plan, learning and growing with each problem so they can face the future with optimism. Well, of course! That's Superhuman! The question is how do you learn all these good things, right?

Coping is not a process that comes easy or natural to anyone (although skilled copers make it look easy). It requires a conscientious, determined effort to *learn about specific ways of coping* with diverse stresses *long before the troubles arrive*, an openness to many solutions, careful observation of many peoples' coping experiences, the courage to try different kinds of solutions, and a willingness to honestly evaluate the effectiveness of your efforts to handle stressful situations.

Now, let's get familiar with a wide variety of theoretically sound ways of handling stress. Since there are so many sources or causes of stress, there will be many possible "cures" or means of relief. Moreover, your stress-reduction techniques need to be tailored to you personally. The only way to know if some self-help method will work for you is to try it. That may seem overwhelming but you need to be familiar with many approaches because you will face many different kinds of stress in your lifetime. The more competent you are with many alternative solutions to problems, the better your chances of winning your battles with stress. Do not try to control stress with cigarettes, alcohol, excessive eating, shopping, gambling, excessive TV or music, etc.

Some treatment methods will probably work for you whether you understand where your stress came from or not. A quick, easy solution is great... sometimes. For instance, a relaxation technique or tranquillizing drugs will slow and calm you down. If the stress is shortlived, a little relaxation may be all you need. However, if the threat you face is persistent, relaxation or drugs, either legal or illegal, deal only with surface symptoms, they do not remove or alter the underlying threatening causes. So, when the relaxation or drug effect wears off, the original stress usually comes back. And, you are back where you started. As with behaviours, many stresses cannot be mastered without understanding the causes and history of the emotions. The treatment you need may have to be tailored to your specific problem (which includes your unique underlying sources of anxiesty, if any). Miller and Smith (1993) provide tests to determine the source and type of stress you are experiencing, then they suggest techniques for your type of stress. It may be reasonable, though, to try a quick, easy method first and see if it works.

REVIEW QUESTIONS

Short Answer Type Questions

1. Define stress.
2. Differentiate strain over stress.
3. Define anxiety.
4. Name some of the theories, which focuses n stress, anxiety etc.,
5. Name some other emotions, which are closely related to stress.

Essay Type Questions

1. Culminate the conclusions drawn out of the new researches conducted on stress/ anxiety.
2. Suggest some practical ways to cope with stress, anxiety and fear.

CHAPTER 9

TECHNOLOGY AND DISASTER MANAGEMENT

TECHNOLOGY AND DISASTER MANAGEMENT

Under the theme "Space benefits for humanity in the twenty-first century", the Third United Nations Conference on the Exploration and Peaceful Uses of Outer Space (UNISPACE III) was held in Vienna from 19 to 30 July 1999. In its resolution 1, the Conference adopted The Space Millennium: Vienna Declaration on Space and Human Development, that was subsequently endorsed by the General Assembly in its resolution 54/68. The Vienna Declaration recommended 33 specific actions that should be taken to enable space technologies to contribute to the solution of global challenges of the new millennium. One of the recommendations put forward was the need "to implement an integrated, global system, especially through international cooperation, to manage natural disaster mitigation, relief and prevention efforts, especially of an international nature, through Earth observation, communications and other space-based services, making maximum use of existing capabilities and filling gaps in worldwide satellite coverage".

The use of space-based solutions and information has increased significantly since UNISPACE-III. The use of such technologies has been proven useful in the risk assessment, mitigation and preparedness phases of disaster management. As the global community learnt from the tsunami event of December 2004, space technologies have a central role to play in providing early warning to communities that are at risk. But in order for developing countries to be able to incorporate the use of space technology-based solutions there is a need to increase awareness, build national capacity and also develop solutions that are customised and appropriate to the needs of the developing world. This was the main goal of the space technology and disaster management programme carried out by the Office for Outer Space Affairs, between 2000 - 2004.

The Office organized a series of regional workshops on the use of space technology for disaster management bringing the results of the regional workshops to an international workshop, held in Munich, Germany, in October 2004. At that workshop, 170 participants from 51 countries agreed on a global strategy that would help developing countries to gain access to and be able to use space technology for disaster management, a strategy put forward as the Munich Vision: a Global Strategy for Improved Risk Reduction and Disaster Management Using Space Technology (A/AC.105/837, annex).

Participants recognized that space-based technologies such as Earth observation satellites, communication satellites, meteorological satellites and global navigation satellite systems (GNSS) played an important role in risk reduction and disaster management and made a number of recommendations in the areas of capacity development and knowledge-building; data access, data availability and information extraction; enhancing awareness; and national, regional and global coordination.

The recommendations and conclusions put forward by the participants of the various workshops, including the final workshop in Munich, were taken into consideration by the ad hoc expert group that was studying the proposal of a coordinating entity that should be created and that would be a "one-stop shop" to provide support to the disaster management community at large, that would be a platform for fostering alliances and that would also contribute to bridging the gap between the disaster management and space communities. Subsequently, by its resolution 61/110 of 14 December 2006, the General Assembly decided to establish the proposed United Nations Platform for Space-based Information for Disaster Management and Emergency Response (UN-SPIDER) as a programme within the United Nations to provide universal access to all countries and all relevant international and regional organizations to all types of space-based information and services relevant to disaster management to support the full disaster management cycle by being a gateway to space information for disaster management support, serving as a bridge to connect the disaster management and space communities and being a facilitator of capacity-building and institutional strengthening, in particular for developing countries

Computer Attack

A computer attack may be defined as actions directed against computer systems to disrupt equipment operations, change processing control, or corrupt stored data. Different attack methods target different vulnerabilities and involve different types of weapons and several may be within the current capabilities of some terrorist groups. Three different methods of attack are identified in this report, based on the effects of the weapons used. However, as technology evolves, distinctions between these methods may begin to blur.

A physical attack involves conventional weapons directed against a computer facility or its transmission lines;

An electronic attack (EA) involves the use the power of electromagnetic energy as a weapon, more commonly as an electromagnetic pulse (EMP) to overload computer circuitry, but also in a less violent form, to insert a stream of malicious digital code directly into an enemy microwave radio transmission; and

A computer network attack (CNA), usually involves malicious code used as a weapon to infect enemy computers to exploit a weakness in software, in the system configuration, or in the computer security practices of an organization or computer user. Other forms of CNA are enabled when an attacker uses stolen information to enter restricted computer systems.

Officials have stated that while CNA and EA threats are "less likely" than physical attacks, they could actually prove more damaging because they involve disruptive technologies that might generate unpredictable consequences or give an adversary unexpected advantages.

Characteristics of Physical Attack

A physical attack disrupts the reliability of computer equipment and availability of data. Physical attack is implemented either through use of conventional weapons, creating heat, blast, and fragmentation, or through direct manipulation of wiring or equipment, usually after gaining unauthorized physical access.

In 1991, during Operation Desert Storm, the U.S. military reportedly disrupted Iraqi communications and computer centres by sending cruise missiles to scatter carbon filaments that short circuited power supply lines. Also, the Al Qaeda attacks directed against the World Trade Center and the Pentagon on September 11, 2001, destroyed many important computer databases and disrupted civilian and military financial and communications systems that were linked globally. The temporary loss of communications links and important data added to the effects of the physical attack by closing financial markets for up to a week.

Characteristics of Electronic Attack (EA)

Electronic attack, most commonly referred to as an Electromagnetic Pulse (EMP), disrupts the reliability of electronic equipment through generating instantaneous high energy that overloads circuit boards, transistors, and other electronics. EMP effects can penetrate computer facility walls where they can erase electronic memory, upset software, or permanently disable all electronic components. Some assert that little has been done by the private sector to protect against the threat from electromagnetic pulse and that commercial electronic systems in the United States could be severely damaged by limited range, small-scale, or portable electromagnetic pulse devices. Some military experts have stated that the United States is perhaps the nation most vulnerable to electromagnetic pulse attack.

Characteristics of Cyber Attack (CNA)

A computer network attack (CNA), or "cyber attack," disrupts the integrity or authenticity of data, usually through malicious code that alters program logic that controls data, leading to errors in output. Computer hackers opportunistically scan the Internet looking for computer systems that are mis-configured or lacking necessary security software. Once infected with malicious code, a computer can be remotely controlled by a hacker who may, via the Internet, send commands to spy on the contents of that computer or attack and disrupt other computers.

Cyber attacks usually require that the targeted computer have some pre-existing system flaw, such as a software error, a lack of antivirus protection, or a faulty system configuration, for the malicious code to exploit. However, as technology evolves, this distinguishing requirement of CNA may begin to fade. For example, some forms of EA can now cause effects nearly identical to some forms of CNA. For example, at controlled power levels, the transmissions between targeted microwave radio towers can be hijacked and specially designed viruses, or altered code, can be inserted directly into the adversary's digital network.

Possible Effects of Cyber Terrorism

As yet, no coordinated or widespread cyber attack has had a crippling effect on the U.S. infrastructure. However, while the number of random Internet cyber attacks has been increasing, the data collected to measure the trends for cyber attacks cannot be used to accurately determine if a terrorist group, or terrorist-sponsoring state, has initiated any of them.

Terrorist Capabilities for Cyber Attack

Extensive planning and pre-operational surveillance by hackers are important characteristics that precede a cyber attack directed at an organization. Some experts estimate that advanced or structured cyber attacks against multiple systems and networks, including target surveillance and testing of sophisticated new hacker tools, might require from two to four years of preparation, while a complex coordinated cyber attack, causing mass disruption against integrated, heterogeneous systems may require 6 to 10 years of preparation. This characteristic, where hackers devote much time to detailed and extensive planning before launching a cyber attack, has also been described as a "hallmark" of previous physical terrorist attacks and bombings launched by Al Qaeda.

Attractiveness of Cyber Terrorism

It is difficult to determine the level of interest, or the capabilities of international terrorist groups to launch an effective cyber attack. A 1999 report by The Center for the Study of Terrorism and Irregular Warfare at the Naval Postgraduate School concluded that it is likely that any severe cyber attacks experienced in the near future by industrialized nations will be used by terrorist groups simply to supplement the more traditional physical terrorist attacks. Some observers have stated that Al Qaeda does not see cyber terrorism as important for achieving its goals, preferring attacks which inflict human casualties. Other observers believe that the groups most likely to consider and employ cyber attack and cyber terrorism are the terrorist groups operating in post-industrial societies (such as Europe and the United States), rather than international terrorist groups that operate in developing regions where there is limited access to high technology. However, other sources report that Al Qaeda has taken steps to improve organizational secrecy through more active and clever use of technology and evidence suggests that Al Qaeda terrorists used the Internet extensively to plan their operations for September 11, 2001 attack.

Lower Risk

Tighter physical security measures now widely in place throughout the United States may encourage terrorist groups in the future to explore cyber attack as way to lower the risk of detection for their operations. Also, linkages between networked computers could expand the effects of a cyber attack. Therefore, a cyber attack directed against only a few vulnerable computers could multiply its effects by corrupting important information that is transmitted to other downstream businesses.

Less Dramatic

However, other security observers believe that terrorist organizations might be reluctant to launch a cyber attack because it would result in less immediate drama and have a lower psychological impact than a more conventional act of destruction, such as a bombing. These observers believe that unless a cyber attack can be made to result in actual physical damage or bloodshed, the President lifted all terrorism related sanctions that had been imposed on Iraq, taking it off the terrorism list, but only de facto.

OTHER LATEST TECHNOLOGICAL EQUIPMENTS

TSUNAMI WARNING SYSTEMS

Tsunamis are one of the most destructive forces in nature and can cause much loss of life, injury, and property damage. Tsunamis are usually produced by the uplift of the sea floor from a large magnitude subduction zone earthquake. Most tsunamis are created in the Pacific Ocean, because the largest number of subduction zones is found there. The effects of a tsunami can be local or distant. There has been a significant improvement in upgradation of Tsunami Warning Systems all over the world, due to the stupendous advancements in the field of science and technology. Its Evolution is as follows.

CENS (Community Emergency Notification System)

A system that gives public safety officials the ability to send an outgoing telephone message to every phone number within a specified warning area or evacuation zone.

CREST (Consolidated Reporting of Earthquakes and Tsunamis)

A project funded through the National Tsunami Hazard Program to upgrade regional seismic networks in Alaska, Washington, Oregon, California, and Hawaii and provide real-time seismic information from these networks to the tsunami warning centres.

CUBE (Caltech USGS Broadcast of Earthquakes)

This system, designed for southern California, provides preliminary earthquake epicenters and magnitudes (above a defined threshold) within minutes of the earthquake's occurrence.

DART (Deep Ocean Assessment and Reporting of Tsunamis)

DART is a real time distant tsunami detector system developed by NOAA's Pacific Marine Environmental Laboratory (PMEL). PMEL is installing the systems in the open ocean off Alaska, Oregon and Washington. The system uses sensitive water-depth detection equipment, underwater modems, satellite telemetry and advanced signal processing to detect and measure tsunami waves in the open ocean. Its purpose is to confirm that a potentially destructive tsunami has indeed been produced.

EAS (Emergency Alert System)

The EAS, which replaced the emergency broadcast system, is the primary method for state and local officials to notify the public of an emergency, using the broadcast industry system.

EMWIN (Emergency Managers Weather Information Network)

The Emergency Managers Weather Information Network (EMWIN) is a satellite or Internet service developed by the National Weather Service and FEMA and operated by the National Weather Service and NOAA. EMWIN receives forecasts, warnings, and climate data from NOAA Weather Wire and prioritizes it by message type. The system provides end users with direct access to weather and warning information without reliance on landlines, multiple layers of human intervention or recurring subscriber fees.

GPS (Global Positioning System)

GPS is a technology that uses satellites to determine the latitude and longitude of a position anywhere in the world.

ITIC (International Tsunami Information Center)

ITIC was established in 1965 and monitors international activities of the Pacific Tsunami Warning Center and assists with many of the activities of ICG/ITSU, the International Coordination Group for the Tsunami Warning System in the Pacific.

NOAA (National Oceanic and Atmospheric Administration)

NOAA is a federal agency under the Department of Commerce responsible for tsunami warnings and monitoring.

NWS (National Weather Service)

The branch of NOAA which operates the tsunami warning centres and disseminates warnings.

PTWC (Pacific Tsunami Warning Center)

Established in 1948 and located in Ewa Beach near Honolulu, the PTWC is responsible for issuing warnings to Hawaii, to U.S. interests in the Pacific other than the West Coast and Alaska and to countries located throughout the Pacific.

RACE (Rapid Alert Cascadia Earthquake)

This system, designed for Oregon and Washington, provides preliminary earthquake epicenters and magnitudes (above a defined threshold) within minutes of the earthquake's occurrence.

REDI (Rapid Earthquake Data Integration)

This system, designed for northern California, provides preliminary earthquake epicenters and magnitudes (above a defined threshold) within minutes of the earthquake's occurrence.

SAWS (Simultaneous Announcement Wireless System)

SAWS is a dedicated system of transmitters and receivers installed by local authorities for all types of messages.

THRUST (Tsunami Hazard Reduction Using System Technology)

Sponsored by the Office for U.S. Foreign Disaster Assistance/Agency for International Development, THRUST is a comprehensive programme to mitigate tsunami hazards in developing countries.

WC/ATWC (West Coast/Alaska Tsunami Warning Center)

Established in 1967 originally to issue warnings to Alaska of local tsunami events. WC/ATWC is now responsible for issuing warnings for any event likely to impact either Alaska, the West Coast of the US, or the Pacific coast of Canada.

Audio Evacuation Systems

An audio evacuation system or voice evacuation system is a type of fire alarm notification system. In addition to, or in place of, sirens, horns, bells and alarm tones, an audio evacuation system plays a voice message with evacuation instructions. These messages can be customised for various types of installations and multilingual capabilities are usually available.

The rationale behind audio evacuation systems is, though conventional fire alarm notification devices alert occupants of a building of the presence of an emergency, they do not provide detailed information to the occupants, such evacuation routes or instructions. The problem lies in buildings where there are a large amount of frequently changing occupants who are not necessarily familiar with the locations of emergency exits or stairwells. These types of buildings are designated in model building codes as "areas of assembly", such as buildings with a capacity of 300 or more people, but voice evacuation rules usually only apply when the occupant load exceeds 1000. Areas of assembly include churches, movie theatres, auditoriums, department stores, restaurants, shopping malls, airports and museums. Additionally, such a system is usually integrated with a fire telephone or paging system, which permits the fire department or building manager to give specific evacuation instructions pertinent to current conditions in real time.

Many audio evacuation systems permit multiple messages. For instance, "non fire" messages can be programmed for situations such as a hazardous material spill, gas leaks, security breaches, severe weather, etc.

In the United States, audio evacuation is now required in many jurisdictions for new structures that are classified as an area of assembly, as well as in new high rise buildings and skyscrapers. Retrofitting older structures is not required, although new fire alarm installations can be required to have audio capabilities. Similar trends are occurring in other countries as well.

Geographical Information Systems

GIS are computer-based tools for mapping and analyzing features and events. A GIS stores information about the world as a collection of thematic layers that can be linked together by geography. It integrates common database operations, such as query and statistical with maps.

A GIS may also be used to enter, manipulate, mange, analyse and visualize geographic data.

Remote Sensing

This technology provides the means to map the characteristics of an area, and monitor its condition at regular intervals, from a distance. Using remote sensing data, it is therefore possible to map or classify features over areas ranging from continental-scale, to individual sites, at a variety of time intervals.

Remote Sensing – GIS Integration

Remote Sensing products may be integrated with other datasets in a GIS to perform further analysis. Some examples include

- Monitoring and modelling ecosystem condition.
- Flood Hazard Mapping
- Mapping the impact and extent of fires.
- Mapping and monitoring sedimentary movement
- Landcover – including wetlands – mapping and classification
- Modelling impacts of land development and land degradation or erosion

Laser Scanning

Monitoring displacements and deformations of natural and anthropogenic spatial structures and objects represent one of the most intricate areas in geodetic surveying. The knowledge about types, characteristics and scales of structural deformations is essential when defining their nature and for the consequent verification of potential permanent damage possibilities or eventual destruction of structures. In traditional surveying, different deformation analysis approaches have evolved (e.g., Delft, Fredericton, Hannover, Karlsruhe, München. All these methods are aimed at ensuring a safe operation and usage of these structures. The second relevant aspect is closely connected with the cost-effective construction and management. The expenses of conceivable restoration may go beyond bounds; therefore, the causes for the occurrence of deformation should be discovered and prevented on time.

In recent years, ***Terrestrial Laser Scanning (TLS)*** has become increasingly used in different engineering surveying applications, including in the field of displacement and deformation monitoring. Despite the growing number of the presented solutions, the millimetre domain in displacement detection is still a very open area of investigation. The ability to perform a rapid and dense measurement of huge amounts of object points is a tempting advantage of TLS in comparison to other sensor technologies and point-wise monitoring approaches, where deformation evaluation is limited to few discrete and well signalized points. In contrast to the lower precision of individual sampled points which may preclude their use in high precision monitoring tasks, the effective detection of deformations on the entire object covering is possible by proper modelling of the object's surfaces exploiting the high data redundancy. TLS is a remote sensing measurement technology; therefore, the direct object accessibility is not required and the influence of installation of control points or other sensor compositions onto the observed object is minimized.

In the process of long term displacement and deformation determination and analysis, the quality and stability of the chosen reference system, *i.e.*, geodetic datum, plays a vital role. The geodetic datum is realized on the basis of geodetic points which should be stabilized on geologically stable ground if deformation parameters (translations, rotations and other structural distortions, defined on the basis of the comparison of 3D surface models from TLS data) are not to be subdued by their movements. Therefore, the connection of the TLS and other geodetic surveying technologies becomes inevitable. By integrating TLS with these surveying techniques into a multi-sensor composition, the weaknesses of individual measurement methods involved can be overcome, while their intrinsic advantages could be used for a complete expression of deformations on the entire surface of the structures in question.

Atmospheric Water Generator

An Atmospheric Water Generator (AWG), or atmospheric condenser, is a developing piece of technology with the intent of producing pure drinking water from the humidity of the surrounding air. An AWG operates in a manner very similar to that of a refrigerated dehumidifier: air is passed through a cooled coil, causing water to condense. The amount of water that can be produced depends on the humidity, the volume of air passing through the coils and the size of the machine.

The device is used in situations where pure drinking water is otherwise difficult to obtain or where the population demands are greater than the water tables can sustain or the water table has been or is contaminated, or for natural disaster relief. An AWG uses refrigeration techniques optimised to condense water from air. Blower driven air is drawn into the system through an electrostatic filter. In the machine's exterior housing, a compressor circulates refrigerant through a coil array located in the path of the air providing a temperature differential between the air and coil surface, resulting in condensation.

The condensation is funnelled into a holding tank. A level switch in the holding tank controls the water making cycle. Water is pump circulated in an ozone generating UV light chamber to kill bacteria and then through high and low density charcoal filters to remove solids and oxygenates. It is finally collected back in the holding tank. The water filtration cycle is both flow and time controlled. Water is dispensed by tap valve diversion.

The actual amount of water produced depends on relative humidity and ambient air temperature. Relative humidity measures the amount of water vapour present in the air at a given temperature. The higher the relative humidity and air temperature, the more effective most all of these devices are. Typically these refrigeration-based devices do not work efficiently when the temperature gets below 15.5°C (60°F) or the relative humidity drops below 30 per cent.

Considerations

- Needs no water source, only air.
- Can generate from 20 litres to over 250,000 litres or more in 24 hours.
- Is designed for maximum cost efficiency.
- Contains no harmful minerals or chemicals.
- Can be powered by solar, wind, dyno or aqua electrical generation systems.

A wide range of atmospheric generators are available from a home/office unit producing 28 litres a day, to 1200 litres and even more than 500,000 litres per day for industrial bottling plants.

Details

The cost effectiveness of an atmospheric water generator depends on the capacity of the machine as well as on humidity and temperature conditions.

Besides such machines can be powered by alternative energy like solar, wind or even gas or oil fired generators which can be of great help especially when such machines are put into operation for relief efforts.

THE AIRCRAFT GATEWAY PROCESSOR (AGP)

The Aircraft Gateway Processor (AGP) is an Aircraft Survivability Equipment (ASE) controller contained within a single, flight qualified Line Replaceable Unit. It is designed to integrate federated ASE sensors and countermeasures to provide a combined threat picture and prioritized tactical response per the user-programmed Pre-Flight Message (PFM). The AGP evolved from the Integrated ASE Controller in the combat-proven Helicopter Integrated Defensive Aids System (HIDAS) and has been selected by Boeing for integration into the Block II AH64D Apache and by the UK MOD for front-linecombat helicopters.

Key Benefits

- **Enhanced platform survivability and reduced crew workload**
  - Via increased situational awareness of the threat environment and initiation of optimized countermeasure responses
- **Prioritized threats shown on a single Multi Function Display (MFD)**
  - With co-ordinated audio warnings to prevent simultaneous reporting to the crew
- **Mission configurable**
  - By means of user-defined PFM
- **Data Recording**
  - Threat information is captured for post-flight analysis
- **Flexible architecture**
  - AGP allows for the addition of new and enhanced sensors and countermeasures without re-qualification of aircraft Operational Flight Programs (OFPs).

MOBILE ELECTRONIC WARFARE PLATFORM

The MEWP is a highly mobile integrated solution for communications and non-communications tactical EW missions. The modular solution is configured to provide Electronic Surveillance (ES) or Electronic Attack (EA) as required by the specific needs of the customer. The MEWP is a self-contained unit with integral EW sub-systems, communications, power unit and environmental control. The MEWP is installed in a self-contained module that includes all the elements required to perform the designated mission enabling it to operate independently of the carrying vehicle.

The flexibility of the containerised design enables a variety of military vehicles to house the module. Therefore, any customer preference can be considered and the possibility of reducing acquisition and ownership cost through fleet commonality is increased.

A MEWP is designed to be highly mobile and rapidly deployable.

Key Features

- Fully integrated situational awareness
- Integrated support and attack
- Utilisation of threat databases
- Multiple signal jamming
- Capable of networked operations
- Real-time data link connectivity
- Off-line analysis and playback facility
- Expandable architecture
- Highly mobile, reliable and sustainable.

REVIEW QUESTIONS

Short Answer Type Questions

1. Differentiate the characteristics of physical attack over electronic attack.
2. Define computer attack.
3. What is the need to have a Tsunami Warning Systems?
4. Write a note on ITIC.
5. Differentiate Global Positioning Systems over EMWIN.
6. Write a note on audio-evacuation systems.
7. What are all the advantages that one can drawn out of integrating remote sensing and GIS technology?
8. Write the usage of TLS?
9. Write a note on AWG?
10. List down key advantages of using AGP.

Essay Type Questions

1. Explain why cyber terrorism and/or attack is considered to the most vulnerable form of technological disasters,
2. Enumerate the evolution of Tsunami Warning System I detail.
3. Explain the other latest technological equipments and its uses for combating terrorism.

CHAPTER 10 APPLICATIONS IN DISASTER MANAGEMENT

"Biological weapons that target selected ethnic groups could become part of the terrorists' arsenal..." and, "The threat from biological weapons has outstripped that from chemical and nuclear arms because of the 'riotous' progress of biotechnology." Such media provides an interesting perspective on the unique challenges associated with efforts to address the threat of bioterrorism.

On the one hand, much of the media's recent coverage successfully captured the BMA reports two fundamental theses that: 1) developments in science – and biotechnology, in particular – are making possible disturbing, new opportunities for the weaponization of biological agents and bioterrorism; and 2) without greater focus and commitment by governments around the world, such developments have the potential to rapidly outpace the international community's ability to respond to and manage associated dangers. On the other hand, the coverage tended to focus on the report's discussion of worst case bio-attack scenarios and highlight the report's most dramatic – but least immediately realistic – examples of possible bioterrorism (such as attacks that make use of genetically engineered agents capable of selectively targeting specific ethnic groups). The result of such coverage is that many in the public are left with the correct impression that bioterrorism is a real danger, but also with an incorrect impression concerning the actual scope and nature of the existing threat.

BIO TERRORISM

The widespread attention that bioterrorism receives today is both significant and new. Up until the past decade, the prospect of someone other than a state using biological weapons was largely confined to the realm of fiction and a small cadre of biowarfare experts. The use of the toxic chemical sarin by the Japanese cult Aum Shinrikyo in the Tokyo subway system in 1995 drew the attention of both policymakers and counterterrorism experts to the possibility that at least some terrorists and other non-state actors may indeed be willing and able to engage in mass-casualty attacks using unconventional weapons. However, it was only in late 2001, when an as yet unidentified perpetrator sent weapons-grade preparations of Bacillus anthracis – the organism that causes anthrax – through the mail, that the world's citizens became keenly aware of the notion that violent non-state actors might seek to use harmful biological agents in terrorist acts.

The 2001 "anthrax attacks" (as they are widely known) were not by any means the first bioterrorism incidents. In 1984, for instance, the Rajneeshees – a religious cult located in Oregon in the United States – contaminated salad bars with the non-lethal pathogen Salmonella enterotica serotype Typhimurium causing more than 750 people to fall ill. Occurring as close as they did to the attacks on September 11, however, the anthrax attacks solidified in a dramatic fashion many of the fears that had accompanied earlier revelations about the advanced level of the secret Soviet biological weapons program and the Aum cult's attempts to develop biological weapons. The intense media and public interest surrounding the 2001 anthrax attacks had predictable effects. What was already a major security issue in the United States quickly achieved the status of a global threat as policymakers worldwide were galvanized to address the possibility of bioterrorism. Amidst the hype, bioterrorism simulations were run, research quickly funded and vaccine production commenced. One would assume that a thorough understanding of the threat underlies the difficult policy decisions associated with such preventive and response-related measures, which often involve resource limitations and tradeoffs between programmes. Yet this has repeatedly been shown not to be the case. At every level – from the local to the national to the international – the approach to countering bioterrorism has often been partial, piecemeal and distorted by political or parochial institutional concerns.

Previous Commission papers have dealt well with general, high-level issues surrounding biological weapons; here we focus on a specific subset of those issues – that relating to non-state actors and biological weapons – and look at the specific policy questions that arise in this context. The comprehensive assessment of the threat posed by bioterrorism is essential for policymakers working to identify and prioritize opportunities for reducing the global risk of such attacks. The first section of the document seeks to ground the discussion empirically by reviewing the specific nature of bioterrorism, highlighting recognizable trends in its modern history and identifying key lessons and developments from the historical record that might signal how bioterrorism will likely manifest itself in the 21st century. The second section of the document begins by considering how threat assessment may be applied practically to bioterrorism, and broadly evaluating the current set of constraints and incentives for bioterrorism according to this threat assessment framework. The paper concludes by identifying a number of specific "opportunities" policymakers have to reduce the threat of bioterrorism by strengthening the constraints and weakening the incentives identified earlier.

Framing the Problem

The first essential step in assessing any type of threat is to properly define the scope and nature of what is to be assessed. Thus, bioterrorism is defined as "the use by nonstate actors of microorganisms (pathogens) or the products of living organisms (toxins) to inflict harm on a wider population."

Three important issues with policy relevance flow from this definition:

- First, we avoid the contentious academic and political debates surrounding the nature of "terrorists" and "terrorism" by focusing on the central issue faced by policymakers: the use by non-state actors of biological weapons. Therefore, for present purposes we sacrifice ontological accuracy for policy utility and consider bioterrorism in its broadest possible sense to include acts perpetrated by criminals, insurgents and violent non-state actors of all stripes, in addition to those perpetrators that can be properly labelled as terrorists. In doing so, it must not forgotten that in the narrower context of terrorism proper the terror aspect is the most important; in other words, the intent of perpetrators is often to cause psychological as well as physical harm to the target society.

- Second, non-state actors will not necessarily use biological weapons only to cause mass death; biological weapons can be used for a variety of other purposes from the strategic to the tactical. Examples include using pathogens to incapacitate a target population (such as the Rajneeshee cult, who only wanted to make local residents too ill to vote in a local election) or to contaminate an area in order to cause economic loss and general social disruption.

- Third, humans are not the only targets of bioterrorism: crops and livestock can be attacked with bio-agents, or can be used to disseminate biological agents to human populations (socalled agro-terrorism) and there is even the potential that microorganisms could be used to attack physical infrastructure, for example by degrading plastics.

The following characteristics of bioterrorism are important for policymakers to be aware of:

- The primary biological agents considered suitable for bioterrorism include:
  - Bacterial organisms, such as those that cause anthrax, plague and tularemia.
  - Viruses, including those that lead to smallpox and ebola.
  - Toxins, including botulinum toxin (derived from a bacterium), ricin (derived from the castor bean plant) and saxitoxin (derived from marine animals). It should be noted that toxins are not alive and cannot multiply – they therefore share several traits associated with chemical agents.

Biological agents are not biological weapons. Merely possessing biological agents with the theoretical potential to cause harm is insufficient; the toxins or microorganisms need to be "weaponized", i.e. prepared and disseminated effectively to their target. Having a beaker filled with a solution containing B. ***anthracis*** represents only a minor hazard. On the other hand, drying, milling and inserting the same quantity of B. anthracis into a device that can deliver fine powder of spores over a large area enables the biological agent to infect large numbers of people. So, the agent must not only be capable of inflicting harm but must also be deliverable to its intended target before it can constitute a weapon of mass destruction.

The substantial incubation period (1 day to 2 weeks) associated with most biological agents between exposure to the infectious agent and the onset of symptoms is unique among weapons types. This is a double-edged sword. Although it provides a window of opportunity to respond and treat the infection and inoculate vulnerable populations, it also hampers law enforcement efforts by allowing the perpetrators to distance themselves geographically from the site of initial agent release thereby making it easier for them to conceal their identity.

Biological weapons are also the only weapon type that can actually perpetuate itself and continue causing harm far in excess of the initial amount of agent used. Here a distinction must be drawn between non-contagious (e.g. anthrax and all toxins) and contagious (e.g. plague and smallpox) biological weapons. At least theoretically, highly contagious and lethal pathogens can present an even greater danger than nuclear weapons in that they are not limited to the geographical target area and can continue to spread indefinitely.

Preparedness can make all the difference to the outcome of a bioterrorist attack. Unlike weapons with more immediate effects, such as explosives, there is the possibility to mitigate the effects of a biological attack through measures, including rapid detection, treatment with antibiotics, vaccination and quarantine. One simulation of an anthrax attack conducted by the Center for Nonproliferation Studies, for example, showed that the difference in the ultimate mortality figures between a poorly coordinated and ill-prepared response and a polished and efficient response was 120,000 as opposed to 35,000 deaths.

Threat Assessment

The basic argument presented in this paper is that inadequate threat assessment leads to sub-optimal policy decisions. The following section outlines a basic threat assessment framework for thinking about bioterrorism holistically and introduces some basic tools that can guide policy decisions in each of the framework's aspects.

The first essential realization is that the threat of bioterrorism cannot be evaluated exclusively in terms of the hazards posed by the various biological agents themselves or in terms of the likelihood of an attack taking place. It is almost trite to say that even the most dangerous pathogen presents little threat in terms of bioterrorism if there is no-one willing or able to use it.

Conversely, even the most diabolical actors require a biological agent capable of causing the harm and terror they might seek.

So, an initial construction of a bioterrorist threat can be denoted as follows:

BIOTERRORIST THREAT = CONSEQUENCES OF ATTACK x LIKELIHOOD OF ATTACK

STATISTICAL SEISMOLOGY AND ITS APPLICATION

This helps in formulating a procedure for estimating the consequence of an earthquake prediction on statistical estimates of seismic risk. Several examples, using this procedure, indicate the following general conclusions: if a prediction with a confidence level of 1.0 significantly affects the risk at a site, then the same prediction at smaller confidence levels will also affect the risk. If an earthquake is predicted in a high risk zone, it can be important for an entire adjacent low risk zone; a prediction for the adjacent low risk zone may not affect the high risk zone at all. Finally, a prediction for a region which may significantly affect the amplitudes of shaking that can be expected in the next year may have no importance for structures which are designed (or planned) with a 50 or more year lifetime, depending on the size of the predicted earthquakes.

These conclusions are drawn from a hypothetical, yet plausible, case study in the Los Angeles, California, region, where hypothetical predictions are considered for events on the San Andreas fault, the Sierra Madre fault and a region of about 4300 km^2 covering the most populated region of the Los Angeles basin. For the background seismicity model used in this study, the threshold of a significant (to the seismic risk) prediction for 1-yr risk is M = 5 on the San Andreas fault, M = on the Sierra Madre fault, and M = 4 in the Los Angeles zone. For the 50-yr risk, the thresholds of significance are M = 7, M = 5 and M = 6, respectively, for the same three zones.

GIS and Epidemiology

Understanding the determinants of a disease and its spread from person to person and community to community, has become increasingly global (ESRI White Paper, 1999). GIS plays a vital tool in strengthening the whole process of epidemiological surveillance information management and analysis. GIS provides excellent means for visualising and analysing epidemiological data, revealing trends, dependencies and inter-relationships that would be more difficult to discover in tabular formats. Public health resources, specific diseases and other health events can be mapped in relation to their surrounding environment and existing health and social infrastructures. Such information when mapped together creates a powerful tool for monitoring and management of diseases and public health programmes.

The underlying factors likely to lead to increased incidence of diseases, including adverse environmental, behavioural and socio-economic conditions, need to be monitored regularly. By tracking the sources of diseases and the movement of contagions, health agencies can respond more effectively to the outbreaks of epidemics by identifying populations at risk.

Software packages such as BodyViewer by GeoHealth, help medical personnel visualise clinical data. Integration of clinical information is accomplished by linking unique codes directly to a graphical representation of the human body and to the geographical location where the patient has originated (ESRI White Paper, 1999). Such geoclinical information system is a useful tool when evaluating environmental risks and exposures.

Advantages of GIS

GIS has several advantages over conventional methods used in health planning, management and research. Data management: GIS can be used to capture, store, handle and geographically integrate large amounts of information from different sources, programmes and sectors; including epidemiological surveillance, census, environment and others. Surveillance of diseases requires continuous and systematic collection and analysis of data. A GIS can eliminate the duplication of effort involved in data collection across an organisation and hence substantially reduce the cost involved in it. GIS serves as a common platform for convergence of multi-disease surveillance activities. Each data record has to be geo-referenced to a desired level of accuracy. Standardised geo-referencing of epidemiological data facilitates structured approaches to data management (Weekly Epidemiological Record, 1999). Once the basic structure is ready, it is easy to convert it to surveillance system for any other disease, by replacing data of one disease with data of another disease (Srivastava & Nagpal, 2000).

GIS provides access to additional information from a wide variety of sources. Global positioning systems (GPS) can be used to obtain locations of point features on a map, such as wells or septic tanks, precisely. GIS can process aerial or satellite imageries to allow information such as temperature, soil types and landuse to be easily integrated and spatial correlations between potential risk factors and the occurrence of diseases to be determined (Weekly Epidemiological Record, 1999). High resolution satellite imageries and aerial photographs can be used to obtain accurate and up to date maps of any region. Latest, accurate, low-cast maps are essential for epidemiological surveillance. Temporal satellite imageries can be used to monitor landuse and landcover changes over time.

Visualisation

GIS offers powerful tools to present spatial information to the level of individual occurrence and conduct predictive modelling. It determines geographical distribution and variation of diseases and their prevalence and incidence. For example, in studying the surveillance of poliomyelitis in India, it is important to find out which type of polio is occurring in which parts of the country, as this has important implications for the disease eradication strategy employed (Balaji, 2000). GIS can help in generating thematic maps - ranged colour maps or proportional symbol maps to denote the intensity of a disease or a vector. In comparison with tables and charts, maps developed using GIS can be extremely effective means for communicating messages clearly even to those who are not familiar with technology. GIS keeps track of the geographical locations of service providers, customers, resources and health plans and programmes. It allows policy makers to easily understand and visualise the problems in relation to the resources and effectively target resources to those communities in need. GIS permits dynamic link between databases and maps so that data updates are automatically reflected on the maps.

Overlay Analysis

GIS can overlay different pieces of information. This helps in decision making and medical research through multicriteria modelling (for example, in understanding the association between prevalence of certain diseases and specific geographic features).

Buffer Analysis

GIS can create buffer zones around selected features. For example, a radius of 10 km around a hospital to depict its catchment area or 1 km around a pollution site or 5 m on both sides of sewerage to indicate the spread of hazardous material. The user can specify the size of the buffer and then combine this information with disease incidence data to determine how many cases fall within the buffer. Buffer or proximity analysis can be used to map the impact zones of vector breeding sites, where control activity needs to be strengthened (Srivastava & Nagpal, 2000).

Network Analysis

GIS provides the ability to quickly access the geo-demographic dynamics of an organisation's existing service area in contrast to the likely demand for services at a new location (ESRI White Paper, 1999). It can identify catchment areas of health centres and also locate suitable site for a new health facility. Health services delivered at home (e.g. polio vaccination) can be scheduled in a more efficient manner by analysing transportation factors and street patterns and by recommending the most efficient route. GIS provides accurate and timely information about where health services are located and instructions and maps on how to get there.

Statistical Analysis

GIS can carry out specific calculations, for example, proportion of population falling within a certain radius of a health centre or dam. It can also calculate distances and areas, for example, distance of a community to a health centre, and area covered by a particular health programme.

Query

GIS allows interactive queries for extracting information contained within the map, table or graph. It can answer queries of location, condition, trends, spatial patterns and modelling.

Extrapolation

GIS provides a range of extrapolation techniques. For example, vector distribution in inaccessible and unsampled areas can be mapped using GIS.

Web GIS

One of the recent advancements in GIS technology is web-based GIS. Health data is stored in a central server which can be accessed from various terminals connected to the server through internet or intranet. Statistical and epidemiological methods need to be developed to protect individual confidentiality while accessing data (Richards et al., 1999). Internet based GIS technology eliminates the traditional method of flow of information and the information is instantly available across the globe. Dynamic maps published on the web allow patients to locate the most convenient services to their home or work easily.

Applications of GIS in Health

GIS is being used by public health administrators and professionals, including policy makers, statisticians, epidemiologists, regional and district medical officers (Weekly Epidemiological Record, 1999). Some of its applications in public health are mentioned below:

- Find out geographical distribution and variation of diseases
- Analyse spatial and temporal trends
- Identify gaps in immunisations
- Map populations at risk and stratify risk factors
- Document health care needs of a community and assess resource allocations
- Forecast epidemics
- Plan and target interventions
- Monitor diseases and interventions over time

- Manage patient care environments, materials, supplies and human resources
- Monitor the utilisation of health centres
- Route health workers, equipments and supplies to service locations
- Publish health information using maps on the Internet
- Locate the nearest health facility.

Thus, GIS aids in faster and better health mapping and analysis than the conventional methods. It gives health professionals quick and easy access to large volumes of data. It provides a variety of dynamic analysis tools and display techniques for monitoring and management of epidemics. GIS has a vital role to play in the future. The possibilities that can be explored are limitless, depending on the skill and imaginative use of the researchers and the willingness of health sector management to resource its implementation. Health administrators, professionals and researchers need training and user support in GIS technology, data and epidemiological methods in order to use GIS properly and effectively.

MASS CASUALTY MANAGEMENT

The national government is the ultimate authority in emergency management as part of its overall responsibilities for the safety and security. Depending on the size and seriousness of the incident the government is responsible for implementing national coordination structures, approving extraordinary resources, calling up the military, assuming extraordinary powers and for activating international systems of cooperation and aid.

A complex Partnership

A variety of Ministries, agencies and other organizations have roles to play in emergencies, with the Ministry of Health taking on a major one. Although the names and responsibilities vary from country to country, these will likely include: the Ministries/Offices of the Interior, Security, Communications and Environment; the various branches of the military; Civil Defense agencies; Red Cross/Red Crescent, the private sector, and so on. Given the mix of roles and responsibilities, some form of a coordinating structure (or structures) should be in place. These may have names like: Emergency Management Council or Cabinet Emergency Committee (comprising the head of state and key ministers); National Interdepartmental Emergency

Committee (top-level civil servants); and National Disaster Recovery Committee (a wider grouping which may include non-governmental as well as government figures).

These structures should have formal roles laid out in National Emergency Management plans and policies. Many countries also have a permanently staffed national Emergency Management Agency (or similarly named system) which assumes command, control and coordination responsibilities when large-scale disasters or emergencies occur. No matter what forms that government and public administration take, national emergency management systems should include:

- Identification of lines of authority, from the national to the local level
- Financial arrangements for funding emergency work
- Arrangements to ensure that government and community activities are maintained (for example, creation of parallel or "hardened" communications systems to take over if normal voice or data transfer systems are affected)
- National stockpiling of appropriate resources (including provincial or state and local prepositioning of stockpiles)
- Database of national experts for advice on specific problems
- Protocols and formal arrangements for coordinated efforts with other countries, or between provincial/state governments within the country.

REVIEW QUESTIONS

Short Answer Type Questions

1. What do you understand by the term bioterrorism?
2. State at least two important characteristics of bioterrorism.
3. How bioterrorism threat can be assessed.
4. What is meant by statistical seismology?
5. List down some of the advantages of GIS.
6. Write a note on web based GIS.
7. Bring out some of the application of GIS in health sector.

Essay Type Questions

1. Explain in detail about bioterrorism and how it can be prevented.
2. Explain the significance of statistical seismology and its application in managing disasters.
3. Elaborately explain the application of GIS and epidemiology in disaster management.
4. Explain the need for managing mass casualty programme along with its significance.

CHAPTER 11

MANAGEMENT OF DISASTERS IN INDIA

INTRODUCTION

India has been traditionally vulnerable to natural disasters on account of its unique geo-climatic conditions. Floods, droughts, cyclones, earthquakes and landslides have been a recurrent phenomena. About 60% of the landmass is prone to earthquakes of various intensities; over 40 million hectares is prone to floods; about 8% of the total area is prone to cyclones and 68% of the area is susceptible to drought. In the decade 1990-2000, an average of about 4344 people lost their lives and about 30 million people were affected by disasters every year. The loss in terms of private, community and public assets has been astronomical.

At the global level, there has been considerable concern over natural disasters. Even as substantial scientific and material progress is made, the loss of lives and property due to disasters has not decreased. In fact, the human toll and economic losses have mounted. It was in this background that the United Nations General Assembly, in 1989, declared the decade 1990-2000 as the International Decade for Natural Disaster Reduction with the objective to reduce loss of lives and property and restrict socio-economic damage through concerted international action, specially in developing countries.

The super cyclone in Orissa in October, 1999 and the Bhuj earthquake in Gujarat in January, 2001 underscored the need to adopt a multi dimensional endeavour involving diverse scientific, engineering, financial and social processes; the need to adopt multi disciplinary and multi sectoral approach and incorporation of risk reduction in the developmental plans and strategies.

Over the past couple of years, the Government of India has brought about a paradigm shift in the approach to disaster management. The new approach proceeds from the conviction that development cannot be sustainable unless disaster mitigation is built into the development process. Another corner stone of the approach is that mitigation has to be multi-disciplinary spanning across all sectors of development. The new policy also emanates from the belief that investments in mitigation are much more cost effective than expenditure on relief and rehabilitation.

Disaster management occupies an important place in this country's policy framework as it is the poor and the under-privileged who are worst affected on account of calamities/disasters.

The steps being taken by the Government emanate from the approach outlined above. The approach has been translated into a National Disaster Framework [a roadmap] covering institutional mechanisms, disaster prevention strategy, early warning system, disaster mitigation, preparedness and response and human resource development. The expected inputs, areas of intervention and agencies to be involved at the National, State and district levels have been identified and listed in the roadmap. This roadmap has been shared with all the State Governments and Union Territory Administrations. Ministries and Departments of Government of India, and the State Governments/UT Administrations have been advised to develop their respective roadmaps taking the national roadmap as a broad guideline. There is, therefore, now a common strategy underpinning the action being taken by all the participating organisations/stakeholders.

The changed approach is being put into effect through:

(a) Institutional changes

(b) Enunciation of policy

(c) Legal and techno-legal framework

(d) Mainstreaming Mitigation into Development process

(e) Funding mechanism

(f) Specific schemes addressing mitigation

(g) Preparedness measures

(h) Capacity building

(i) Human Resource Development and, above all, community participation.

INSTITUTIONAL AND POLICY FRAMEWORK

The institutional and policy mechanisms for carrying out response, relief and ehabilitation have been well-established since Independence. These mechanisms have proved to be robust and effective insofar as response, relief and rehabilitation are concerned. The changed policy/approach, however, mandates a priority to pre-disaster aspects of mitigation, prevention and preparedness and new institutional mechanisms are being put in place to address the policy change.

Mitigation, preparedness and response are multi-disciplinary functions, involving a number of Ministries/Departments. Institutional mechanisms which would facilitate this inter-disciplinary approach are being put in place. It is proposed to create Disaster Management Authorities, both at the National and State levels, with representatives from the relevant Ministries/Departments to bring about this coordinated and multi-disciplinary with experts covering a large number of branches. The National Emergency Management Authority is proposed to be constituted. The organization will be multi-disciplinary with experts covering a large number of branches. The National Emergency Management Authority is proposed as a combined Secretariat/Directorate structure – a structure which will be an integral part of the Government while, at the same time, retaining the flexibility of a filed organization. The Authority will be headed by an officer of the rank of Secretary/ Special Secretary to the Government in the Ministry of Home Affairs with representatives from the Ministries/Departments of Health, Water Resources, Environment & Forest, Agriculture, Railways, Atomic Energy, Defence, Chemicals, Science & Technology, Telecommunication, Urban Employment and Poverty alleviation, Rural Development and Indian Meteorological Department as Members. The authority would meet as often as required and review the Status of warning systems, mitigation measure and disaster preparedness. When a disaster strikes, the Authority will coordinate disaster management activities.

The Authority will be responsible for:

- Providing necessary support and assistance to State Governments by way of resource data, macro-management of emergency response, specialized emergency response teams, sharing of disaster related data base etc.
- Coordinating/mandating Government's policies for disaster reduction/ mitigation.
- Ensuring adequate preparedness at all levels
- Coordinating response to a disaster when it strikes

- Assisting the Provincial Government in coordinating post disaster relief and rehabilitation
- Coordinating resources of all National Government Department/agencies involved.
- Monitor and introduce a culture of building requisite features of disaster mitigation in all development plans and programmes.
- Any other issues of work, which may be entrusted to it by the Government.

The States have also been asked to set up Disaster Management Authorities under the Chief Minister with Ministers of relevant Departments [Water Resources, Agriculture, Drinking Water Supply, Environment & Forests, Urban Development, Home, Rural Development etc.] as members. 10 States and UTs – Tamil Nadu, Arunachal Pradesh, Uttaranchal, Orissa, Gujarat, Kerala, Nagaland, Delhi, A&N administration and Chandigarh Administration have notified the authority. The other States are in the process of setting up similar authorities.

Re-structuring of the Relief Department in the States

At the State level, the work of post calamity relief was being handled by the Departments of Relief & Rehabilitation. The Government of India is working with the State Governments to restructure the Departments of Relief & Rehabilitation into Departments of Disaster Management with an enhanced area of responsibility to include mitigation and preparedness apart from their present responsibilities of relief and rehabilitation. The changeover has already happened in 11 States/UTs - Andhra Pradesh, Arunachal Pradesh, Bihar, Himachal Pradesh, Rajasthan Tamil Nadu, Uttaranchal, Nagaland, Andaman & Nicobar Administration, Sikkim and Lakshadweep. The change is under process in other States.

The States have been advised to restructure/re-group the officers/staff within the Department of Disaster Management with definite functions to pursue the holistic approach to disaster management. The four functional groups to be assigned with specific tasks within the departments are as indicted below:

- ***Functional Group 1: Hazard Mitigation***
- ***Functional Group 2: Preparedness and Capacity Building***
- ***Functional Group 3: Relief and Response***
- ***Functional Group 4: Administration and Finance***

At the district level, the District Magistrate who is the chief coordinator will be the focal point for coordinating all activities relating to prevention, mitigation and preparedness apart from his existing responsibilities pertaining to response and relief. The District Coordination and Relief Committee is being reconstituted/ re-designated into Disaster Management Committees with officers from relevant departments being added as members. Because of its enhanced mandate of mitigation and prevention, the district heads of the departments engaged in development are now being included in the Committee so that mitigation and prevention is mainstreamed into the district plan. The existing system of drawing up preparedness and response plans will continue. There will, however, also be a long term mitigation plan. District Disaster Management Committees have already been constituted in 256 districts and are in the process of being constituted in the remaining districts.

Similarly, sub-divisional and Block/Taluka level Disaster Management Committees are also being constituted. At the village level Disaster Management Committees and Disaster Management Teams are being constituted. Each village in multi-hazard prone district will have a Disaster Management Plan. The process of drafting the plans at all levels has already begun. The Disaster Management Committee which draws up the plans consists of elected representatives at the village level, local authorities; Government functionaries including doctors/paramedics of primary health centres located in the village, primary school teachers etc. The plan encompasses prevention, mitigation and preparedness measures.

The Disaster Management Teams at the village level will consist of members of youth organisations like Nehru Yuvak Kendra and other non-governmental organisations as well as able bodied volunteers from the village. The teams are provided basic training in evacuation, evacuation, search and rescue, first aid trauma counseling etc. The Disaster Management Committee will review the disaster management plan at least once in a year. It would also generate awareness among the people in the village about dos' and don'ts for specific hazards depending on the vulnerability of the village. A large number of village level Disaster Management Committees and Disaster Management Teams have already been constituted.

Disaster Management Policy

Disaster management is a multidisciplinary activity involving a number of a number of Departments/agencies spanning across all sectors of development. Where a number of Departments/agencies are involved, it is essential to have a policy in place, as it serves as a framework for action by all the relevant departments/agencies. A National policy on disaster management has been drafted, and is in the process of consultations. In the line with the changed focus, the policy proposes to integrate disaster mitigation into development planning. The policy shall inform all spheres of Central Government activity and shall enjoin upon all existing sectoral policies.

The broad objective of the policy are to minimize the loss of lives and social, private and community assets because of natural or man-made disasters and contribute to sustainable development and better standards of living for all, more specifically for the poor and vulnerable section by ensuring that the developments gains are not lost through natural calamities/disaster.

The policy notes that State Governments are primarily responsible for disaster management including prevention and mitigation, while the Government of India provides assistance where necessary as per the norms laid down from time to time and proposes that this overall framework may continue. However, since response to a disaster requires coordination of resources available across all the Departments of the Government, the policy mandates that the Central Government will, in conjunction with the State Governments, seek to ensure that such a coordination mechanism is laid down through an appropriate chain of command so that mobilization of resources is facilitated.

The broad features of the draft national policy on disaster management are enunciated below:

(i) A holistic and pro-active approach towards prevention, mitigation and preparedness will be adopted for disaster management.

(ii) Each Ministry/Department of the Central/State Government will set apart an appropriate quantum of funds under the Plan for specific schemes/projects addressing vulnerability reduction and preparedness.

The basic responsibility for management of disasters is that of the State Government concerned. The role of the National government is supportive, in terms of supplementation of physical and financial resources and complementary measures in sectors like transport, and interstate movement of food grains. The national government also sets out the policy climate and draws lessons from disasters.

The lessons learned are communicated to States and national initiatives are made possible. The Union Department of Agriculture and Cooperation (DAC) is the nodal Department-An Additional Secretary in the DAC is designated as the Central Relief Commissioner. He provides the focal point for interaction with the State Governments, and other Departments and agencies of the Union Government and for the implementation of the decision of the Union Government. Now, as a national initiative, the representatives of the communities and the NGOs are invited in the operational and policy processes so as to achieve greater impact of mitigation and preparedness measures. For example, CARE (India) coordinates the Government of India NGO Committee and Disaster Mitigation Institute is invited to join in dissemination of information and awareness programmes and different task forces constituted for disaster management related activities.

The Department of Agriculture and Cooperation in the Agriculture Ministry is the nodal Department for all matters concerning natural disasters relief at the Centre. In the DAC, the Relief Commissioner functions as the nodal officer to coordinate relief operations for all natural disasters.

The Central Relief Commissioner receives information relating to forecast/warning of the natural calamity from the Director-General, India Meteorological Department (IMD) or from the Central Water Commission on a continuing basis. Besides, he also monitors the developments taking place and provides the necessary feedback, through the Agriculture Secretary to the Agriculture Minister, Prime Minister and the Cabinet.

CABINET COMMITTEE

The Cabinet may set up a committee for effective implementation of relief measures in the wake of natural disaster. The Secretary in the Ministry of Agriculture acts as the Secretary of this committee. In the absence of such a committee, all the matters related to the relief shall be reported to the Cabinet Secretary.

National Crisis Management Committee (NCMC)

Under the chairmanship of the Cabinet Secretary, the NCMC has been constituted in the Cabinet Secretariat. The other members of this committee include the Secretary to Prime Minister, Secretaries in the Ministries of Home Affairs, Defence, Research and Analysis Wing and Agriculture and Cooperation along with Director Intelligence Bureau and an officer of Cabinet Secretariat. The NCMC gives direction to the crisis management group as deemed necessary.

Crisis Management Group (CMC)

A group under the chairmanship of the Central Relief Commissioner comprising the senior officers from the various ministries and other concerned departments formed to review every year—contingency plans formulated by the Central Ministries/ Departments; to review the measures required for dealing with a natural disaster, to coordinate the activities of the Central Ministries and the State Governments in relation to disaster preparedness and relief and to obtain information from the nodal officers on measures relating to the above. The Joint Secretary (NDM) and Additional Central Relief Commissioner is the convener of CMC. The CMC meets every six months.

At the State level, the State Relief Commissioner (or Secretary, Department of Revenue) supervises and controls relief operations through Collectors or Deputy Commissioners, who are the main functionaries to coordinate the relief operation at district level.

State

As pointed out earlier, the Central Government only supplements the efforts of the State Governments. The State Governments are autonomous in organising relief operations in the event of natural disaster and in the long-term preparedness/ rehabilitation measures.

The States have Relief Commissioners who are in charge of the relief measures in the wake of natural disasters in their respective States. In the absence of the Relief Commissioner, the Chief Secretary or an Officer nominated by him is in overall charge of the Relief operations in the concerned State.

The Chief Secretary is the head of the State Administration. The State Headquarters has, in addition, a number of secretaries, heads of the various departments handling specific subjects under the overall supervision and coordination of the Chief Secretary. At the level of the State Government, natural disasters are usually the responsibility of the Revenue Department or the Relief Department. While important policy decisions are taken at the State Headquarters by the Cabinet of the State headed by the Chief Minister, day-to-day decisions involving policy matters are taken or exercised by the Secretary in the Department.

State Crisis Management Group

There is a State Crisis Management Group (SCMG) under the Chairmanship of Chief Secretary/Relief Commissioner of Chief Secretary/Relief Revenue/Relief, Home. Civil Supplies, Power, Irrigation, Water Supply, Panchayat (local self-government), Agriculture Forests, Rural Development, Health, Planning, Public Works and Finance.

District

States are further divided into districts, each headed by the District Collector (also known as the District Magistrate or Deputy Commissioner). It is the District Collector who is the focal point at the District level of directing, supervising and monitoring relief measures for disaster and for the preparation of District level plans.

Earthquake Occurrences

India has large part of its land area liable to wide range of probable maximum seismic intensities where shallow earthquakes of magnitudes of 5.0 or more on Richter scale, have been known to occur in the historical past or recorded in the last about 100 years. IMD has prepared a catalogue of all such known earthquakes which is continually updated. The largest earthquake magnitude in India has been 8.7 which has its origin in the Shillong Plateau in 1897. This and the 1950 quake in Sadiya region have been so intense that the rivers changed their courses, ground elevations got changed permanently and stones were thrown upward.

Cyclone Occurrences

Over the warm water (sea surface temperature greater than 260°C or 270°C) in the tropical ocean, little away from the equator within the belt of 30°N and 30°S, the occurrence of tropical cyclone is almost a worldwide phenomenon. However, their characteristics like frequency, intensity and coastal impact vary from region to region. But these have been the deadliest when crossing the coast bordering the north Bay of Bengal (coastal areas of Andhra Pradesh, Orissa, West Bengal and Bangladesh), mainly because of the serious storm surge problem in this area.

On the average, about 5-6 tropical cyclones form in the Bay of Bengal and the Arabian Sea every year, out of which 2 or 3 may be severe. More cyclones form in the Bay of Bengal than in the Arabian Sea. The ratio is 4:1. There are two definite seasons of tropical cyclones in the North Indian Ocean. One is from May to June and the other is from mid-September to mid-December. May, June, October and November are known for severe storms.

INDIA'S NATURAL DISASTER PRONENESS – AN OVERVIEW

On the basis of geographic and climatic considerations, India can be divided into 5 Zones according to its disaster proneness to natural disasters:

1. Northern Mountain Region Including Foot Hills: This region is prone to strong Snow Storms leading to Land slides and strong Cold waves and also is Earthquake prone belt with violent subterranean Volcanic activity.
2. Indo-gangetic Plains: Heavy rains during monsoon make these plains vulnerable to Floods.
3. Deccan Plateau: A Drought prone area.

4. The Western Desert: A Drought prone area.

5. Coastal Areas: They are prone to Sea erosion, Cyclones and Tidal waves.

India's Disaster Ridden History

- About 60 per cent of India's land mass is prone to Earth Quakes.
- Over 40 million Hectares are prone to Floods.
- Nearly 3 lakh sq kms are at risk of Cyclones.
- The Earth quake in Bhuj killed 14,000 people.
- Cyclone in Orissa took away 10,000 lives.
- Between 1990 and 2000 an average of about 3400 people lost their lives annually.
- About 3 crore people were affected by Disasters every year.

About 17,000 people perished by the Tsunami on 26 December 04. This is reason enough for Governments to give more^pnonty to Disaster Management but it has not been the case so far.

The lack of minimum health services and basic health education are aggravating factors which could make a disaster out of an emergency and a complex emergency out of social tension.

Disaster Risk Management – Review and Evaluation of the Plan

Initial risk management plans will never be perfect. Practice, experience and actual loss results will necessitate changes in the plan and contribute information to allow possible different decisions to be made in dealing with the risks being faced.

Risk analysis results and management plans should be updated periodically. There are two primary reasons for this:

1. To evaluate whether the previously selected security controls are still applicable and effective, and
2. To evaluate the possible risk level changes in the business environment. For example, information risks are a good example of rapidly changing business environment.

Limitations

If risks are improperly assessed and prioritised, time can be wasted in dealing with risk of losses that are not likely to occur. Spending too much time assessing and managing unlikely risks can divert resources that could be used more profitably. Unlikely events do occur but if the risk is unlikely enough to occur it may be better to simply retain the risk and deal with the result if the loss does in fact occur.

Prioritising too highly the risk management processes could be an organisation from ever completing a project or even getting started. This is especially true if other work is suspended until the risk management process is considered complete.

It is also important to keep in mind the distinction between risk and uncertainty. Risk can be measured by impacts and probability.

Risk Analysis

Risk analysis is the science of risks and their probability and evaluation. The term cindynics (from the Greek kindunos, "danger") has been proposed for this field. This term is used in France, but has not been widely adopted in the English-speaking world. Probabilistic risk assessment is the analysis strategy usually employed in science and engineering.

Risk Analysis and the Risk Workshop

As part of the risk management process risk analysis for each project should be performed. The data of which would be based on risk discussion workshops to identify potential issues and risks ahead of time before these were to pose cost and/ or schedule negative impacts.

The risk workshops should be chaired by a small group ideally between 6 to 10 individuals from the various departmental functions (e.g. project manager, construction manager, site superintendent and representatives from operations, procurement, [project] controls, etc.) so as to cover every risk element from different perspectives.

The outcome of the risk analysis would be the creation/ review of the risk register to identify and quantify risk elements to the project and their potential impact.

Given that risk management is a continuous and iterative process, the risk workshop members would regroup on at regular intervals and project milestones to review the risk register mitigation plans, make changes to it as appropriate and following those changes re-run the risk model. By constantly monitoring risks these can be successfully mitigated resulting in a cost and schedule savings with a positive impact on the project.

THE HISTORIC MOVEMENT – DISASTER MANAGEMENT ACT, 2005

The President of India gave his assent to the Disaster Management Bill 2005 on January 9, 2006. The Act comprising 79 sections and 11 chapters is capable of effectively managing the disaster and matters related to it. The objectives as stated in the statement of purpose and preamble are as follows:

An Overview of the Act

Definitions

Section 2 of the Act defines 'Disaster' as a catastrophe, mishap, calamity or grave occurrence in any area, arising from either natural or man made causes, or by accident or negligence which results in substantial loss of life or human suffering, or damage to and destruction of property or damage to or degradation of environment, and is of such a nature or magnitude as to be beyond the coping capacity of the community of the affected area.

'Disaster Management' is defined as a continuous and integrated process of planning, organizing, coordinating and implementing measures which are necessary or expedient to prevent danger or threat of any disaster, mitigation or reduce the risk or severity or consequences of any disaster, capacity-building and preparedness to deal with any disaster, prompt response to any threatening disaster situation or disaster, assessing the severity or magnitude of effects of any disaster, evacuation, rescue and relief, rehabilitation and reconstruction.

National Disaster Management Authority

The Act empowers the Central Government to appoint the National Disaster Management Authority with the Prime Minister of India as the Chairperson and such number of other members, not exceeding nine. The Central Government is to provide the National Authority with such officers, consultants and employees, as it considers necessary for carrying out the functions of the National Authority. The National Authority has the responsibility to lay down, approve the policies, plans and guidelines for disaster management prepared by various departments of Government of India to ensure timely and effective response to disaster.

National Executive Committee

To assist the National Authority an advisory committee called the National Executive Committee consisting of experts in the field of disaster management having practical experience of disaster management at the National, State and District level. The National Executive Committee is further empowered to constitute one or more sub-committees, for the efficient discharge of its functions. The Committee is entrusted to prepare a national plan for disaster management which is to be reviewed and updated annually.

National Plan

The National Plan shall include the prevention of disasters, the integration of mitigation measures in the development plans, the preparedness and capacity building to effectively respond to any threatening disaster situations or disaster, the roles and responsibilities of different Ministries or Departments of the Government of India. The National Authority is to recommend guidelines for the minimum standards of relief to be provided to persons affected by disaster like the minimum requirements to be provided in the relief camps in relation to shelter, food, drinking water, medical cover and sanitation, the special provisions to be made for widows and orphans, assistance on account of loss of life as also assistance on account of damage to houses and for restoration of means of livelihood and such other relief as may be necessary. In cases of disasters of severe magnitude, the National Authority may recommend relief in repayment of loans or for grant of fresh loans to the persons affected by disaster on such concessional terms as may be appropriate.

State Disaster Management Authority

Similar to National Authority at the Centre, the State Government is to establish a State Disaster Management Authority for the State. The State Authority is to be headed by the Chief Minister of the State as the Chairperson and such number of other members, not exceeding nine. The State Authority is empowered as and when it considers necessary to constitute an advisory committee, consisting of experts in the field of disaster management. The State Authority is supposed to lay down the State disaster management policy, approve the State Plan in accordance with the guidelines laid down by the National Authority.

State Executive Committee

The State Executive Committee is empowered to control and restrict, vehicular traffic to, from or within, the vulnerable or affected area, control and restrict the entry of any person, his movement within and departure from, a vulnerable or affected area, remove debris, conduct search and carry out rescue operations, provide shelter, food, drinking water, essential provisions, healthcare and services in accordance with the standards laid down by the National Authority and State Authority.

District Disaster Management Authority

Every State Government, in turn, is to establish a District Disaster Management Authority for every district in the State with the District Collector as the Chairperson and such number of other members, not exceeding seven. The District Authority is to act as the district planning, coordinating and implementing body for disaster management and take all measures for the purposes of disaster management in the district in accordance with the guidelines laid down by the National Authority and the State Authority.

Central Government and International Agencies

The Central Government is empowered to further measures as it deems necessary or expedient for the purpose of disaster management like deployment of naval, military and air forces, other armed forces of the Union or any other civilian personnel as may be required for the purposes of this Act, coordination with the United Nations agencies, international organizations and governments of foreign countries for the purposes of this Act, and establish institutions for research, training, and developmental programmes in the field of disaster management.

National Institute of Disaster Management

The Central Government is empowered to constitute an institute to be called the National Institute of Disaster Management. The institute functions within the broad policies and guidelines laid down by the National Authority and is responsible for planning and promoting training and research in the area of disaster management, documentation and development of national level information base relating to disaster management policies, prevention mechanisms and mitigation measures.

National Disaster Response Force

A National Disaster Response Force for the purpose of specialist response to a threatening disaster situation or disaster is to be constituted. The general superintendence, direction and control of the Force shall be vested and exercised by the National Authority and the command and supervision of the Force shall vest in an officer to be appointed by the Central Government as the Director General of the National Disaster Response Force.

National Disaster Response Fund

The National Disaster Response Fund to meet any threatening disaster situation or disaster is to be constituted. The Fund is made available to the National Executive Committee to be applied to meet the expenses for emergency response, relief and rehabilitation in accordance with the guidelines laid down by the Central Government in consultation with the National Authority.

Civil and Criminal Liabilities

The Act imposes punishments to persons for contravening the provisions of this Act, 2005 such as obstructing or abandoning, refusing to comply with any of the provisions of this Act, making false claims, misappropriation of money or materials or false warning, etc. The punishment in such cases could be imprisonment or fine or both.

Role of Media and the Act

The National Authority, the State Authority, or a District Authority is empowered to recommend the Government to give direction to any authority or person in control of any audio or audiovisual media or such other means of communication as may be available to carry any warning or advisories regarding any threatening disaster situation or disaster, and the said means of communication and media as designated shall comply with such direction.

REVIEW QUESTIONS

Short Answer Type Questions

1. State how the Government of India has brought about a paradigm shift in the approach to disaster management.
2. In what ways, the change process is put into effect
3. What is the role of district magistrate in managing disasters.
4. State the functions of taluk level disaster management comitee.
5. Write a note on crisis management group.
6. Write a note on the Disaster Management Act, 2005.

Essay Type Questions

1. Analyze the disaster management policy of India in detail along with its pros and cons.
2. With the help of statistical data, explore the India's disaster proneness.
3. Compare and contrast the risk analysis and risk workshop
4. Highlight the points to be focused on the Disaster Management Act, 2005.

CHAPTER 12

THE FUTURE OF DISASTER MANAGEMENT

There is an emphasis now on global security and terrorism. Humanitarian aid specialists, through working with disasters on a daily basis, are convinced that risk reduction is a worthwhile investment. "There's no doubt in our minds that spending money now on good mitigation and preparedness activities more than pays off." It is firmly believed that risk reduction is a worthwhile investment. The World Bank undertook a study attempting to determine the added value of disaster prevention to a development project, and concluded that the return on investments was 'very substantial'. DIPECHO, like all other donors included in this report, has not undertaken any formal cost-benefit analyses.

However, despite such lack of concrete proof that disaster risk reduction is an investment and not a cost. 'The perception of ECHO is that DIPECHO brings added value.' The SDC's Humanitarian Aid department is also convinced that risk reduction 'pays'. Moreover it is informed that it does not suffer from 'donor reluctance' to fund risk reduction programmes. We must know where we should put our money ... We are convinced that disaster prevention and preparedness is cost effective but we can't prove it. But we're definitely convinced.

There also appears to be growing concern regarding the economic impact of disasters outside humanitarian aid departments and across donor organisations as a whole. As Freeman et al. observe, 'The need to formally include disaster losses in the planning process has been recognised by the World Bank, the United Nations (UNDP), the Inter- American Development Bank [and others].' In Latin American and Caribbean countries in particular, there has been recognition of the 'value of disaster reduction measures in reducing and alleviating serious economic disruptions and thus in determining a country's path towards economic growth'. The IADB was motivated to invest in risk reduction following the immense losses caused by hurricanes Mitch and George, the earthquake in Colombia and the effects of El Nino in 1998 and the Venezuela floods and El Salvador earthquake of 1999. Keipi (Sustainable Development Department, IADB) explains, the IADB developed a greater sense of urgency to do prevention so that countries do not get in debt and the poverty mdex does not soar.'

'Changes do not come about because people are killed, changes come about as a result of financial losses.' With such evidence of donor conviction that risk reduction is a worthwhile investment in vulnerable countries, the fundamental question is why it struggles to obtain a higher priority within relief and more significantly, development assistance.

Differing priorities of communities and high-level decision makers relief specialists endeavouring to tackle the issue of disaster prevention face a major constraint. The attempt of humanitarian aid departments to undertake risk reduction initiatives is set against a backdrop of rising numbers of disasters and hence an increased pressure to respond. Our contacts in CIDA informed us that CIDA allocates 7-8 per cent of its humanitarian budget to risk reduction and Hodge (IHA, CIDA) stated, 'Given the needs that there are and the demands that are placed on the humanitarian aid budget that's as far as we are able to go.' Borns is facing similar tensions within OFDA: '...good [disaster risk reduction] more than pays off ... the only real limitation is that when push comes to shove are you going to do mitigation or are you going to respond?'.

Disaster Planning

Disaster recovery planning is effectively the preparation of those steps that will be necessary for recovery from a disaster or other crisis situation.

Importance of Disaster Recovery Plan: The plan itself is the core, of the whole planning exercise, and is of critical importance. It is vital, therefore, that if you are to manage an incident successfully, the plan itself must be of the highest quality and be up to date.

Creation of Disaster Recovery Plan: There are number of options, ranging from consultancy to software. However, probably the most common these days is the use of disaster recovery plan templates. This helps keep the exercise relatively simple.

Data Recovery: This is process of salvaging data from damaged, failed, wrecked or inaccessible storage media when cannot be accessed through normal means.

Recognition of the Value of Disaster Risk Reduction

The scale of human needs right now in the world today is so overwhelming, simply meeting humanitarian needs exceeds all the systems we have in place ... the humanitarian situation is so acute that governments, agencies and donors may argue that they should not put funds into something perceived as having a limited impact on people.

The answer to this problem is to mainstream risk reduction into development. Hodge argued that the struggle for resources within CIDA's IHA Division is '...partly why we want to have it mainstreamed into development thinking ... it makes more sense in terms of the actions that can be taken on and the amount of energy and human resources the agency can devote to it'. She also believes that mainstreaming the issue will increase the financial resources allocated for it: '...within our ... small budget and the pressures that we have on our overall humanitarian resources.'

However, while there are constraints to humanitarian aid divisions investing more in risk reduction, the same is true for development divisions. The need to engage with other important issues was frequently given as a reason why more development finances could not, or should not, be invested in risk reduction. Whether the current level of priority awarded to disaster risk reduction vis-a-vis other development needs is a 'misrepresentation' is a fundamental question. In the IADB's natural disaster action plan it is stated: 'Local communities, already stressed by their daily struggle for better employment, health, basic education and other needs, have not pressured their local and national leaders to do more to reduce their vulnerability to disaster.' Moreover, as highlighted by Red Cross Vulnerability and Capacity Assessments (VCA) in Palestine and Bangladesh, even when an NGO or donor priorities risk reduction within its agenda, often the community can have a different perception of what its primary needs actually are. This was noted by IHA.

Most of the projects visited were relevant at the local level because the target communities were vulnerable to natural hazards and needed disaster preparedness training. However, only two projects seemed to be demand-driven, i.e. they responded to identified community needs and interests ... Beneficiaries of the four other projects indicated that their top priorities would be health care, housing, employment, etc. while disaster preparedness would be relatively less important. It is not surprising that a 'vulnerable' community finding it difficult to survive on a daily basis focuses on its immediate requirements rather than on out-of-the-ordinary occurrences. As Peppiart observes, investing in disaster preparedness is often an 'unaffordable luxury' for the very poor.

However, at a macro-level, amongst those with an ability to decide on the emphasis needed to reduce a community's long-term vulnerability, is a similar attitude of non-engagement with the issue acceptable? Clearly, and as the research revealed, non-engagement can be due to a number of valid development issues 'competing' with natural disasters. With reference to a recent Low Development Country (LDC) conference, out of 49 LDCs, many are disaster prone and losses are at their highest. However, at the LDC conference the agenda was about trade and debt, not disaster risk. This is what the Finance Ministers are saying is their priority. Conflict is also increasingly competing with natural disasters.

Conflict is perceived as being the major threat to development [and so] natural hazards always seem peripheral. Undeniably these are important issues. However, it cannot be denied that invalid political priorities also play a role in pushing risk reduction down the agenda. One contact asserted that disaster risk reduction is sometimes ignored or delayed in application because of 'confusing, conflicting and unacceptable priorities as expressed by the affected country'. For instance, let us raise the question that, how much money some countries have allocated to their military in recent years in comparison with disaster risk reduction, where natural disasters have killed many thousands but relatively few have died as a result of conflict.

It is interesting to note that, whereas risk reduction is constantly fighting to 'prove its worth', politicians do not often raise the question of 'cost-benefit analysis' regarding proposed emergency relief programmes. This is probably due to the high 'visibility' of relief work, and the profile a government can acquire through being seen to respond to major disasters, can all contribute to a government prioritising it over risk reduction. As another contact observed, if there happens to be a disaster during a politician's term of office then much aid will be received and a politician can be seen to be responding. This will increase the chance of re-election, while prevention investments — especially in a four-year Government period — may not reap such glamorous rewards.

The research highlighted that there is a need for more concrete evidence of the cost-effectiveness of risk reduction. This is required to help convince development sectors that investing in disaster preventive action is worthwhile. It is likely that if [cost-benefit and cost-effectiveness] tools become the 'norm' in project assessment then there will be a significant increase in risk reduction projects since favourable benefits, over costs, are likely to emerge from such economic appraisal despite believing risk reduction to be 'common sense'. Moreover it is also argued the need for cost-benefit analyses, stating that currently the 'economic rationale' for risk reduction is not strong enough to convince the development specialists and, critically, the economists (including those working on PRSPs in developing countries) that risk reduction pays.

Cost-benefit models are notoriously difficult to apply to disasters and much needs to be done to develop and adapt them. However, the alternative is to wait for another major disaster (s) to provide the rationale for engaging more extensively in risk reduction. He says, 'If we woke up and there was no Tokyo, this would change the landscape of international assistance for disasters.'

Be Imaginative

'We have to do disaster risk reduction but understand the context we are working in'. Moreover, while trying to promote the issue, other valid development needs must be considered: 'The development package has a limit at the moment and everyone is trying to throw something new into the pot.' Issue must be tackled 'Imaginatively': The pot is not likely to increase so much. Therefore, we should probably concentrate on being more effective and imaginative within it.

In practice, this means building risk reduction initiatives into the existing context, agenda and priorities of developmental strategies. 'Risk management must be a formal component of development planning for countries with high natural catastrophe exposure'. This has to be demand driven by disaster-prone countries as country priorities are a key driver in determining the focus of donor programmes. Recognising this, the IADB is actively engaged with national "decision-makers."

Dialogue meetings' with Ministry of Finance officials — and others — from the countries within its region of operation. One recent meeting, as aforementioned, was on the subject of local risk management. It is absolutely necessary that the officials need to understand and be convinced of the importance of risk reduction as they are significant players in defining country strategies.

There may be a need to demonstrate the links between disasters and particular development issues. For instance, 'In southern Africa HIV/AIDS is increasing the vulnerability of poor communities to a whole range of disasters such as food insecurity.'

The UNDP's forthcoming World Vulnerability Index may assist with identification of high-risk countries.

Some donors are using the issue of climate change to increase awareness of, and attention to, the need for disaster risk reduction. However, several of our contacts observed a danger in using climate change as a 'hook' in this way. This relates to overfocusing on environmental vulnerabilities to disasters, while neglecting other causes of vulnerability such as social, economic and political factors. Therefore, when using the threat of climate change to promote disaster risk reduction, the focus must always be on assessing all forms of vulnerability to hazards and the need to address these if communities are to cope with current events let alone with any intensification of hazards attributed to climate change. (Interestingly, CIDA is using its Climate Change Working Group to promote the integration of risk reduction into development planning.

The rich world's scant investment in natural disaster risk reduction is illogical and indefensible. Rich nations, when facing a threat to their security or well-being, mobilise and invest massive resources to protect their interests. They do not do the same for poor countries threatened by disaster, although they frequently plough major resources into relief and recovery operations once a disaster has struck. It would make more economic sense for rich nations to invest greater resources in risk reduction with vulnerable countries. In light of increasingly fragile social, political, economic and natural environments, the longer we delay in addressing risk reduction and preparedness, the greater the impact, scale and cost of emergencies'.

It would also make greater moral sense for the rich world to help prevent needless loss of life from disasters in the developing world than simply to provide aid and sympathy after disaster strikes. Yet a society's sense of the morality or otherwise of such a situation will depend upon its values and principles of justice and equity influencing its perception of duty and responsibility for others. The Millennium Development Goals (MDGs) are a positive step towards achieving a more just and equitable world. However, whilst policy makers are currently considering the inclusion of a humanitarian aid goal within the MDGs, disaster reduction itself is not given adequate attention. Therefore, it is crucial that, as donors increasingly focus their interventions to meet these goals, they recognise and account for the serious threat that disasters pose to them.

If risk reduction is to acquire a higher political profile, it must be thoroughly integrated into development policy and practice. As our research shows, many representatives of donor agencies say this themselves and are affirmed by other organisations and independent experts. Therefore, this report is aimed primarily at development sectors of donor organisations where greatest progress needs to be made in terms of understanding, owning and addressing risk reduction within the context of their work. The development and widespread use of a practical tool, such as a checklist, is a positive step towards this. However, humanitarian/relief sectors have a dual responsibility. They must seek to mitigate disaster risks where possible within relief interventions and they may need to take the lead in promoting and developing a strong corporate understanding of the issue within a donor organisation.

We readily acknowledge that the failure to 'mainstream' disaster risk reduction into development has long been the subject of discussion among the risk reduction community. We do not claim to have made a new discovery here. However, this report has identified the main impediments to mainstreaming and proposed some practical steps towards overcoming them.

We hope this will encourage new and more effective risk reduction action by donors and other organisations, particularly:

- Moves to integrate risk reduction into all development programming in disaster-prone countries, including the development of tools for community-based risk assessment and to aid development professionals in their analysis and reduction of risks.
- Support given to individuals and units focused on making the above happen.
- Advocacy to help remove the underlying causes of vulnerability.

Unless these and other actions are taken as a matter of urgency, preventable disasters will continue to undermine the efforts of poor people to escape poverty and the efforts of rich countries to help them. More investment in risk reduction as a 'mainstreamed' component of relief and development interventions, on the other hand, will save lives, safeguard development efforts and add value to them. There is no valid reason why this investment cannot be made.

Government Policy and Practice on Natural Disaster Risk Reduction: During the period in which Tearfund met or spoke with donors, organisations and experts to discuss disaster risk reduction policy and practice, several of Tearfund's partners met with their own local municipalities and/or national governments to do the same. The comments made by officials within the Bangladesh, Honduras, India and Malawi governments provide evidence of both progress and difficulties in the field of risk reduction at southern government level. It is interesting to note the synergies between the problems outlined by these officials and those presented by donors as detailed in this report.

With the exception of India, the comments were collated by Tearfund partners working in these countries. Comments were selected on the basis of relevance to the research project's objectives. Some of the comments have received minor editing to assist in providing clarity of expression.

Bangladesh

The government of Bangladesh, since its independence in 1971, has established a separate ministry called the Ministry of Relief, which was then turned into the Ministry of Relief and Rehabilitation in the late seventies. After a number of disasters, the government created a separate bureau (the Disaster Management Bureau) in 1992 in order to speed up its activities in pre- and post-disaster periods. The government has also created a strong National Disaster Management Council, which meets at least twice in a year. Apart from this, there are Disaster Management Committees at district, subdistrict (upazila) and union (last tier of local government administration) levels.

Honduras — The Municipality of Brus Laguna (BRL)

Coordinating the Municipal Emergency Committee (CODEM) and building its capacity to reduce the risk of storms, urricanes, fires, etc. planning to coordinate Local Emergency Committees. The Municipality of Juan Francisco Bulnes (JBF): Preventing deforestation on river banks and beaches, natural disaster training in some communities. The Municipality of Puerto Lempira (PLP): This Municipality has created the Municipal Environment Unit (UMA) and managed local watersheds to secure quality and supply of water.

India

The Government of Gujarat (GoG) has a vision of building a state which has the capacity, capability and resources to cope with natural disasters. Keeping this in mind, the government has focused not only on structural aspects but also on non-structural aspects of disaster mitigation and preparedness. The disaster management activities of GoG include retrofitting of hazardous buildings, strict enforcement of building codes for new construction and reconstruction of buildings, simplification of General Development Control Regulations, demolition of unsafe buildings in high seismic zone areas, construction of water harvesting structures for water storage, revision in syllabus of colleges to include disaster mitigation components, etc. Apart from this, the government aims to provide information to various respondents like government officials and staff, civil society and individuals, regarding disaster preparedness. For this, it has directed its efforts on disaster management capacity building through education, information sharing and dissemination, hazard-related research and training.

Other National Organisations

Australia

Australia has the federal government agency Emergency Management Australia (EMA) as the key federal co-ordinating and advisory body for emergency management. Each state has their own State Emergency Service. The Emergency Call Service provides emergency telephone numbers to state Police, Fire and Ambulance services and arrangements in place for state and federal cooperation.

Canada

Public Safety Canada is Canada's national emergency management agency. Each province has a mandate to set up their Emergency Management Organisations. PSC also coordinates and supports the efforts of federal organisations ensuring national security and the safety of Canadians. They also work with other levels of government, first responders, community groups, the private sector (operators of critical infrastructure) and other nations.

PSC's work is based on a wide range of policies and legislation. Through the Public Safety and Emergency Preparedness Act which defines the powers, duties and functions of PSEPC are outlined. Other acts are specific to fields such as corrections, emergency management, law enforcement and national security.

Germany

In Germany the Federal Government controls the German Katastrophenschutz (disaster relief) or Zivilschutz (civil defence) programmes. Particularly the German fire department and the Technisches Hilfswerk (Federal Agency for Technical Relief, THW) are part of these programmes. Also the German Armed Forces (Bundeswehr) can be deployed for disaster relief operations.

New Zealand

In New Zealand the Ministry of Civil Defence and Emergency Management has statutory authority for controlling any state of emergency declared by central government. Local government bodies such as city and regional councils have their own emergency management agencies to control localised states of emergency, but these all defer to the MCDEM in the event of a national state of emergency. The Wellington Emergency Management Office utilise a building that has been proposed to built with its own water, electricity/ communications and sewerage facilities to ensure operations in the event of an emergency or disaster.

Russia

In Russia the Ministry of Extraordinary Situations (EMERCOM) is engaged in fire fighting, Civil Defence, Search and Rescue, rescue services after natural and human-made disasters.

United Kingdom

The United Kingdom adjusted its focus on emergency management following the 2000 UK fuel protests, severe UK flooding in the same year and the 2001 UK foot and mouth crisis. This resulted in the creation of the Civil Contingencies Act 2004 which legislated the responsibilities of all category one responders regarding an emergency response. The United Kingdom's management of the CCA is through the Civil Contingencies Secretariat through regional disaster centres and at the local authority level.

United States of America

Under the Department of Homeland Security (DHS), the Federal Emergency Management Agency (FEMA) is lead agency for emergency management. The HAZUS software package developed by FEMA is central in the risk assessment process in the country. The United States and its territories are covered by one of ten regions for FEMA's emergency management purposes. Tribal, state, county and local governments develop emergency management programmes/ departments and operate hierarchically within each region. Emergencies are managed at the mostlocal level possible, utilising mutual aid agreements with adjacent jurisdictions. If the emergency is terrorist related or if declared an "Incident of National Significance", the Secretary of Homeland Security will initiate the National Response Plan (NRP). Under this plan the involvement of federal resources will be made possible, integrating in with the local, county, state, or tribal entities. Management will continue to be handled at the lowest possible level utilising the National Incident Management System (NIMS).

The Citizen Corps is an organisation of volunteer service programmes, administered locally and coordinated nationally by DHS, which seek to mitigate disaster and prepare the population for emergency response through public education, training, and outreach. Community Emergency Response Teams are a Citizen Corps programme focused on disaster preparedness and teaching basic disaster response skills. These volunteer teams are utilised to provide emergency support when disaster overwhelms the conventional emergency services.

VARIOUS ONGOING STRATEGIES

In order to get themselves protected from the hazardous situations, peoples all around the world have started inventing and adopting various innovative strategies according to the changing geographical conditions. Some of the major innovative strategies are analyzed hereunder.

Blast Shelter

A blast shelter is a place where people can go to protect themselves from bomb blasts. It differs from a fallout shelter, in that its main purpose is to protect from shock waves and overpressure, instead of from radioactive precipitation, as a fallout shelter does. It is also possible for a shelter to protect from both blast and fallout.

Types of Blast Shelters

Since, according to the Federation of American Scientists, the blast is the main cause of death from nuclear weapons, blast shelters are a vital form of protection from nuclear attack and are employed in civil defence.

There are above-ground, below-ground, dedicated, dual-purpose, and potential blast shelters. Dedicated blast shelters are built specifically for the purpose of blast protection. Dual-purpose blast shelters are existing structures with blast protective properties that have been modified to accommodate people in their seeking protection from blast. Potential blast shelters are existing structures or geological features exhibiting blast protective properties that have potential to be used for protection from blast.

Its Design

Blast shelters deflect the blast wave from nearby explosions to prevent ear and internal injuries to people sheltering in the bunker. While frame buildings collapse from as little as 3 psi (20 kPa) of overpressure, blast shelters are regularly constructed to survive several hundred psi. This substantially decreases the likelihood that a bomb can harm the structure.

The basic plan is to provide a structure that is very strong in compression. The actual strength specification must be done individually, based on the nature and probability of the threat. A typical specification for heavy civil defence shelter in Europe during the Cold war was an overhead explosion of a 500 kiloton weapon at the height of 500 metres. Such a weapon would be used to attack soft targets (factories, administrative centres, communications) in the area.

Only the heaviest bedrock-shelters would stand a chance of surviving.

Most expedient blast shelters are civil engineering structures that contain large buried tubes or pipes such as sewage or rapid transit tunnels. Even these, nonetheless, require several additions to serve properly: blast doors, air-filtration and ventilation equipment, secondary exits/and air-proofing.

The doors must be at least as strong as the walls. The usual design is a trap-door, to minimise the size and expense. In dual-purpose shelters, which have a secondary peace time use, the door may be normal. To reduce the weight, the door is normally constructed of steel, with a fitted steel lintel and frame welded to the steel-reinforcement of the concrete. The shelter should be located so that there is no combustible material directly outside it.

Air-raid Shelter

Air-raid shelters are structures for the protection of the civil population as well as military personnel against enemy attacks (Bombing) from the air. They are similar to bunkers in many regards, though they are not designed against ground attack (many have been successfully used as defensive structures in such situations anyway).

Air raid shelters were built specifically to serve as protection against enemy air raids. However, pre-existing edifices designed for other functions, such as underground stations (tube or subway stations), tunnels, or cellars in houses, basements in larger establishments, and railway arches, were also utilised.

These structures, being below ground or almost so, and being especially strengthened to support the weight of the buildings above them, were therefore particularly suitable to safeguard people during air raids. A commonly used home-made shelter was known as the Anderson shelter which would be built with beds, in the garden to protect from air raids.

The Cellars

Cellars in Continental Europe have always been much more important than they have in the United Kingdom, and especially in Germany almost all houses and apartment blocks have been and are still being built with cellars. For this reason, air-raid precautions during World War II in Germany could be much more readily organised by the authorities than it was possible to do so in the UK.

All that was necessary was to ascertain that cellars were being prepared to accommodate all the residents of a building; that all the cellar hatch and window protections were in place; access to the cellars was safe in the event of an air raid; once inside, the occupants were secure for any incidents other than direct hits during the air raid; and that the means of escape in case of a real emergency were easily available.

The Basements

Basements, the storeys beneath the larger kinds of premises and establishments, also became available for the use of air raid shelters. In this way, basements under factory premises, schools, hospitals, department stores and other businesses were utilised. What had to be kept in mind, however, was that heavy machinery and materials, water storage facilities above the shelter, and insufficient support structures, such as pillars and beams beneath the shelter ceiling, did not aggravate the situation and endanger the lives of the occupants in the basements further.

When Wilkinson's Lemonade factory in North Shields received a direct hit on Saturday, 3rd May 1941 during a German attack on the northeast coast of England, 107 occupants lost their lives when the ceiling of the basement in which they were sheltering, and the heavy machinery above it, collapsed.

Railway Arches and Subways

Railway arches and subways, too, were being utilised in the UK for air raid protection at all times during World War II.

Railway arches were deep, curved structures of brick or concrete, set into the vertical sidewalls of railway lines, that had been intended originally for commercial depots, etc. The arches were covered usually with wooden or brick screen or curtain-walls, thus giving a considerable amount of protection against air raids - provided, of course, that railway lines were not the prime target of the attack at the particular time and so being more likely to suffer from direct hits.

Each arch could accommodate anything from 60 to 150 or so persons. However, fewer people could find shelter at night as sleeping areas for the occupants took up more of the space available — a limitation applying to any other type of shelter as well. Subways (so-called in British usage to denote underpasses) were actual thoroughfares also in the shape of arches, normally allowing passage underneath railway lines.

Underground Stations

People were keen to get on with their lives as normally as possible whatever hardships they encountered outside the tube shelters. Nevertheless, Londoners preferred to use the Underground stations to any other shelters because they felt safest there and were willing to show determination to continue to use the tube stations and tunnels.

The government soon realised the extent of this popular resolve and that the underground, after all, could be the answer to the lack of available shelters and cellars in London. Businesses (for example Plessey Ltd.) were allowed to use the underground stations and unopened tunnels, government offices were installed in others and the anti-aircraft centre for London used a station as its headquarters.

However, tube stations and tunnels were still vulnerable to a direct hit and several such incidents did occur.

Other Tunnels

Many other types of tunnels were adapted for shelters to protect the civil population and the military and administrative establishments in the UK during the war. Some had been built many years before, some had been part of an ancient defence system and some had belonged to commercial enterprises, such as coal mining.

The Victoria tunnels at Newcastle upon Tyne, for example, completed as long ago as 1842 and used for transporting coal from the collieries to the river Tyne, had been closed in 1860 and remained so until 1939. 12 m deep in places, the tunnels, stretching in parts beneath the city of Newcastle, were converted to air raid shelters with a capacity for 9,000 people.

The large medieval labyrinth of tunnels beneath Dover Castle had been built originally as part of the defensive system of the approaches to England, extended over the centuries and further excavated and reinforced during World Wars I and II, until it was capable of accommodating large parts of the secret defence systems protecting the British Isles.

On 26 May 1940, it became the headquarters under Vice Admiral Bertram Ramsay of "Operation Dynamo", from where the rescue and evacuation of up to 338,000 troops from France directed.

Street Communal Shelter

In the United Kingdom, it was being recognised early that public shelters in open spaces, especially near streets, were gently needed for pedestrians and drivers and passengers in passing vehicles, etc. The programme of building street communal shelters commenced in March 1940, the government supplying the materials and being the moving force behind the scheme and private builders executing the work under the supervision of surveyors.

These shelters consisted of 14-inch brick walls and one-foot thick reinforced concrete roofs, similarly to, but much larger than, the private shelters in backyards and gardens being introduced slightly later. The communal shelters were usually intended to accommodate about fifty persons and were divided into various sections by interior walls with openings connecting the different sections. Sections were normally furnished with six bunks.

The construction work then went on rapidly, until the resources of concrete and bricks began to be depleted due to the excessive demand placed on them so suddenly. Also at around the same time rumours of accidents started to circulate, such as on one occasion people being drowned due to a burst main filling up the shelter with water. It was then that these shelters began to become highly unpopular and shortly afterwards householders were being encouraged to build or have built private shelters on their properties, or within their houses, with materials being supplied by the government.

Anderson Shelter

The Anderson shelter was designed in 1938 by William Paterson and Oscar Carl (Karl) Kerrison in response to a request from the Home Office. It was named after Sir John Anderson, then Lord Privy Seal with special responsibility for preparing air-raid precautions immediately prior to the outbreak of World War II, and it was he who then initiated the development of the shelter. After evaluation by Dr. David Anderson, Bertram Lawrence Hurst and Sir Henry Jupp, of the Institution of Civil Engineers, the design was released for production.

Anderson shelters were designed to accommodate up to six people. The main principle of protection was based on curved and straight galvanised corrugated steel panels.

Six curved panels were bolted together at the top, so forming the main body of the shelter, three straight sheets on either side and two more straight panels were fixed to each end, one containing the door — a total of fourteen panels. A small drainage sump was often incorporated in the floor to collect rainwater seeping into the shelter. The shelters were 6 ft (1.8 m) high, 4 ft 6 in (1.4 m) wide, and 6 ft 6 in (2 m) long. They were buried 4 ft (1.2 m) deep in the soil and then covered with a minimum of 15 in (0.4 m) of soil above the roof. The earth banks could be planted with vegetables and flowers, that at tinies could be quite an appealing sight and in this way would become the subject of competitions of the best-planted shelter among householders in the neighbourhood. The internal fitting out of the shelter was left to the owner and so there were wide variations in comfort.

Anderson shelters were issued free to all householders who earned less than £250 a year, and those with a higher income were charged £ 150,000 shelters of this type were distributed from February 1939 to the outbreak of war. During the war, a further 2.1 million were erected.

Because of the large number made and their robustness, many Anderson shelters still survive. Many were dug up after the war and converted into storage sheds for use in gardens and allotments.

Morrison Shelter

Morrison shelters, officially termed Table (Morrison) Indoor Shelters, were designed by John Baker and named after Herbert Morrison, the Minister of Home Security at the time. It was the result of the realisation that due to the lack of house cellars to was necessary to develop an effective type of indoor shelter. The shelters came in assembly kits, to be bolted together inside the home. They were approximately 6 ft 6 in (2 m) long, 4 ft 1-2 m) wide and 2 ft 6 in (0.75 m) high, had a solid 1/8 in (3 mm) steel plate "table" top, welded wire mesh sides, and metal lath "mattress"- type floor. Altogether it had 359 parts d had 3 tools supplied with the pack.

One of the first structures to be designed using Baker's theory of plastic structural analysis, it was designed to absorb the impact of debris falling on the top of the shelter. The sides could be removed to permit it being used as a table. 500,000 Morrisons had been distributed by the end of 1941, with a further 100,000 being added in 1943 to prepare the population for the expected German V-l flying bomb (doodlebug) attacks.

In one examination of 44 severely damaged houses where three people had been killed, 13 seriously injured and 16 slightly injured out of a total of 136 people who had occupied Morrison shelters, it was found that the fatalities had occurred in a house which had suffered a direct hit. Some of the severely injured were in shelters sited incorrectly within the houses.

Military Citadels under London

There are several bunkers and tunnels under key government buildings, built to withstand air raids, although the scale of this is unknown because the government does not freely release this information.

The Hochbunker

Hochbunker(s), or "high-rise" bunkers or (blockhouses), were a peculiarly German type of construction, designed to relieve the pressure. German authorities were facing to accommodate additional numbers of the population in high-density housing areas, as well as pedestrians on the streets during air raids. In contrast to any other shelters, these buildings were indeed considered completely bomb-proof. They also had the advantage of being built upward — much more cheaply than downward by excavation. There were no equivalents of hochbunkers in the cities of the Allied countries.

Hochbunkers consisted usually of large concrete blocks above ground of thicknesses between 1 m and 1.5 m, huge lintels above doorways and openings and they often had a constant interior temperature of 7 to 10°C, thus being perfectly suitable for laboratory utilisation during and after the war. They had been designated to protect people, administrative centres, important archives and works of art.

Their structures took many forms, square blocks, but also lower and longer rectangular shapes, including triangles, straight towers of a square plan rising to great heights, as well as round tower-like edifices, even pyramidal constructions. Some of the circular towers contained helical floors that gradually curved their way upward within the circular walls. Many of these structures may still be seen to this day. They have been converted into offices, storage space and some have even been adopted for hotels, hospitals and schools, as well as many other peacetime purposes.

The cost of demolishing these edifices after the war would have been enormous, as the attempts at breaking up one of the six so-called Flak Towers of Vienna proved, hochbunkers which during the war had anti-aircraft batteries at their top platforms. Only a crack could be achieved in one of the walls, before the attempt had to be abandoned. The Pallasstrasse air-raid shelter, Schoneberg has a post-war block of flats built over the shelter. During the Cold War the shelter was in use as a NATO food-store.

Brick-built Shelter

Brick-built shelters with reinforced concrete roofs were often constructed in backyards and gardens in the UK.

Military air-raid shelters included blast pens at airfields for the security of aircrews and aircraft maintenance personnel away from the main airbase buildings.

Few shelters could have been considered ultimately safe in a case of a direct bomb-hit. The German authorities claimed that hochbunkers were totally bomb-proof, but none were hit any of the 41 Grand Slam bunker busters dropped by the end of World War II. Two were dropped on the bunkerwerft Valentin submarine pens near Bremen, Penetrating 4 to 7 metres of reinforced concrete and bringing the roof down.

More recently, the penetration by laser-guided "smart bombs" of the Amiriyah shelter during the 1991 Gulf War showed how vulnerable reinforced concrete blockhouses are to direct hits from bunker-buster bombs.

However, the air-raid shelters are built to protect the civilian population, so protection against a direct hit is of secondary value. The most important dangers are the blast and shrapnel. It is unlikely that any military enemy would intentionally target a civilian shelter, even if it were carpet bombing a city.

Air-raid Shelters in Modern Times

As said above, air-raid shelters, such as the Anderson, can still be found in back gardens, in which they are commonly used as sheds, or (on the roof which is covered with earth) as vegetables patches. Some are left empty or are filled with debris.

A notable country still having its air-raid /nuclear blast/ fallout shelter is Switzerland. Many houses still have enormous concrete doors deep in the basement, these doors which are around 40 cm thick. Inside these shelters, an air supply system can be found. Currently, many people use these shelters as safes (to hold financial documents) or as storages for priceless documents, such as pictures of wedding days, or a child's school work, or as a cellar. In many cases structures are the most secure of a house, because of the shelter's ceiling. The ceiling of this shelter is also made of thick concrete, which, in the event of the house collapsing, should, in theory, not come down with it.

Blast Pen

A blast pen was a specially-constructed E-shaped double bay at British RAF World War 2 fighter stations, being either 150 feet or 190 feet wide and 80 feet front-to-back, accommodating aircraft for safe-keeping against bomb blasts and splinters during enemy air-attacks.

Although the pens were open to the sky the projecting sidewalls preserved the aircraft from lateral damage, with 12-inch thick, 9-feet high concrete centres and banked-up earth on either side, forming a roughly triangular section 18-feet wide at their base. The longer spine section behind the parking areas usually encloses a narrow corridor for aircrew and servicing personnel to use as an air raid shelters.

Examples may still be seen at the present Kenley Aerodrome and at North Weald aerodrome in Essex close to "The Squadron" bar, some pens have had their second bay removed over the years, thus becoming U-shaped.

Blockhouse

In military science, a blockhouse is a small, isolated fort in the form of a single building. It is intended to serve as a defensive strongpoint against any enemy which does not possess siege equipment or, in modern times, artillery. If a fortification is intended to protect against such weapons as well, it is more likely to qualify as castle or, in modern times, a bunker.

Age of Exploration

Originally blockhouses were often constructed as part of a large plan, to "block" access to vital points in the scheme. But from the Age of Exploration to the nineteenth century standard patterns of blockhouses were constructed for defence in frontier areas, particularly South Africa, New Zealand, Canada, and the United States.

Blockhouses may be made of masonry where available, but were commonly made from very heavy timbers, sometimes even logs arranged in the manner of a log cabin. They were usually two or even three floors, with all storeys being provided with embrasures or loopholes and the uppermost storey would be roofed. If the structure was of timber, usually the upper storey would project outward from the lower so the upper storey defenders could fire on enemy attacking the lower storey, or perhaps pour water on any fires. When the structure had very one storey, its loopholes were often placed close to the ceiling, with a bench lining the walls inside for defenders to stand on, so that attackers could not easily reach the loopholes.

Blockhouses were normally entered via a sturdy, barred door at ground level. Most blockhouses were roughly square in plan, but some of the more elaborate ones were hexagonal or octagonal, to provide better all-around fire. In some cases, blockhouses became the basis for complete forts, by building a palisade with the blockhouse at one corner and possibly a second tower at the opposite corner. Many historical stone blockhouses have survived and a few timber ones have been restored at historical sites. In New Zealand, a number of one storey timber blockhouses survive from the Maori Wars, while stone blockhouses from the Boer War are relatively common in South Africa.

Concrete Blockhouses

During the First and Second World Wars many types of blockhouses were built, when time allowed usually constructed of reinforced concrete. The major difference between a modern blockhouse and a bunker is that a bunker is constructed mostly below ground level while a blockhouse is constructed mostly above ground level.

Some blockhouses like those constructed in England in 1940 were built for traditional fortification reasons, often hexagonal in shape and were called pillboxes. Between 20 and 30 thousand were built in Britain during World War II in preparation for a possible German attack.

In London the Admiralty Citadel is one of the most sturdy above ground structures built during World War II. It was constructed in 1940-1941 as a bomb-proof operations centre for the Admiralty, with foundations nine metres deep and a concrete roof six metres thick. It too was intended to serve as a strong point in defending against the feared invasion.

In Berlin and other cities, during World War II, some massive blockhouses were built as air-raid shelters and anti-aircraft artillery platforms. They were called Hochbunker "High hunkers" and those which functioned as anti-aircraft artillery platforms were also called Flak Towers. Some were over 6 stories high. Several survive to this day because the cost of demolition would be prohibitive.

Afghanistan 2006

Blockhouses and Sangars have become a feature of the 2006 conflict in Afghanistan, being used by the British coalition forces, amongst others, as strong points to control the contested Southern provinces. These positions have served to draw out the Taliban, who have taken to attacking repeatedly in numbers.

Bunker

A bunker is a defensive military fortification. Bunkers are mostly below ground, compared to blockhouses which are mostly above ground. They were used extensively in World War I and World War II. During the Cold War, massive bunker complexes were built to house both strategic (command and control) infrastructure as well as government personnel and stores for the event of a nuclear war. During that time, bunkers became a part of American culture with people building backyard fallout shelters, though these were not intended to protect against direct attacks as bunkers normally would.

Trench Bunker

This type of bunker or blockhouse is a small concrete box, partly dug into the ground, which is usually a part of a trench system. Such bunkers givc the defending soldiers better protection than the open trench and also include top protection against aerial attack (grenades, mortar shells). The front bunker of a trench system usually includes machine guns or mortars and forms a dominant shooting post. The rear bunkers are usually used as command posts or Tactical Operations Centre (TOC), for storage and as field hospitals to attend to wounded soldiers. Many mines in France were transformed into bunkers by both the Germans and the French in World War I and World War II.

Pillbox

Dug-in guard posts (with loopholes through which to fire guns) and made from concrete are also known as "pillboxes". The originally jocular name arose from their perceived similarity to the cylindrical boxes in which medicinal pills were once sold. They are in effect a trench firing step hardened to protect against small-arms fire and grenades and raised a little to improve the field of fire.

Their use seems to have developed during the period of the First World War when defence in depth using the Machine Gun Corps was being perfected. However, most of those seen in Britain, having been leftover from the 1940 invasion scare, are designed for use by riflemen rather than for machine gunners.

The concrete nature of pillboxes means that they are a feature of prepared positions and their original use is likely to have been in the Hindenburg Line. This is likely to have been the time when they acquired their incongruous English name.

The Oxford English Dictionary's earliest record of the use of the word pillbox in connection with a defensive post is from 13 September 1917, after the German withdrawal onto the Hindenburg Line.

Pillboxes are often camouflaged in order to conceal their location and to maximise the element of surprise. They may be part of a trench system, form an interlocking line of defence with other pillboxes by providing covering fire to each other (defence in depth), or they may be placed to guard strategic structures such as bridges and jetties.

Industrial Bunker

Typical industrial bunkers include mining sites, food storage areas, dumps for materials, data storage and sometimes living quarters. They were built mainly by nations like Germany during World War II to protect important industries from x aerial x bombardment.

Personal Shelter

Experts in preparedness for war recommend purchasing and stockpiling the materials for an expedient blast or fallout shelter and then constructing it only if war appears very likely. In real wars, such materials almost immediately become unavailable as emergency construction depletes stocks. The storage needed is modest, and the materials are inexpensive in peacetime and easy to inspect and maintain.

When a house is purpose-built with a bunker, the normal location is a reinforced below-grade bathroom with large Cabinets.

Today some vendors, provide true bunkers engineered to provide good protection to individual families at modest cost. One common design approach uses fibre-reinforced plastic shells. Compressive protection may be provided by inexpensive earth arching. The overburden is designed to shield from radiation. To prevent the shelter from floating to the surface in high groundwater, some designs have a skirt held-down with the overburden.

Design

Blast Protection: Bunkers deflect the blast wave from nearby explosions to prevent ear and internal injuries to people sheltering in the bunker. While frame buildings collapse from as little as 3 psi (0.2 bar) of overpressure, bunkers are regularly constructed to survive several hundred psi (over 10 bar). This substantially decreases the likelihood that a bomb can harm the structure.

The basic plan is to provide a structure that is very strong in physical compression. The most common purpose-built structure is a buried, steel reinforced concrete vault or arch. Most expedient (makeshift) blast shelters are civil engineering structures that contain large buried tubes or pipes such as sewage or rapid transit tunnels. Improvised purpose-built blast shelters normally use earthen arches or vaults. To form these, a narrow (1-2 metre) flexible tent of thin wood is placed in a deep trench (usually the apex is below grade) and then covered with cloth or plastic and then covered with 1-2 metres of tamped earth.

Famous Installations

Famous bunkers include NORAD's underground facility at Cheyenne Mountain and the Canadian set of so-called Diefenbunkers. The Soviet Union maintained huge bunkers (one of the secondary uses of the very deeply dug Moscow Subway system was as nuclear shelters) and in Albania, Enver Hoxha dotted the country with hundreds of thousands of bunkers. Dictators and potentates like Saddam Hussein often spend massive sums building fortresses beneath their palaces. Osama bin Laden at one time was also rumoured to be hiding in massive 'underground fortresses' in Tora Bora, though these would only be natural features strengthened and extended to some degree.

Earth Sheltering

Earth sheltering is the architectural practice of using earth against building walls for external thermal mass, to reduce heat loss and to maintain easily a steady indoor air temperature. Earth sheltering is popular among advocates of passive solar and sustainable architecture, but the idea has been around for nearly as long as humans have been constructing their own shelter.

Living within earth shelters has been a large part of human history. The connection to earth shelter dwellings began with the utilisation of caves and over time evolving technologies led to the construction of customised earth dwellings. Today, earth shelter construction is a rare practice, especially in the USA. During the energy crisis and the oil embargo of 1973, along with the back to the land movement, there was a surge of interest in earth shelter/underground home construction in an effort towards self-sufficient living. However, progress has been slow and earth shelter construction is often viewed by architects, engineers and the public alike as an unconventional method of building. Techniques of earth sheltering have not yet become common knowledge and much of society still remains unaware of the process or benefits of this type of building construction.

Types of Construction

- Earth Berming: Earth is piled up against exterior and packed, sloping down away from the house roof may, or may not be, fully earth covered and windows/ openings may occur on one or more sides of the shelter. Due to the building being above grade, less moisture problems are associated with earth berming in comparison to underground/fully recessed construction.

- In-hill Construction: The house is set into a slope or hillside. The most practical application is using a hill facing towards the equator (south in the Northern Hemisphere and north in the Southern Hemisphere). There is only one exposed wall in this type of earth sheltering, the wall facing out of the hill, all other walls are embedded within the earth/hill.

  Underground/ Fully Recessed Construction: The ground is excavated, and the house is set in below grade. It can also be referred to as an Atrium style due to the common atrium/courtyard constructed in the middle of the shelter to provide adequate light and ventilation.

Benefits

The benefits of earth sheltering are numerous. They include: taking advantage of the earth as a thermal mass, offering extra protection from the natural elements, energy savings, providing substantial privacy, efficient use of land in urban settings, shelters requires low maintenance and earth sheltering commonly takes advantage of passive solar building design.

The earth's mass absorbs and retains heat. Overtime, this heat is released to surrounding areas, such as an earth shelter. Because of the high density of the earth, change in the earth's temperature occurs slowly. This is known as 'thermal lag.' Because of this principle, the earth provides a fairly constant temperature for the underground shelters, even when the outdoor temperature undergoes great fluctuation. In most of the United States, the average temperature of the earth once well below the frost line is around 55 to 57 degrees Fahrenheit (13 to 14 degrees Celsius). The depth of frost lines vary from region to region. Thus, at the base of a deep earth term, the house is heated against an exterior temperature gradient of perhaps ten to fifteen degrees, instead of against a steeper temperature grade where air is on the outside of the wall instead of earth. In the summer, the temperature gradient actually helps to cool the house.

The reduction of air infiltration within an earth shelter can be highly profitable. Because three walls of the structure are mainly surrounded by earth, very little surface area is exposed to the outside air. This alleviates the problem of warm air escaping the house through gaps around windows and doors. Furthermore, the earth walls protect against the cold winter winds which might otherwise penetrate these gaps. However, this can also become a potential indoor air quality problem. The installation of vents is key.

As a result of the thermal mass of the structure, the thermal lag of the earth, the protection against unwanted air infiltration and the combined use of passive solar techniques, the need for extra heating and cooling is minimal. Therefore, there is a drastic reduction of energy consumption required for the home compared to homes of standard construction.

Earth shelters also provide privacy from neighbours, as well as soundproofing. The ground provides acoustic protection against outside noise. This is a major benefit in urban areas or along highways with constant traffic. In urban areas, one of the other major benefits of underground sheltering is the efficient use of land. Many houses can sit below grade without spoiling the habitat above ground. Each house can have both a house and a lawn/garden within the same site.

LESSONS FROM THE YOKOHAMA STRATEGY FOR THE FUTURE

The 1994 Yokohama Strategy acknowledges that disaster risk reduction should encompass other disaster situations such as environmental and technological hazards. Those hazards include environmental emergencies resulting from conflicts, which are unfortunately on the increase, particularly in developing countries. Military conflicts always imply human suffering and may have severe environmental consequences. Since 1999, UNEP has undertaken a number of assessments to determine the environmental risks from conflicts. Following the Balkans crisis, in 1999, UNEP assessed and analysed the state of the environment in the Balkans region, identified regional environmental trends and provided early warning information on environmental threats caused by the crisis. UNEP has since been working in the region to determine the environmental risks from the Kosovo conflict and a number of assessment reports (Albania, Bosnia and Herzegovina, Serbia and Montenegro, the former Yugoslav Republic of Macedonia) have been produced covering various impacts on the environmental resources and institutional capacities for environmental management and protection. Following assessment activities, a series of workshops and seminars are provided to help build capacities for environmental management and protection and to enhance the integration of environmental considerations into the reconstruction and recovery process.

To Conclude: Need of Positive Interest among University, Research Institutions

UGC can start disaster management courses and research in allied departments of the universities on a priority basis. Such experiences can be pooled and shared. J.C. Pant in his keynote address at the opening session of the Workshop on Disaster Prevention, held at NIRD, Hyderabad on 19th-20th December, 2000 remarked: "Coming back to the main theme of disaster management, I would like to highlight the role of the elite and intellectual segments of our society. Every disaster is a unique event and every kind of data emerging out of it needs to be meticulously recorded for posterity. The scientific community, the technologists, the social scientists and other branches of knowledge need to be mobilised at short notice to record data and carry out necessary studies whenever a disaster strikes. This gives rise to a need for laying out a structure for initiating the learning exercise, at short notice, which can be used to collect data whenever a disaster strikes, in order to generate knowledge which may prevent future disasters as well as prepare people to face them in a better manner whenever they recur. This learning process has to be traced backward to know about the causes of various kinds of disasters, which is only possible through a process of networking of such knowledge as is available throughout the world today." We have decided to broadly network knowledge in three groups:

(i) Knowledge relating to natural disasters;

(ii) Knowledge relating to non-natural disasters; and .

(iii) Knowledge relating to biological disasters.

This will also involve identifying centres of excellence in different fields of knowledge and technology which would need to collaborate to develop the required networks of knowledge. A small task force of eminent persons in the field of science and technology is working in this area and we hope to give concrete shape to this concept in the near future. This would help the country to prevent and reduce the occurrence of disasters and mitigate their impact whenever they strike. This exercise of harnessing science and technology in aid of disaster management promises to be an exciting venture which would hopefully usher in a comparatively safer world in the near future.

The whole process of preparation of disaster management plans initiated by the High Powered Committee is laying special emphasis on taking timely preventive measures by incorporating them into the very development planning system. This, in a manner of speaking, is promising to generate a nation-building exercise, which will involve the poorest of the poor in their own development. This will also need the willing cooperation of the elite of our society, working in close collaboration people's organisations at all levels to plan for safe and better future.

REVIEW QUESTIONS

Short Answer Type Questions

1. Write a note on disaster planning.
2. By being imaginative, what are all the advantages we can gain over disasters.
3. Write note on blast shelters.
4. Write note on the cellars.
5. What do you understand by the term 'the hochbunker'.
6. Differentiate trench bunker over industrial bunker.
7. What is meant by blast pen and bring out its significance?
8. What is called as 'pill box'?
9. State any two advantages of earth sheltering.
10. Write a note on "the yokohoma strategy'.

Essay Type Questions

1. Critically analyse the importance of disaster planning in recognition of disaster rik reduction.
2. Compare and contrast the existence and purpose of various national organizations all around the world towards disaster planning for the future.
3. Critically analyze the various ongoing strategies for the future, adopted by the peoples all over the globe.

ANNEXURE

THE DISASTER MANAGEMENT ACT, 2005

An Act to provide for the effective management of disasters and for matters connected therewith or incidental thereto.

BE it enacted by Parliament in the Fifty-sixth Year of the Republic of India as follows:-

@

CHAPTER I

%

PRELIMINARY

!

CHAPTER I

PRELIMINARY

@

1.

%

Short title, extent and commencement.

!

1. Short title, extent and commencement.

(1) This Act may be called the Disaster Management Act, 2005.

(2) It extends to the whole of India.

(3) It shall come into force on such date as the Central Government may, by notification in the Official Gazette appoint; and different dates may be appointed for different provisions of this Act and for different States, and any reference to commencement in any provision of this Act in relation to any State shall be construed as a reference to the commencement of that provision in that State.

@

2.

%

Definitions.

!

2. Definitions.-In this Act, unless the context otherwise requires,-

(a) "affected area" means an area or part of the country affected by a disaster;

(b) "capacity-building" includes-

(i) identification of existing resources and resources to be acquired or created;

(ii) acquiring or creating resources identified under sub-clause (i);

(iii) organisation and training of personnel and coordination of such training for effective management of disasters;

(c) "Central Government" means the Ministry or Department of the Government of India having administrative control of disaster management;

(d) "disaster" means a catastrophe, mishap, calamity or grave occurrence in any area, arising from natural or man made causes, or by accident or negligence which results in substantial loss of life or human suffering or damage to, and destruction of, property, or damage to, or degradation of, environment, and is of such a nature or magnitude as to be beyond the coping capacity of the community of the affected area;

(e) "disaster management" means a continuous and integrated process of planning, organising, coordinating and implementing measures which are necessary or expedient for-

(i) prevention of danger or threat of any disaster;

(ii) mitigation or reduction of risk of any disaster or its severity or consequences;

(iii) capacity-building;

(iv) preparedness to deal with any disaster;

(v) prompt response to any threatening disaster situation or disaster;

(vi) assessing the severity or magnitude of effects of any disaster;

(vii) evacuation, rescue and relief;

(viii) rehabilitation and reconstruction;

(f) "District Authority" means the District Disaster Management Authority constituted under sub-section (1) of section 25;

(g) "District Plan" means the plan for disaster management for the district prepared under section 31;

(h) "local authority" includes panchayati raj institutions, municipalities, a district board, cantonment board, town planning authority or Zila Parishad or any other body or authority, by whatever name called, for the time being invested by law, for rendering essential services or, with the control and management of civic services, within a specified local area;

(i) "mitigation" means measures aimed at reducing the risk, impact or effects of a disaster or threatening disaster situation;

(j) "National Authority" means the National Disaster Management Authority established under sub-section (1) of section 3;

(k) "National Executive Committee" means the Executive Committee of the National Authority constituted under sub-section (1) of section 8;

(l) "National Plan" means the plan for disaster management for the whole of the country prepared under section 11;

(m) "preparedness" means the state of readiness to deal with a threatening disaster situation or disaster and the effects thereof;

(n) "prescribed" means prescribed by rules made under this Act;

(o) "reconstruction" means construction or restoration of any property after a disaster;

(p) "resources" includes manpower, services, materials and provisions;

(q) "State Authority" means the State Disaster Management Authority established under sub-section (1) of section 14 and includes the Disaster Management Authority for the Union territory constituted under that section;

(r) "State Executive Committee" means the Executive Committee of a State Authority constituted under sub-section (1) of section 20;

(s) "State Government" means the Department of Government of the State having administrative control of disaster management and includes Administrator of the Union territory appointed by the President under article 239 of the Constitution;

(t) "State Plan" means the plan for disaster management for the whole of the State prepared under section 23.

@

CHAPTER II

%

THE NATIONAL DISASTER MANAGEMENT AUTHORITY

!

CHAPTER II

THE NATIONAL DISASTER MANAGEMENT AUTHORITY

@

3.

%

Establishment of National Disaster Management Authority.

!

3. Establishment of National Disaster Management Authority.

(1) With effect from such date as the Central Government may, by notification in the Official Gazette appoint in this behalf, there shall be established for the purposes of this Act, an authority to be known as the National Disaster Management Authority.

(2) The National Authority shall consist of the Chairperson and such number of other members, not exceeding nine, as may be prescribed by the Central Government and, unless the rules otherwise provide, the National Authority shall consist of the following:-

   (a) the Prime Minister of India, who shall be the Chairperson of the National Authority, ex officio;

   (b) other members, not exceeding nine, to be nominated by the Chairperson of the National Authority.

(3) The Chairperson of the National Authority may designate one of the members nominated under clause (b) of sub-section (2) to be the Vice- Chairperson of the National Authority.

(4) The term of office and conditions of service of members of the National Authority shall be such as may be prescribed.

@

4.

%

Meetings of National Authority.

!

4. Meetings of National Authority.-

(1) The National Authority shall meet as and when necessary and at such time and place as the Chairperson of the National Authority may think fit.

(2) The Chairperson of the National Authority shall preside over the meetings of the National Authority.

(3) If for any reason the Chairperson of the National Authority is unable to attend any meeting of the National Authority, the Vice-Chairperson of the National Authority shall preside over the meeting.

@

5.

%

Appointment of officers and other employees of the National Authority.

!

5. Appointment of officers and other employees of the National Authority: The Central Government shall provide the National Authority with such officers, consultants and employees, as it considers necessary for carrying out the functions of the National Authority.

@

6.

%

Powers and functions of National Authority.

!

6. Powers and functions of National Authority.-

(1) Subject to the provisions of this Act, the National Authority shall have the responsibility for laying down the policies, plans and guidelines for disaster management for ensuring timely and effective response to disaster.

(2) Without prejudice to generality of the provisions contained in subsection (1), the National Authority may -

(a) lay down policies on disaster management;

(b) approve the National Plan;

(c) approve plans prepared by the Ministries or Departments of the Government of India in accordance with the National Plan;

(d) lay down guidelines to be followed by the State Authorities in drawing up the State Plan;

(e) lay down guidelines to be followed by the different Ministries or Departments of the Government of India for the purpose of integrating the measures for prevention of disaster or the mitigation of its effects in their development plans and projects;

(f) coordinate the enforcement and implementation of the policy and plan for disaster management;

(g) recommend provision of funds for the purpose of mitigation;

(h) provide such support to other countries affected by major disasters as may be determined by the Central Government;

(i) take such other measures for the prevention of disaster, or the mitigation, or preparedness and capacity building for dealing with the threatening disaster situation or disaster as it may consider necessary;

(j) lay down broad policies and guidelines for the functioning of the National Institute of Disaster Management.

(3) The Chairperson of the National Authority shall, in the case of emergency, have power to exercise all or any of the powers of the National Authority but exercise of such powers shall be subject to ex post facto ratification by the National Authority.

@

7.

%

Constitution of advisory committee by National Authority.

!

7. Constitution of advisory committee by National Authority.-

(1) The National Authority may constitute an advisory committee consisting of experts in the field of disaster management and having practical experience of disaster management at the national, State or district level to make recommendations on different aspects of disaster management.

(2) The members of the advisory committee shall be paid such allowances as may be prescribed by the Central Government in consultation with the National Authority.

@

8.

%

Constitution of National Executive Committee.

!

8. Constitution of National Executive Committee.-

(1) The Central Government shall, immediately after issue of notification under subsection (1) of section 3, constitute a National Executive Committee to assist the National Authority in the performance of its functions under this Act.

(2) The National Executive Committee shall consist of the following members, namely:

(a) the Secretary to the Government of India in charge of the Ministry or Department of the Central Government having administrative control of the disaster management, who shall be Chairperson, ex officio;

(b) the Secretaries to the Government of India in the Ministries or Departments having administrative control of the agriculture, atomic energy, defence, drinking water supply, environment and forests, finance (expenditure), health, power, rural development, science and technology, space, telecommunication, urban development, water resources and the Chief of the Integrated Defence Staff of the Chiefs of Staff Committee, ex officio.

(3) The Chairperson of the National Executive Committee may invite any other officer of the Central Government or a State Government for taking part in any meeting of the National Executive Committee and shall exercise such powers and perform such functions as may be prescribed by the Central Government in consultation with the National Authority.

(4) The procedure to be followed by the National Executive Committee in exercise of its powers and discharge of its functions shall be such as may be prescribed by the Central Government.

@

9.

%

Constitution of sub-committees.

!

9. Constitution of sub-committees.

(1) The National Executive Committee may, as and when it considers necessary, constitute one or more subcommittees, for the efficient discharge of its functions.

(2) The National Executive Committee shall, from amongst its members, appoint the Chairperson of the sub-committee referred to in sub-section (1).

(3) Any person associated as an expert with any sub-committee may be paid such allowances as may be prescribed by the Central Government.

@

10.

%

Powers and functions of National Executive Committee.

!

10. Powers and functions of National Executive Committee.

(1) The National Executive Committee shall assist the National Authority in the discharge of its functions and have the responsibility for implementing the policies and plans of the National Authority and ensure the compliance of directions issued by the Central Government for the purpose of disaster management in the country.

(2) Without prejudice to the generality of the provisions contained in sub-section (1), the National Executive Committee may -

(a) act as the coordinating and monitoring body for disaster management;

(b) prepare the National Plan to be approved by the National Authority;

(c) coordinate and monitor the implementation of the National Policy;

(d) lay down guidelines for preparing disaster management plans by different Ministries or Departments of the Government of India and the State Authorities;

(e) provide necessary technical assistance to the State Governments and the State Authorities for preparing their disaster management plans in accordance with the guidelines laid down by the National Authority;

(f) monitor the implementation of the National Plan and the plans prepared by the Ministries or Departments of the Government of India;

(g) monitor the implementation of the guidelines laid down by the National Authority for integrating of measures for prevention of disasters and mitigation by the Ministries or Departments in their development plans and projects;

(h) monitor, coordinate and give directions regarding the mitigation and preparedness measures to be taken by different Ministries or Departments and agencies of the Government;

(i) evaluate the preparedness at all governmental levels for the purpose of responding to any threatening disaster situation or disaster and give directions, where necessary, for enhancing such preparedness;

(j) plan and coordinate specialised training programme for disaster management for different levels of officers, employees and voluntary rescue workers;

(k) coordinate response in the event of any threatening disaster situation or disaster;

(l) lay down guidelines for, or give directions to, the concerned Ministries or Departments of the Government of India, the State Governments and the State Authorities regarding measures to be taken by them in response to any threatening disaster situation or disaster;

(m) require any department or agency of the Government to make available to the National Authority or State Authorities such men or material resources as are available with it for the purposes of emergency response, rescue and relief;

(n) advise, assist and coordinate the activities of the Ministries or Departments of the Government of India, State Authorities, statutory bodies, other governmental or non-governmental organisations and others engaged in disaster management;

(o) provide necessary technical assistance or give advice to the State Authorities and District Authorities for carrying out their functions under this Act;

(p) promote general education and awareness in relation to disaster management; and

(q) perform such other functions as the National Authority may require it to perform.

@

11.

%

National Plan.

!

11. National Plan.

(1) There shall be drawn up a plan for disaster management for the whole of the country to be called the National Plan.

(2) The National Plan shall be prepared by the National Executive Committee having regard to the National Policy and in consultation with the State Governments and expert bodies or organisations in the field of disaster management to be approved by the National Authority.

(3) The National Plan shall include-

(a) measures to be taken for the prevention of disasters, or the mitigation of their effects;

(b) measures to be taken for the integration of mitigation measures in the development plans;

(c) measures to be taken for preparedness and capacity building to effectively respond to any threatening disaster situations or disaster;

(d) roles and responsibilities of different Ministries or Departments of the Government of India in respect of measures specified in clauses (a), (b) and (c).

(4) The National Plan shall be reviewed and updated annually.

(5) Appropriate provisions shall be made by the Central Government for financing the measures to be carried out under the National Plan.

(6) Copies of the National Plan referred to in sub-sections (2) and (4) shall be made available to the Ministries or Departments of the Government of India and such Ministries or Departments shall draw up their own plans in accordance with the National Plan.

@

12.

%

Guidelines for minimum standards of relief.

!

12. Guidelines for minimum standards of relief.-The National Authority shall recommend guidelines for the minimum standards of relief to be provided to persons affected by disaster, which shall include,-

(i) the minimum requirements to be provided in the relief camps in relation to shelter, food, drinking water, medical cover and sanitation;

(ii) the special provisions to be made for widows and orphans;

(iii) ex gratia assistance on account of loss of life as also assistance on account of damage to houses and for restoration of means of livelihood;

(iv) such other relief as may be necessary.

@

13.

%

Relief in loan repayment, etc.

!

13. Relief in loan repayment, etc.-The National Authority may, in cases of disasters of severe magnitude, recommend relief in repayment of loans or for grant of fresh loans to the persons affected by disaster on such concessional terms as may be appropriate.

@

CHAPTER III

%

STATE DISASTER MANAGEMENT AUTHORITIES

!

CHAPTER III

STATE DISASTER MANAGEMENT AUTHORITIES

@

14.

%

Establishment of State Disaster Management Authority.

!

14. Establishment of State Disaster Management Authority.-

(1) Every State Government shall, as soon as may be after the issue of the notification under sub-section (1) of section 3, by notification in the Official Gazette, establish a State Disaster Management Authority for the State with such name as may be specified in the notification of the State Government.

(2) A State Authority shall consist of the Chairperson and such number of other members, not exceeding nine, as may be prescribed by the State Government and, unless the rules otherwise provide, the State Authority shall consist of the following members, namely:-

(a) the Chief Minister of the State, who shall be Chairperson, ex officio;

(b) other members, not exceeding eight, to be nominated by the Chairperson of the State Authority;

(c) the Chairperson of the State Executive Committee, ex officio.

(3) The Chairperson of the State Authority may designate one of the members nominated under clause (b) of sub-section (2) to be the Vice- Chairperson of the State Authority.

(4) The Chairperson of the State Executive Committee shall be the Chief Executive Officer of the State Authority, ex officio:

Provided that in the case of a Union territory having Legislative Assembly, except the Union territory of Delhi, the Chief Minister shall be the Chairperson of the Authority established under this section and in case of other Union territories, the Lieutenant Governor or the Administrator shall be the Chairperson of that Authority:

Provided further that the Lieutenant Governor of the Union territory of Delhi shall be the Chairperson and the Chief Minister thereof shall be the Vice-Chairperson of the State Authority.

(5) The term of office and conditions of service of members of the State Authority shall be such as may be prescribed.

@

15.

%

Meetings of the State Authority.

!

15. Meetings of the State Authority.-

(1) The State Authority shall meet as and when necessary and at such time and place as the Chairperson of the State Authority may think fit.

(2) The Chairperson of the State Authority shall preside over the meetings of the State Authority.

(3) If for any reason, the Chairperson of the State Authority is unable to attend the meeting of the State Authority, the Vice-Chairperson of the State Authority shall preside at the meeting.

@

16.

%

Appointment of officers and other employees of State Authority.

!

16. Appointment of officers and other employees of State Authority.-The State Government shall provide the State Authority with such officers, consultants and employees, as it considers necessary, for carrying out the functions of the State Authority.

@

17.

%

Constitution of advisory committee by the State Authority.

!

17. Constitution of advisory committee by the State Authority.-

(1) A State Authority may, as and when it considers necessary, constitute an advisory committee, consisting of experts in the field of disaster management and having practical experience of disaster management to make recommendations on different aspects of disaster management.

(2) The members of the advisory committee shall be paid such allowances as may be prescribed by the State Government.

@

18.

%

Powers and functions of State Authority.

!

18. Powers and functions of State Authority.

(1) Subject to the provisions of this Act, a State Authority shall have the responsibility for laying down policies and plans for disaster management in the State.

(2) Without prejudice to the generality of provisions contained in subsection (1), the State Authority may-

(a) lay down the State disaster management policy;

(b) approve the State Plan in accordance with the guidelines laid down by the National Authority;

(c) approve the disaster management plans prepared by the departments of the Government of the State;

(d) lay down guidelines to be followed by the departments of the Government of the State for the purposes of integration of measures for prevention of disasters and mitigation in their development plans and projects and provide necessary technical assistance therefor;

(e) coordinate the implementation of the State Plan;

(f) recommend provision of funds for mitigation and preparedness measures;

(g) review the development plans of the different departments of the State and ensure that prevention and mitigation measures are integrated therein;

(h) review the measures being taken for mitigation, capacity building and preparedness by the departments of the Government of the State and issue such guidelines as may be necessary.

(3) The Chairperson of the State Authority shall, in the case of emergency, have power to exercise all or any of the powers of the State Authority but the exercise of such powers shall be subject to ex post facto ratification of the State Authority.

@

19.

%

Guidelines for minimum standard of relief by State Authority.

!

19. Guidelines for minimum standard of relief by State Authority.-The State Authority shall lay down detailed guidelines for providing standards of relief to persons affected by disaster in the State: Provided that such standards shall in no case be less than the minimum standards in the guidelines laid down by the National Authority in this regard.

@

20.

%

Constitution of State Executive Committee.

!

20. Constitution of State Executive Committee.-

(1) The State Government shall, immediately after issue of notification under sub-section (1) of section 14, constitute a State Executive Committee to assist the State Authority in the performance of its functions and to coordinate action in accordance with the guidelines laid down by the State Authority and ensure the compliance of directions issued by the State Government under this Act.

(2) The State Executive Committee shall consist of the following members, namely:

(a) the Chief Secretary to the State Government, who shall be Chairperson, ex officio;

(b) four Secretaries to the Government of the State of such departments as the State Government may think fit, ex officio.

(3) The Chairperson of the State Executive Committee shall exercise such powers and perform such functions as may be prescribed by the State Government and such other powers and functions as may be delegated to him by the State Authority.

(4) The procedure to be followed by the State Executive Committee in exercise of its powers and discharge of its functions shall be such as may be prescribed by the State Government.

@

21.

%

Constitution of sub-committees by State Executive Committee.

!

21. Constitution of sub-committees by State Executive Committee.-

(1) The State Executive Committee may, as and when it considers necessary, constitute one or more sub-committees, for efficient discharge of its functions.

(2) The State Executive Committee shall, from amongst its members, appoint the Chairperson of the sub-committee referred to in sub-section (1).

(3) Any person associated as an expert with any sub-committee may be paid such allowances as may be prescribed by the State Government.

@

22.

%

Functions of the State Executive Committee.

!

22. Functions of the State Executive Committee.

(1) The State Executive Committee shall have the responsibility for implementing the National Plan and State Plan and act as the coordinating and monitoring body for management of disaster in the State.

(2) Without prejudice to the generality of the provisions of subsection (1), the State Executive Committee may-

(a) coordinate and monitor the implementation of the National Policy, the National Plan and the State Plan;

(b) examine the vulnerability of different parts of the State to different forms of disasters and specify measures to be taken for their prevention or mitigation;

(c) lay down guidelines for preparation of disaster management plans by the departments of the Government of the State and the District Authorities;

(d) monitor the implementation of disaster management plans prepared by the departments of the Government of the State and District Authorities;

(e) monitor the implementation of the guidelines laid down by the State Authority for integrating of measures for prevention of disasters and mitigation by the departments in their development plans and projects;

(f) evaluate preparedness at all governmental or non-governmental levels to respond to any threatening disaster situation or disaster and give directions, where necessary, for enhancing such preparedness;

(g) coordinate response in the event of any threatening disaster situation or disaster;

(h) give directions to any Department of the Government of the State or any other authority or body in the State regarding actions to be taken in response to any threatening disaster situation or disaster;

(i) promote general education, awareness and community training in regard to the forms of disasters to which different parts of the State are vulnerable and the measures that may be taken by such community to prevent the disaster, mitigate and respond to such disaster;

(j) advise, assist and coordinate the activities of the Departments of the Government of the State, District Authorities, statutory bodies and other governmental and non-governmental organisations engaged in disaster management;

(k) provide necessary technical assistance or give advice to District Authorities and local authorities for carrying out their functions effectively;

(l) advise the State Government regarding all financial matters in relation to disaster management;

(m) examine the construction, in any local area in the State and, if it is of the opinion that the standards laid for such construction for the prevention of disaster is not being or has not been followed, may direct the District Authority or the local authority, as the case may be, to take such action as may be necessary to secure compliance of such standards;

(n) provide information to the National Authority relating to different aspects of disaster management;

(o) lay down, review and update State level response plans and guidelines and ensure that the district level plans are prepared, reviewed and updated;

(p) ensure that communication systems are in order and the disaster management drills are carried out periodically;

(q) perform such other functions as may be assigned to it by the State Authority or as it may consider necessary.

@

23.

%

State Plan.

!

23. State Plan.

(1) There shall be a plan for disaster management for every State to be called the State Disaster Management Plan.

(2) The State Plan shall be prepared by the State Executive Committee having regard to the guidelines laid down by the National Authority and after such consultation with local authorities, district authorities and the people's representatives as the State Executive Committee may deem fit.

(3) The State Plan prepared by the State Executive Committee under subsection (2) shall be approved by the State Authority.

(4) The State Plan shall include,-

(a) the vulnerability of different parts of the State to different forms of disasters;

(b) the measures to be adopted for prevention and mitigation of disasters;

(c) the manner in which the mitigation measures shall be integrated with the development plans and projects;

(d) the capacity-building and preparedness measures to be taken;

(e) the roles and responsibilities of each Department of the Government of the State in relation to the measures specified in clauses (b), (c) and (d) above;

(f) the roles and responsibilities of different Departments of the Government of the State in responding to any threatening disaster situation or disaster.

(5) The State Plan shall be reviewed and updated annually.

(6) Appropriate provisions shall be made by the State Government for financing for the measures to be carried out under the State Plan.

(7) Copies of the State Plan referred to in sub-sections (2) and (5) shall be made available to the Departments of the Government of the State and such Departments shall draw up their own plans in accordance with the State Plan.

@

24.

%

Powers and functions of State Executive Committee in the event of threatening disaster situation.

!

24. Powers and functions of State Executive Committee in the event of threatening disaster situation.-For the purpose of, assisting and protecting the community affected by disaster or providing relief to such community or, preventing or combating disruption or dealing with the effects of any threatening disaster situation, the State Executive Committee may-

(a) control and restrict, vehicular traffic to, from or within, the vulnerable or affected area;

(b) control and restrict the entry of any person into, his movement within and departure from, a vulnerable or affected area;

(c) remove debris, conduct search and carry out rescue operations;

(d) provide shelter, food, drinking water, essential provisions, healthcare and services in accordance with the standards laid down by the National Authority and State Authority;

(e) give direction to the concerned Department of the Government of the State, any District Authority or other authority, within the local limits of the State to take such measure or steps for rescue, evacuation or providing immediate relief saving lives or property, as may be necessary in its opinion;

(f) require any department of the Government of the State or any other body or authority or person in charge of any relevant resources to make available the resources for the purposes of emergency response, rescue and relief;

(g) require experts and consultants in the field of disasters to provide advice and assistance for rescue and relief;

(h) procure exclusive or preferential use of amenities from any authority or person as and when required;

(i) construct temporary bridges or other necessary structures and demolish unsafe structures which may be hazardous to public;

(j) ensure that non-governmental organisations carry out their activities in an equitable and non-discriminatory manner;

(k) disseminate information to public to deal with any threatening disaster situation or disaster;

(l) take such steps as the Central Government or the State Government may direct in this regard or take such other steps as are required or warranted by the form of any threatening disaster situation or disaster.

@

CHAPTER IV

%

DISTRICT DISASTER MANAGEMENT AUTHORITY

!

CHAPTER IV

DISTRICT DISASTER MANAGEMENT AUTHORITY

@

25.

%

Constitution of District Disaster Management Authority.

!

25. Constitution of District Disaster Management Authority.

(1) Every State Government shall, as soon as may be after issue of notification under sub-section (1) of section 14, by notification in the Official Gazette, establish a District Disaster Management Authority for every district in the State with such name as may be specified in that notification.

(2) The District Authority shall consist of the Chairperson and such number of other members, not exceeding seven, as may be prescribed by the State Government, and unless the rules otherwise provide, it shall consist of the following, namely:

(a) the Collector or District Magistrate or Deputy Commissioner, as the case may be, of the district who shall be Chairperson, ex officio;

(b) the elected representative of the local authority who shall be the co-Chairperson, ex officio:

Provided that in the Tribal Areas, as referred to in the Sixth Schedule to the Constitution, the Chief Executive Member of the district council of autonomous district, shall be the co-Chairperson, ex officio;

(c) the Chief Executive Officer of the District Authority, ex officio;

(d) the Superintendent of Police, ex officio;

(e) the Chief Medical Officer of the district, ex officio;

(f) not exceeding two other district level officers, to be appointed by the State Government.

(3) In any district where zila parishad exists, the Chairperson thereof shall be the co-Chairperson of the District Authority.

(4) The State Government shall appoint an officer not below the rank of Additional Collector or Additional District Magistrate or Additional Deputy Commissioner, as the case may be, of the district to be the Chief Executive Officer of the District Authority to exercise such powers and perform such functions as may be prescribed by the State Government and such other powers and functions as may be delegated to him by the District Authority.

@

26.

%

Powers of Chairperson of District Authority.

!

26. Powers of Chairperson of District Authority.

(1) The Chairperson of the District Authority shall, in addition to presiding over the meetings of the District Authority, exercise and discharge such powers and functions of the District Authority as the District Authority may delegate to him.

(2) The Chairperson of the District Authority shall, in the case of an emergency, have power to exercise all or any of the powers of the District Authority but the exercise of such powers shall be subject to ex post facto ratification of the District Authority.

(3) The District Authority or the Chairperson of the District Authority may, by general or special order, in writing, delegate such of its or his powers and functions, under sub-section (1) or (2), as the case may be, to the Chief Executive Officer of the District Authority, subject to such conditions and limitations, if any, as it or he deems fit.

@

27.

%

Meetings.

!

27. Meetings.-The District Authority shall meet as and when necessary and at such time and place as the Chairperson may think fit.

@

28.

%

Constitution of advisory committees and other committees.

!

28. Constitution of advisory committees and other committees.

(1) The District Authority may, as and when it considers necessary, constitute one or more advisory committees and other committees for the efficient discharge of its functions.

(2) The District Authority shall, from amongst its members, appoint the Chairperson of the Committee referred to in sub-section (1).

(3) Any person associated as an expert with any committee or subcommittee constituted under sub-section (1) may be paid such allowances as may be prescribed by the State Government.

@

29.

%

Appointment of officers and other employees of District Authority.

!

29. Appointment of officers and other employees of District Authority.- The State Government shall provide the District Authority with such officers, consultants and other employees as it considers necessary for carrying out the functions of District Authority.

@

30.

%

Powers and functions of District Authority.

!

30. Powers and functions of District Authority.

(1) The District Authority shall act as the district planning, coordinating and implementing body for disaster management and take all measures for the purposes of disaster management in the district in accordance with the guidelines laid down by the National Authority and the State Authority.

(2) Without prejudice to the generality of the provisions of subsection (1), the District Authority may-

(i) prepare a disaster management plan including district response plan for the district;

(ii) coordinate and monitor the implementation of the National Policy, State Policy, National Plan, State Plan and District Plan;

(iii) ensure that the areas in the district vulnerable to disasters are identified and measures for the prevention of disasters and the mitigation of its effects are undertaken by the departments of the Government at the district level as well as by the local authorities;

(iv) ensure that the guidelines for prevention of disasters, mitigation of its effects, preparedness and response measures as laid down by the National Authority and the State Authority are followed by all departments of the Government at the district level and the local authorities in the district;

(v) give directions to different authorities at the district level and local authorities to take such other measures for the prevention or mitigation of disasters as may be necessary;

(vi) lay down guidelines for prevention of disaster management plans by the department of the Government at the districts level and local authorities in the district;

(vii) monitor the implementation of disaster management plans prepared by the Departments of the Government at the district level;

(viii) lay down guidelines to be followed by the Departments of the Government at the district level for purposes of integration of measures for prevention of disasters and mitigation in their development plans and projects and provide necessary technical assistance therefor;

(ix) monitor the implementation of measures referred to in clause (viii);

(x) review the state of capabilities for responding to any disaster or threatening disaster situation in the district and give directions to the relevant departments or authorities at the district level for their upgradation as may be necessary;

(xi) review the preparedness measures and give directions to the concerned departments at the district level or other concerned authorities where necessary for bringing the preparedness measures to the levels required for responding effectively to any disaster or threatening disaster situation;

(xii) organise and coordinate specialised training programmes for different levels of officers, employees and voluntary rescue workers in the district;

(xiii) facilitate community training and awareness programmes for prevention of disaster or mitigation with the support of localauthorities, governmental and non-governmental organisations;

(xiv) set up, maintain, review and upgrade the mechanism for early warnings and dissemination of proper information to public;

(xv) prepare, review and update district level response plan and guidelines;

(xvi) coordinate response to any threatening disaster situation or disaster;

(xvii) ensure that the Departments of the Government at the district level and the local authorities prepare their response plans in accordance with the district response plan;

(xviii) lay down guidelines for, or give direction to, the concerned Department of the Government at the district level or any other authorities within the local limits of the district to take measures to respond effectively to any threatening disaster situation or disaster;

(xix) advise, assist and coordinate the activities of the Departments of the Government at the district level, statutory bodies and other governmental and non-governmental organisations in the district engaged in the disaster management;

(xx) coordinate with, and give guidelines to, local authorities in the district to ensure that measures for the prevention or mitigation of threatening disaster situation or disaster in the district are carried out promptly and effectively;

(xxi) provide necessary technical assistance or give advise to the local authorities in the district for carrying out their functions;

(xxii) review development plans prepared by the Departments of the Government at the district level, statutory authorities or local authorities with a view to make necessary provisions therein for prevention of disaster or mitigation;

(xxiii) examine the construction in any area in the district and, if it is of the opinion that the standards for the prevention of disaster or mitigation laid down for such construction is not being or has not been followed, may direct the concerned authority to take such action as may be necessary to secure compliance of such standards;

(xxiv) identify buildings and places which could, in the event of any threatening disaster situation or disaster, be used as relief centersor camps and make arrangements for water supply and sanitation in such buildings or places;

(xxv) establish stockpiles of relief and rescue materials or ensure preparedness to make such materials available at a short notice;

(xxvi) provide information to the State Authority relating to different aspects of disaster management;

(xxvii) encourage the involvement of non-governmental organisations and voluntary social-welfare institutions working at the grassroots level in the district for disaster management;

(xxviii) ensure communication systems are in order, and disaster management drills are carried out periodically;

(xxix) perform such other functions as the State Government or State Authority may assign to it or as it deems necessary for disaster management in the District.

@

31.

%

District Plan.

!

31. District Plan.

(1) There shall be a plan for disaster management for every district of the State.

(2) The District Plan shall be prepared by the District Authority, after consultation with the local authorities and having regard to the National Plan and the State Plan, to be approved by the State Authority.

(3) The District Plan shall include-

(a) the areas in the district vulnerable to different forms of disasters;

(b) the measures to be taken, for prevention and mitigation of disaster, by the Departments of the Government at the district level and local authorities in the district;

(c) the capacity-building and preparedness measures required to be taken by the Departments of the Government at the district level and the local authorities in the district to respond to any threatening disaster situation or disaster;

(d) the response plans and procedures, in the event of a disaster, providing for- (i) allocation of responsibilities to the Departments of the Government at the district level and the local authorities in the district; (ii) prompt response to disaster and relief thereof; (iii) procurement of essential resources; (iv) establishment of communication links; and (v) the dissemination of information to the public; (e) such other matters as may be required by the State Authority.

(4) The District Plan shall be reviewed and updated annually.

(5) The copies of the District Plan referred to in sub-sections (2) and (4) shall be made available to the Departments of the Government in the district.

(6) The District Authority shall send a copy of the District Plan to the State Authority which shall forward it to the State Government.

(7) The District Authority shall, review from time to time, the implementation of the Plan and issue such instructions to different departments of the Government in the district as it may deem necessary for the implementation thereof.

@

32.

%

Plans by different authorities at district level and their

implementation.

!

32. Plans by different authorities at district level and their implementation.-Every office of the Government of India and of the State Government at the district level and the local authorities shall, subject to the supervision of the District Authority, -

(a) prepare a disaster management plan setting out the following, namely:

(i) provisions for prevention and mitigation measures as provided for in the District Plan and as is assigned to the department or agency concerned;

(ii) provisions for taking measures relating to capacity-building and preparedness as laid down in the District Plan;

(iii) the response plans and procedures, in the event of, any threatening disaster situation or disaster;

(b) coordinate the preparation and the implementation of its plan with those of the other organisations at the district level including local authority, communities and other stakeholders;

(c) regularly review and update the plan; and

(d) submit a copy of its disaster management plan, and of any amendment thereto, to the District Authority.

@

33.

%

Requisition by the District Authority.

!

33. Requisition by the District Authority.-The District Authority may by order require any officer or any Department at the district level or any local authority to take such measures for the prevention or mitigation of disaster, or to effectively respond to it, as may be necessary, and such officer or department shall be bound to carry out such order.

@

34.

%

Powers and functions of District Authority in the event of any

threatening disaster situation or disaster.

!

34. Powers and functions of District Authority in the event of any threatening disaster situation or disaster.-For the purpose of assisting, protecting or providing relief to the community, in response to any threatening disaster situation or disaster, the District Authority may-

(a) give directions for the release and use of resources available with any Department of the Government and the local authority in the district;

(b) control and restrict vehicular traffic to, from and within, the vulnerable or affected area;

(c) control and restrict the entry of any person into, his movement within and departure from, a vulnerable or affected area;

(d) remove debris, conduct search and carry out rescue operations;

(e) provide shelter, food, drinking water and essential provisions, healthcare and services;

(f) establish emergency communication systems in the affected area;

(g) make arrangements for the disposal of the unclaimed dead bodies;

(h) recommend to any Department of the Government of the State or any authority or body under that Government at the district level to take such measures as are necessary in its opinion;

(i) require experts and consultants in the relevant fields to advise and assist as it may deem necessary;

(j) procure exclusive or preferential use of amenities from any authority or person;

(k) construct temporary bridges or other necessary structures and demolish structures which may be hazardous to public or aggravate the effects of the disaster;

(l) ensure that the non-governmental organisations carry out their activities in an equitable and non-discriminatory manner;

(m) take such other steps as may be required or warranted to be taken in such a situation.

@

CHAPTER V

%

MEASURES BY THE GOVERNMENT FOR DISASTER MANAGEMENT

!

CHAPTER V

MEASURES BY THE GOVERNMENT FOR DISASTER MANAGEMENT

@

35.

%

Central Government to take measures.

!

35. Central Government to take measures.

(1) Subject to the provisions of this Act, the Central Government shall take all such measures as it deems necessary or expedient for the purpose of disaster management.

(2) In particular and without prejudice to the generality of the provisions of sub-section (1), the measures which the Central Government may take under that sub-section include measures with respect to all or any of the following matters, namely:

(a) coordination of actions of the Ministries or Departments of the Government of India, State Governments, National Authority, State Authorities, governmental and non-governmental organisations in relation to disaster management;

(b) ensure the integration of measures for prevention of disasters and mitigation by Ministries or Departments of the Government of India into their development plans and projects;

(c) ensure appropriate allocation of funds for prevention of disaster, mitigation, capacity-building and preparedness by the Ministries or Departments of the Government of India;

(d) ensure that the Ministries or Departments of the Government of India take necessary measures for preparedness to promptly and effectively respond to any threatening disaster situation or disaster;

(e) cooperation and assistance to State Governments, as requested by them or otherwise deemed appropriate by it;

(f) deployment of naval, military and air forces, other armed forces of the Union or any other civilian personnel as may be required for the purposes of this Act;

(g) coordination with the United Nations agencies, international organisations and governments of foreign countries for the purposes of this Act;

(h) establish institutions for research, training, and developmental programmes in the field of disaster management;

(i) such other matters as it deems necessary or expedient for the purpose of securing effective implementation of the provisions of this Act.

(3) The Central Government may extend such support to other countries affected by major disaster as it may deem appropriate.

@

36.

%

Responsibilities of Ministries or Departments of Government of India.

!

36. Responsibilities of Ministries or Departments of Government of India.-It shall be the responsibility of every Ministry or Department of the Government of India to -

(a) take measures necessary for prevention of disasters, mitigation, preparedness and capacity-building in accordance with the guidelines laid down by the National Authority;

(b) integrate into its development plans and projects, the measures for prevention or mitigation of disasters in accordance with the guidelines laid down by the National Authority;

(c) respond effectively and promptly to any threatening disaster situation or disaster in accordance with the guidelines of the National Authority or the directions of the National Executive Committee in this behalf;

(d) review the enactments administered by it, its policies, rules and regulations, with a view to incorporate therein the provisions necessary for prevention of disasters, mitigation or preparedness;

(e) allocate funds for measures for prevention of disaster, mitigation, capacity-building and preparedness;

(f) provide assistance to the National Authority and State Governments for-

(i) drawing up mitigation, preparedness and response plans, capacitybuilding, data collection and identification and training of personnel in relation to disaster management;

(ii) carrying out rescue and relief operations in the affected area;

(iii) assessing the damage from any disaster;

(iv) carrying out rehabilitation and reconstruction;

(g) make available its resources to the National Executive Committee or a State Executive Committee for the purposes of responding promptly and effectively to any threatening disaster situation or disaster, including measures for-

(i) providing emergency communication in a vulnerable or affected area;

(ii) transporting personnel and relief goods to and from the affected area;

(iii) providing evacuation, rescue, temporary shelter or other immediate relief;

(iv) setting up temporary bridges, jetties and landing places;

(v) providing, drinking water, essential provisions, healthcare, and services in an affected area;

(h) take such other actions as it may consider necessary for disaster management.

@

37.

%

Disaster management plans of Ministries or Departments of Government of

India.

!

37. Disaster management plans of Ministries or Departments of Government of India.

(1) Every Ministry or Department of the Government of India shall

(a) prepare a disaster management plan specifying the following particulars, namely:

(i) the measures to be taken by it for prevention and mitigation of disasters in accordance with the National Plan;

(ii) the specifications regarding integration of mitigation measures in its development plans in accordance with the guidelines of the National Authority and the National Executive Committee;

(iii) its roles and responsibilities in relation to preparedness and capacity-building to deal with any threatening disaster situation or disaster;

(iv) its roles and responsibilities in regard to promptly and effectively responding to any threatening disaster situation or disaster;

(v) the present status of its preparedness to perform the roles and responsibilities specified in sub-clauses (iii) and (iv);

(vi) the measures required to be taken in order to enable it to perform its responsibilities specified in sub-clauses (iii) and (iv);

(b) review and update annually the plan referred to in clause (a);

(c) forward a copy of the plan referred to in clause (a) or clause (b), as the case may be, to the Central Government which Government shall forward a copy thereof to the National Authority for its approval.

(2) Every Ministry or Department of the Government of India shall-

(a) make, while preparing disaster management plan under clause (a) of sub-section (1), provisions for financing the activities specified therein;

(b) furnish a status report regarding the implementation of the plan referred to in clause (a) of sub-section (1) to the National Authority, as and when required by it.

@

38.

%

State Government to take measures.

!

38. State Government to take measures.

(1) Subject to the provisions of this Act, each State Government shall take all measures specified in the guidelines laid down by the National Authority and such further measures as it deems necessary or expedient, for the purpose of disaster management.

(2) The measures which the State Government may take under sub-section (1) include measures with respect to all or any of the following matters, namely:

(a) coordination of actions of different departments of the Government of the State, the State Authority, District Authorities, local authority and other non-governmental organisations;

(b) cooperation and assistance in the disaster management to the National Authority and National Executive Committee, the State Authority and the State Executive Committee, and the District Authorities;

(c) cooperation with, and assistance to, the Ministries or Departments of the Government of India in disaster management, as requested by them or otherwise deemed appropriate by it;

(d) allocation of funds for measures for prevention of disaster, mitigation, capacity-building and preparedness by the departments of the Government of the State in accordance with the provisions of the State Plan and the District Plans;

(e) ensure that the integration of measures for prevention of disaster or mitigation by the departments of the Government of the State in their development plans and projects;

(f) integrate in the State development plan, measures to reduce or mitigate the vulnerability of different parts of the State to different disasters;

(g) ensure the preparation of disaster management plans by different departments of the State in accordance with the guidelines laid down by the National Authority and the State Authority;

(h) establishment of adequate warning systems up to the level of vulnerable communities;

(i) ensure that different departments of the Government of the State and the District Authorities take appropriate preparedness measures;

(j) ensure that in a threatening disaster situation or disaster, the resources of different departments of the Government of the State are made available to the National Executive Committee or the State Executive Committee or the District Authorities, as the case may be, for the purposes of effective response, rescue and relief in any threatening disaster situation or disaster;

(k) provide rehabilitation and reconstruction assistance to the victims of any disaster; and

(l) such other matters as it deems necessary or expedient for the purpose of securing effective implementation of provisions of this Act.

@

39.

%

Responsibilities of departments of the State Government.

!

39. Responsibilities of departments of the State Government.-It shall be the responsibility of every department of the Government of a State to-

(a) take measures necessary for prevention of disasters, mitigation, preparedness and capacity-building in accordance with the guidelines laid down by the National Authority and the State Authority;

(b) integrate into its development plans and projects, the measures for prevention of disaster and mitigation;

(c) allocate funds for prevention of disaster, mitigation, capacitybuilding and preparedness;

(d) respond effectively and promptly to any threatening disaster situation or disaster in accordance with the State Plan, and in accordance with the guidelines or directions of the National Executive Committee and the State Executive Committee;

(e) review the enactments administered by it, its policies, rules and regulations with a view to incorporate therein the provisions necessary for prevention of disasters, mitigation or preparedness;

(f) provide assistance, as required, by the National Executive Committee, the State Executive Committee and District Authorities, for-

(i) drawing up mitigation, preparedness and response plans, capacitybuilding, data collection and identification and training of personnel in relation to disaster management;

(ii) assessing the damage from any disaster;

(iii) carrying out rehabilitation and reconstruction;

(g) make provision for resources in consultation with the State Authority for the implementation of the District Plan by its authorities at the district level;

(h) make available its resources to the National Executive Committee or the State Executive Committee or the District Authorities for the purposes of responding promptly and effectively to any disaster in the State, including measures for-

(i) providing emergency communication with a vulnerable or affected area;

(ii) transporting personnel and relief goods to and from the affected area;

(iii) providing evacuation, rescue, temporary shelter or other immediate relief;

(iv) carrying out evacuation of persons or live-stock from an area of any threatening disaster situation or disaster;

(v) setting up temporary bridges, jetties and landing places;

(vi) providing drinking water, essential provisions, healthcare and services in an affected area;

(i) such other actions as may be necessary for disaster management.

@

40.

%

Disaster management plan of departments of State.

!

40. Disaster management plan of departments of State.

(1) Every department of the State Government, in conformity with the guidelines laid down by the State Authority, shall-

(a) prepare a disaster management plan which shall lay down the following:

(i) the types of disasters to which different parts of the State are vulnerable;

(ii) integration of strategies for the prevention of disaster or the mitigation of its effects or both with the development plans and programmes by the department;

(iii) the roles and responsibilities of the department of the State in the event of any threatening disaster situation or disaster and emergency support function it is required to perform;

(iv) present status of its preparedness to perform such roles or responsibilities or emergency support function under sub-clause (iii);

(v) the capacity-building and preparedness measures proposed to be put into effect in order to enable the Ministries or Departments of the Government of India to discharge their responsibilities under section 37;

(b) annually review and update the plan referred to in clause (a); and

(c) furnish a copy of the plan referred to in clause (a) or clause (b), as the case may be, to the State Authority.

(2) Every department of the State Government, while preparing the plan under sub-section (1), shall make provisions for financing the activities specified therein.

(3) Every department of the State Government shall furnish an implementation status report to the State Executive Committee regarding the implementation of the disaster management plan referred to in subsection (1).

@

CHAPTER VI

%

LOCAL AUTHORITIES

!

CHAPTER VI

LOCAL AUTHORITIES

@

41.

%

Functions of the local authority.

!

41. Functions of the local authority.

(1) Subject to the directions of the District Authority, a local authority shall-

(a) ensure that its officers and employees are trained for disaster management;

(b) ensure that resources relating to disaster management are so maintained as to be readily available for use in the event of any threatening disaster situation or disaster;

(c) ensure all construction projects under it or within its jurisdiction conform to the standards and specifications laid down for prevention of disasters and mitigation by the National Authority, State Authority and the District Authority;

(d) carry out relief, rehabilitation and reconstruction activities in the affected area in accordance with the State Plan and the District Plan.

(2) The local authority may take such other measures as may be necessary for the disaster management.

@

CHAPTER VII

%

NATIONAL INSTITUTE OF DISASTER MANAGEMENT

!

CHAPTER VII

NATIONAL INSTITUTE OF DISASTER MANAGEMENT

@

42.

%

National Institute of Disaster Management.

!

42. National Institute of Disaster Management.

(1) With effect from such date as the Central Government may, by notification in the Official Gazette appoint in this behalf, there shall be constituted an institute to be called the National Institute of Disaster Management.

(2) The National Institute of Disaster Management shall consist of such number of members as may be prescribed by the Central Government.

(3) The term of office of, and vacancies among, members of the National Institute of Disaster Management and manner of filling such vacancies shall be such as may be prescribed.

(4) There shall be a governing body of the National Institute of Disaster Management which shall be constituted by the Central Government from amongst the members of the National Institute of Disaster Management in such manner as may be prescribed.

(5) The governing body of the National Institute of Disaster Management shall exercise such powers and discharge such functions as may be prescribed by regulations.

(6) The procedure to be followed in excercise of its powers and discharge of its functions by the governing body, and the term of office of, and the manner of filling vacancies among the members of the governing body, shall be such as may be prescribed by regulations.

(7) Until the regulations are made under this section, the Central Government may make such regulations; and any regulation so made may be altered or rescinded by the National Institute of Disaster Management in exercise of its powers.

(8) Subject to the provisions of this Act, the National Institute of Disaster Management shall function within the broad policies and guidelines laid down by the National Authority and be responsible for planning and promoting training and research in the area of disaster management, documentation and development of national level information base relating to disaster management policies, prevention mechanisms and mitigation measures.

(9) Without prejudice to the generality of the provisions contained in sub-section (8), the National Institute, for the discharge of its functions, may -

(a) develop training modules, undertake research and documentation in disaster management and organise training programmes;

(b) formulate and implement a comprehensive human resource development plan covering all aspects of disaster management;

(c) provide assistance in national level policy formulation;

(d) provide required assistance to the training and research institutes for development of training and research programmes for stakeholders including Government functionaries and undertake training of faculty members of the State level training institutes;

(e) provide assistance to the State Governments and State training institutes in the formulation of State level policies, strategies, disaster management framework and any other assistance as may be required by the State Governments or State training institutes for capacity-building of stakeholders, Government including its functionaries, civil society members, corporate sector and people's elected representatives;

(f) develop educational materials for disaster management including academic and professional courses;

(g) promote awareness among stakeholders including college or school teachers and students, technical personnel and others associated with multi-hazard mitigation, preparedness and response measures;

(h) undertake, organise and facilitate study courses, conferences, lectures, seminars within and outside the country to promote the aforesaid objects;

(i) undertake and provide for publication of journals, research papers and books and establish and maintain libraries in furtherance of the aforesaid objects;

(j) do all such other lawful things as are conducive or incidental to the attainment of the above objects; and

(k) undertake any other function as may be assigned to it by the Central Government.

@

43.

%

Officers and other employees of the National Institute.

!

43. Officers and other employees of the National Institute.-The Central Government shall provide the National Institute of Disaster Management with such officers, consultants and other employees, as it considers necessary, for carrying out its functions.

@

CHAPTER VIII

%

NATIONAL DISASTER RESPONSE FORCE

!

CHAPTER VIII

NATIONAL DISASTER RESPONSE FORCE

@

44.

%

National Disaster Response Force.

!

44. National Disaster Response Force.

(1) There shall be constituted a National Disaster Response Force for the purpose of specialist response to a threatening disaster situation or disaster.

(2) Subject to the provisions of this Act, the Force shall be constituted in such manner and, the conditions of service of the members of the Force, including disciplinary provisions therefor, be such as may be prescribed.

@

45.

%

Control, direction, etc.

!

45. Control, direction, etc. The general superintendence, direction and control of the Force shall be vested and exercised by the National Authority and the command and supervision of the Force shall vest in an officer to be appointed by the Central Government as the Director General of the National Disaster Response Force.

@

CHAPTER IX

%

FINANCE, ACCOUNTS AND AUDIT

!

CHAPTER IX

FINANCE, ACCOUNTS AND AUDIT

@

46.

%

National Disaster Response Fund.

!

46. National Disaster Response Fund.

(1) The Central Government may, by notification in the Official Gazette, constitute a fund to be called the National Disaster Response Fund for meeting any threatening disaster situation or disaster and there shall be credited thereto-

(a) an amount which the Central Government may, after due appropriation made by Parliament by law in this behalf provide;

(b) any grants that may be made by any person or institution for the purpose of disaster management.

(2) The National Disaster Response Fund shall be made available to the National Executive Committee to be applied towards meeting the expenses for emergency response, relief and rehabilitation in accordance with the guidelines laid down by the Central Government in consultation with the National Authority.

@

47.

%

National Disaster Mitigation Fund.

!

47. National Disaster Mitigation Fund.

(1) The Central Government may, by notification in the Official Gazette, constitute a Fund to be called the National Disaster Mitigation Fund for projects exclusively for the purpose of mitigation and there shall be credited thereto such amount which the Central Government may, after due appropriation made by Parliament by law in this behalf, provide.

(2) The National Disaster Mitigation Fund shall be applied by the National Authority.

@

48.

%

Establishment of funds by State Government.

!

48. Establishment of funds by State Government.

(1) The State Government shall, immediately after notifications issued for constituting the State Authority and the District Authorities, establish for the purposes of this Act the following funds, namely:

(a) the fund to be called the State Disaster Response Fund;

(b) the fund to be called the District Disaster Response Fund;

(c) the fund to be called the State Disaster Mitigation Fund;

(d) the fund to be called the District Disaster Mitigation Fund.

(2) The State Government shall ensure that the funds established-

(i) under clause (a) of sub-section (1) is available to the State Executive Committee;

(ii) under sub-clause (c) of sub-section (1) is available to the State Authority;

(iii) under clauses (b) and (d) of sub-section (1) are available to the District Authority.

@

49.

%

Allocation of funds by Ministries and Departments.

!

49. Allocation of funds by Ministries and Departments.

(1) Every Ministry or Department of the Government of India shall make provisions, in its annual budget, for funds for the purposes of carrying out the activities and programmes set out in its disaster management plan.

(2) The provisions of sub-section (1) shall, mutatis mutandis, apply to departments of the Government of the State.

@

50.

%

Emergency procurement and accounting.

!

50. Emergency procurement and accounting.-Where by reason of any threatening disaster situation or disaster, the National Authority or the State Authority or the District Authority is satisfied that immediate procurement of provisions or materials or the immediate application of resources are necessary for rescue or relief,-

(a) it may authorise the concerned department or authority to make the emergency procurement and in such case, the standard procedure requiring inviting of tenders shall be deemed to be waived;

(b) a certificate about utilisation of provisions or materials by the controlling officer authorised by the National Authority, State Authority or District Authority, as the case may be, shall be deemed to be a valid document or voucher for the purpose of accounting of emergency, procurement of such provisions or materials.

@

CHAPTER X

%

OFFENCES AND PENALTIES

!

CHAPTER X

OFFENCES AND PENALTIES

@

51.

%

Punishment for obstruction, etc.

!

51. Punishment for obstruction, etc.-Whoever, without reasonable cause-

(a) obstructs any officer or employee of the Central Government or the State Government, or a person authorised by the National Authority or State Authority or District Authority in the discharge of his functions under this Act; or

(b) refuses to comply with any direction given by or on behalf of the Central Government or the State Government or the National Executive Committee or the State Executive Committee or the District Authority under this Act, shall on conviction be punishable with imprisonment for a term which may extend to one year or with fine, or with both, and if such obstruction or refusal to comply with directions results in loss of lives or imminent danger thereof, shall on conviction be punishable with imprisonment for a term which may extend to two years.

@

52.

%

Punishment for false claim.

!

52. Punishment for false claim.-Whoever knowingly makes a claim which he knows or has reason to believe to be false for obtaining any relief, assistance, repair, reconstruction or other benefits consequent to disaster from any officer of the Central Government, the State Government, the National Authority, the State Authority or the District Authority, shall, on conviction be punishable with imprisonment for a term which may extend to two years, and also with fine.

@

53.

%

Punishment for misappropriation of money or materials, etc.

!

53. Punishment for misappropriation of money or materials, etc.- Whoever, being entrusted with any money or materials, or otherwise being, in custody of, or dominion over, any money or goods, meant for providing relief in any threatening disaster situation or disaster, misappropriates or appropriates for his own use or disposes of such money or materials or any part thereof or wilfully compels any other person so to do, shall on conviction be punishable with imprisonment for a term which may extend to two years, and also with fine.

@

54.

%

Punishment for false warning.

!

54. Punishment for false warning.-Whoever makes or circulates a false alarm or warning as to disaster or its severity or magnitude, leading to panic, shall on conviction, be punishable with imprisonment which may extend to one year or with fine.

@

55.

%

Offences by Departments of the Government.

!

55. Offences by Departments of the Government.

(1) Where an offence under this Act has been committed by any Department of the Government, the head of the Department shall be deemed to be guilty of the offence and shall be liable to be proceeded against and punished accordingly unless he proves that the offence was committed without his knowledge or that he exercised all due diligence to prevent the commission of such offence.

(2) Notwithstanding anything contained in sub-section (1), where an offence under this Act has been committed by a Department of the Government and it is proved that the offence has been committed with the consent or connivance of, or is attributable to any neglect on the part of, any officer, other than the head of the Department, such officer shall be deemed to be guilty of that offence and sall be liable to be proceeded against and punished accordingly.

@

56.

%

Failure of officer in duty or his connivance at the contravention of the provisions of this Act.

!

56. Failure of officer in duty or his connivance at the contravention of the provisions of this Act.-Any officer, on whom any duty has been imposed by or under this Act and who ceases or refuses to perform or withdraws himself from the duties of his office shall, unless he has obtained the express written permission of his official superior or has other lawful excuse for so doing, be punishable with imprisonment for a term which may extend to one year or with fine.

@

57.

%

Penalty for contravention of any order regarding requisitioning.

!

57. Penalty for contravention of any order regarding requisitioning.-If any person contravenes any order made under section 65, he shall be punishable with imprisonment for a term which may extend to one year or with fine or with both.

@

58.

%

Offence by companies.

!

58. Offence by companies.

(1) Where an offence under this Act has been committed by a company or body corporate, every person who at the time the offence was committed, was in charge of, and was responsible to, the company, for the conduct of the business of the company, as well as the company, shall be deemed to be guilty of the contravention and shall be liable to be proceeded against and punished accordingly:

Provided that nothing in this sub-section shall render any such person liable to any punishment provided in this Act, if he proves that the offence was committed without his knowledge or that he exercised due diligence to prevent the commission of such offence.

(2) Notwithstanding anything contained in sub-section (1), where an offence under this Act has been committed by a company, and it is proved that the offence was committed with the consent or connivance of or is attributable to any neglect on the part of any director, manager, secretary or other officer of the company, such director, manager, secretary or other officer shall also, be deemed to be guilty of that offence and shall be liable to be proceeded against and punished accordingly.

Explanation.-For the purpose of this section -

(a) "company" means any body corporate and includes a firm or other association of individuals; and

(b) "director", in relation to a firm, means a partner in the firm.

@

59.

%

Previous sanction for prosecution.

!

59. Previous sanction for prosecution.-No prosecution for offences punishable under sections 55 and 56 shall be instituted except with the previous sanction of the Central Government or the State Government, as the case may be, or of any officer authorised in this behalf, by general or special order, by such Government.

@

60.

%

Cognizance of offences.

!

60. Cognizance of offences.-No court shall take cognizance of an offence under this Act except on a complaint made by-

(a) the National Authority, the State Authority, the Central Government, the State Government, the District Authority or any other authority or officer authorised in this behalf by that Authority or Government, as the case may be; or

(b) any person who has given notice of not less than thirty days in the manner prescribed, of the alleged offence and his intention to make a complaint to the National Authority, the State Authority, the Central Government, the State Government, the District Authority or any other authority or officer authorised as aforesaid.".

@

CHAPTER XI

%

MISCELLANEOUS

!

CHAPTER XI

MISCELLANEOUS

@

61.

%

Prohibition against discrimination.

!

61. Prohibition against discrimination.-While providing compensation and relief to the victims of disaster, there shall be no discrimination on the ground of sex, caste, community, descent or religion.

@

62.

%

Power to issue direction by Central Government.

!

62. Power to issue direction by Central Government.-Notwithstanding anything contained in any other law for the time being in force, it shall be lawful for the Central Government to issue direction in writing to the Ministries or Departments of the Government of India, or the National Executive Committee or the State Government,

State Authority, State Executive Committee, statutory bodies or any of its officers or employees, as the case may be, to facilitate or assist in the disaster management and such Ministry or Department or Government or Authority, Executive Committee, statutory body, officer or employee shall be bound to comply with such direction.

@

63.

%

Powers to be made available for rescue operations.

!

63. Powers to be made available for rescue operations.-Any officer or authority of the Union or a State, when requested by the National Executive Committee, any State Executive Committee or District Authority or any person authorised by such Committee or Authority in this behalf, shall make available to that Committee or authority or person, such officers and employees as requested for, to perform any of the functions in connection with the prevention of disaster or mitigation or rescue or relief work.

@

64.

%

Making or amending rules, etc., in certain circumstances.

!

64. Making or amending rules, etc., in certain circumstances.-Subject to the provisions of this Act, if it appears to the National Executive Committee, State Executive Committee or the District Authority, as the case may be, that provisions of any rule, regulation, notification, guideline, instruction, order, scheme or bye-laws, as the case may be, are required to be made or amended for the purposes of prevention of disasters or the mitigation thereof, it may require the amendment of such rules, regulation, notification, guidelines, instruction, order, scheme or bye-laws, as the case may be, for that purpose, and the appropriate department or authority shall take necessary action to comply with the requirements.

@

65.

%

Power of requisition of resources, provisions, vehicles, etc., for
rescue operations, etc.

!

65. Power of requisition of resources, provisions, vehicles, etc., for rescue operations, etc.-

(1) If it appears to the National Executive Committee, State Executive Committee or District Authority or any officer as may be authorised by it in this behalf that-

(a) any resources with any authority or person are needed for the purpose of prompt response;

(b) any premises are needed or likely to be needed for the purpose of rescue operations; or

(c) any vehicle is needed or is likely to be needed for the purposes of transport of' resources from disaster affected areas or transport of resources to the affected area or transport in connection with rescue, rehabilitation or reconstruction, such authority may, by order in writing, requisition such resources or premises or such vehicle, as the case may be, and may make such further orders as may appear to it to be necessary or expedient in connection with the requisitioning.

(2) Whenever any resource, premises or vehicle is requisitioned under sub-section (1), the period of such requisition shall not extend beyond the period for which such resource, premises or vehicle is required for any of the purposes mentioned in that sub-section.

(3) In this section,-

(a) "resources" includes men and material resources;

(b) "services" includes facilities;

(c) "premises" means any land, building or part of a building and includes a hut, shed or other structure or any part thereof;

(d) "vehicle" means any vehicle used or capable of being used for the purpose of transport, whether propelled by mechanical power or otherwise.

@

66.

%

Payment of compensation.

!

66. Payment of compensation.-

(1) Whenever any Committee, Authority or officer referred to in sub-section (1) of section 65, in pursuance of that section requisitions any premises, there shall be paid to the persons interested compensation the amount of which shall be determined by taking into consideration the following, namely:-

(i) the rent payable in respect of the premises, or if no rent is so payable, the rent payable for similar premises in the locality;

(ii) if as consequence of the requisition of the premises the person interested is compelled to change his residence or place of business, the reasonable expenses (if any) incidental to such change:

Provided that where any person interested being aggrieved by the amount of compensation so determined makes an application within the thirty days to the Central Government or the State Government, as the case may be, for referring the matter to an arbitrator, the amount of compensation to be paid shall be such as the arbitrator appointed in this behalf by the Central Government or the State Government, as the case may be, may determine:

Provided further that where there is any dispute as to the title to receive the compensation or as to the apportionment of the amount of compensation, it shall be referred by the Central Government or the State Government, as the case may be, to an arbitrator appointed in this behalf by the Central Government or the State Government, as the case may be, for determination, and shall be determined in accordance with the decision of such arbitrator.

Explanation.-In this sub-section, the expression "person interested" means the person who was in actual possession of the premises requisitioned under section 65 immediately before the requisition, or where no person was in such actual possession, the owner of such premises.

(2) Whenever any Committee, Authority or officer, referred to in subsection (1) of section 65 in pursuance of that section requisitions any vehicle, there shall be paid to the owner thereof compensation the amount of which shall be determined by the Central Government or the State Government, as the case may be, on the basis of the fares or rates prevailing in the locality for the hire of such vehicle:

Provided that where the owner of such vehicle being aggrieved by the amount of compensation so determined makes an application within the prescribed time to the Central Government or the State Government, as the case may be, for referring the matter to an arbitrator, the amount of compensation to be paid shall be such as the arbitrator appointed in this behalf by the Central Government or the State Government, as the case may be, may determine:

Provided further that where immediately before the requisitioning the vehicle or vessel was by virtue of a hire purchase agreement in the possession of a person other than the owner, the amount determined under this sub-section as the total compensation payable in respect of the requisition shall be apportioned between that person and the owner in such manner as they may agree upon, and in default of agreement, in such manner as an arbitrator appointed by the Central Government or the State Government, as the case may be, in this behalf may decide.

@

67.

%

Direction to medial for communication of warnings, etc.

!

67. Direction to medial for communication of warnings, etc.-The National Authority, the State Authority, or a District Authority may recommend to the Government to give direction to any authority or person in control of any audio or audio-visual media or such other means of communication as may be available to carry any warning or advisories regarding any threatening disaster situation or disaster, and the said means of communication and media as designated shall comply with such direction.

@

68.

%

Authentication of orders or decisions.

!

68. Authentication of orders or decisions.-Every order or decision of the National Authority or the National Executive Committee, the State Authority, or the State Executive Committee or the District Authority, shall be authenticated by such officers of the National Authority or the National Executive Committee or, the State Executive Committee, or the District Authority, as may be authorised by it in this behalf.

@

69.

%

Delegation of powers.

!

69. Delegation of powers.-The National Executive Committee, State Executive Committee, as the case may be, by general or special order in writing, may delegate to the Chairperson or any other member or to any officer, subject to such conditions and limitations, if any, as may be specified in the order, such of its powers and functions under this Act as it may deem necessary.

@

70.

%

Annual report.

!

70. Annual report.-

(1) The National Authority shall prepare once every year, in such form and at such time as may be prescribed, an annual report giving a true and full account of its activities during the previous year and copies thereof shall be forwarded to the Central Government and that Government shall cause the same to be laid before both Houses of Parliament within one month of its receipt.

(2) The State Authority shall prepare once in every year, in such form and at such time as may be prescribed, an annual report giving a true and full account of its activities during the previous year and copies thereof shall be forwarded to the State Government and that Government shall cause the same to be laid before each House of the State Legislature where it consists of two Houses, or where such Legislature consists of one House, before that House.

@

71.

%

Bar of jurisdiction of court.

!

71. Bar of jurisdiction of court.-No court (except the Supreme Court or a High Court) shall have jurisdiction to entertain any suit or proceeding in respect of anything done, action taken, orders made, direction, instruction or guidelines issued by the Central Government, National Authority, State Government, State Authority or District Authority in pursuance of any power conferred by, or in relation to its functions, by this Act.

@

72.

%

Act to have overriding effect.

!

72. Act to have overriding effect.-The provisions of this Act, shall have effect, notwithstanding anything inconsistent therewith contained in any other law for the time being in force or in any instrument having effect by virtue of any law other than this Act.

@

73.

%

Action taken in good faith.

!

73. Action taken in good faith.-No suit or prosecution or other proceeding shall lie in any court against the Central Government or the National Authority or the State Government or the State Authority or the District Authority or local authority or any officer or employee of the Central Government or the National Authority or the State Government or the State Authority or the District Authority or local authority or any person working for on behalf of such Government or authority in respect of any work done or purported to have been done or intended to be done in good faith by such authority or Government or such officer or employee or such person under the provisions of this Act or the rules or regulations made thereunder.

@

74.

%

Immunity from legal process.

!

74. Immunity from legal process.-Officers and employees of the Central Government, National Authority, National Executive Committee, State Government, State Authority, State Executive Committee or District Authority shall be immune from legal process in regard to any warning in respect of any impending disaster communicated or disseminated by them in their official capacity or any action taken or direction issued by them in pursuance of such communication or dissemination.

@

75.

%

Power of Central Government to make rules.

!

75. Power of Central Government to make rules.-

(1) The Central Government may, by notification in the Official Gazette, make rules for carrying out the purposes of this Act.

(2) In particular, and without prejudice to the generality of the foregoing power, such rules may provide for all or any of the following matters, namely:

   (a) the composition and number of the members of the National Authority under sub-section (2), and the term of office and conditions of service of members of the National Authority under sub-section (4), of section 3;

   (b) the allowances to be paid to the members of the advisory committec under sub-section (2) of section 7;

(c) the powers and functions of the Chairperson of the National Executive Committee under sub-section (3) of section 8 and the procedure to be followed by the National Executive Committee in exercise of its powers and discharge of its functions under sub-section (4) of section 8;

(d) allowances to be paid to the persons associated with the subcommittee constituted by the National Executive Committee under subsection (3) of section 9;

(e) the number of members of the National Institute of Disaster Management under sub-section (2), the term of the office and vacancies among members and the manner of filling such vacancies under subsection (3) and the manner of constituting the Governing Body of the National Institute of Disaster Management under sub-section (4) of section 42;

(f) the manner of constitution of the Force, the conditions of service of the members of the Force, including disciplinary provisions under sub-section (2) of section 44;

(g) the manner in which notice of the offence and of the intention to make a complaint to the National Authority, the State Authority, the Central Government, the State Government or the other authority or officer under clause (b) of section 60;

(h) the form in which and the time within which annual report is to be prepared under section 70;

(i) any other matter which is to be, or may be, prescribed, or in respect of which provision is to be made by rules.

@

76.

%

Power to make regulations.

!

76. Power to make regulations.-

(1) The National Institute of Disaster Management, with the previous approval of the Central Government may, by notification in the Official Gazette, make regulations consistent with this Act and the rules made thereunder to carry out the purposes of this Act.

(2) In particular, and without prejudice to the generality of the foregoing power, such regulations may provide for all or any of the following matters, namely:

(a) powers and functions to be exercised and dicharged by the governing body;

(b) procedure to be followed by the governing body in exercise of the powers and discharge of its functions;

(c) any other matter for which under this Act provision may be made by the regulations.

@

77.

%

Rules and regulations to be laid before Parliament.

!

77. Rules and regulations to be laid before Parliament.-Every rule made by the Central Government and every regulation made by the National Institute of Disaster Management under this Act shall be laid, as soon as may be after it is made, before each House of Parliament, while it is in session, for a total period of thirty days which may be comprised of one session or in two or more successive sessions, and if, before the expiry of the session immediately following the session or the successive sessions aforesaid, both Houses agree in making any modification in the rule or regulation or both Houses agree that the rule or regulation should not be made, the rule or regulation shall thereafter have effect only in such modified form or be of no effect, as the case may be; so, however, that any such modification or annulment shall be without prejudice to the validity of anything previously done under that rule or regulation.

@

78.

%

Power of State Government to make rules.

!

78. Power of State Government to make rules.-

(1) The State Government may, by notification in the Official Gazette, make rules to carry out the provisions of this Act.

(2) In particular, and without prejudice to the generality of the foregoing power, such rules may provide for all or any of the following matters, namely:

(a) the composition and number of the members of the State Authority under sub-section (2), and the term of office and conditions of service of the members of the State Authority under sub-section (5), of section 14;

(b) the allowances to be paid to the members of the advisory committee under sub-section (2) of section 17;

(c) the powers and functions of the Chairperson of the State Executive Committee under sub-section (3), and the procedure to be followed by the State Executive Committee in exercise of its powers and discharge of its functions under sub-section (4) of section 20;

(d) allowances to be paid to the persons associated with the subcommittee constituted by the State Executive Committee under subsection (3) of section 21;

(e) the composition and the number of members of the District Authority under sub-section (2), and the powers and functions to be exercised anddischarged by the Chief Executive Officer of the District Authority under sub-section (3) of section 25;

(f) allowances payable to the persons associated with any committee constituted by the District Authority as experts under sub-section (3) of section 28;

(g) any other matter which is to be, or may be, prescribed, or in respect of which provision is to be made by rules.

(3) Every rule made by the State Government under this Act shall be laid, as soon as may be after it is made, before each House of the State Legislature where it consists of two Houses, or where such Legislature consists of one House before that House.

@

79.

%

Power to remove difficulties.

!

79. Power to remove difficulties.-

(1) If any difficulty arises in giving effect to the provisions of this Act, the Central Government or the State Government, as the case may be, by notification in the Official Gazette, make order not inconsistent with the provisions of this Act as may appear to it to be necessary or expedient for the removal of the difficulty:

Provided that no such order shall be made after the expiration of two years from the commencement of this Act.

(2) Every order made under this section shall be laid, as soon as may be after it is made, before each House of Parliament or the Legislature, as the case may be.

T. K. VISWANATHAN,

Secy. to the Govt. of India.

{}